D1271902

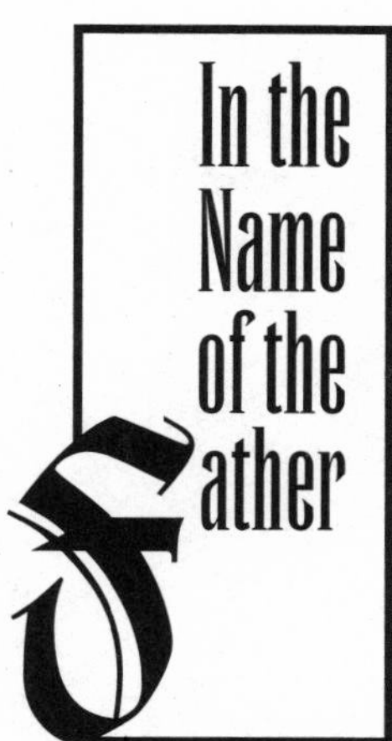
In the
Name
of the
Father

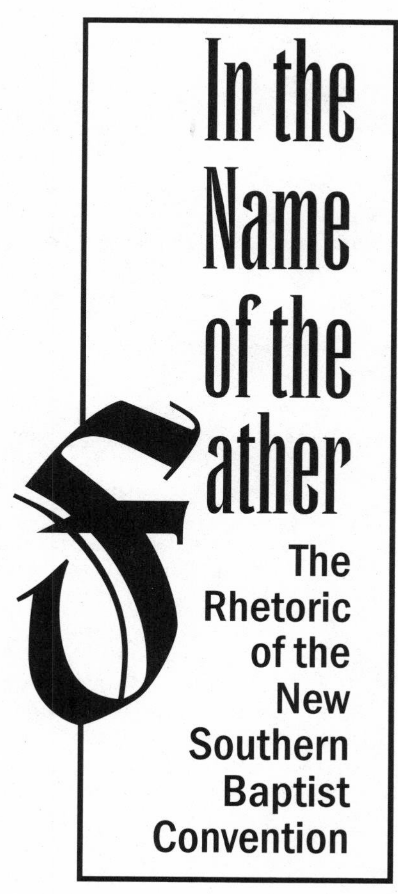

In the Name of the Father

The Rhetoric of the New Southern Baptist Convention

Carl L. Kell
L. Raymond Camp

With a Foreword by Kenneth Chafin

Southern Illinois University Press
Carbondale and Edwardsville

Copyright © 1999 by the Board of Trustees, Southern Illinois University
All rights reserved
Printed in the United States of America

02 01 00 99 4 3 2 1

Publication partially funded by a subvention grant from the College of Humanities and Social Sciences, North Carolina State University.

Library of Congress Cataloging-in-Publication Data
Kell, Carl L.
In the name of the Father : the rhetoric of the new Southern Baptist Convention / Carl L. Kell, L. Raymond Camp ; with a foreword by Kenneth Chafin.
p. cm.

Includes bibliographical references and index.
1. Southern Baptist Convention—History—20th century. 2. Conservatism—Religious aspects—Southern Baptist Convention—History of doctrines—20th century. I. Camp, L. Raymond. II. Title.
BX6462.7.K444 1999
286'.132'09045—dc21 98-35148
ISBN 0-8093-2220-X (hardcover : alk. paper) CIP

The paper used in this publication meets the minimum requirements of American National Standard for Information Sciences—Permanence of Paper for Printed Library Materials, ANSI Z39.48-1984. ♾

To our wives,
Mary Anne and Carolyn,
whose guidance and encouragement have
been both necessary and indispensable

Contents

Illustrations

Following Page 62

Foreword

The thesis of this book is true, and it saddens me. The authors rightly see the inerrancy controversy—the position that holds the Bible is literally true and without error on any subject—in the Southern Baptist Convention (SBC) as the best expression in the twentieth century of the power of the spoken word to change the nature and character of a major Protestant denomination. Their thesis is that it was the fundamentalists' flawless use of rhetoric, in the classical sense, and not their theology or beliefs about the Bible, that allowed them to accomplish their goals.

In the pulpits and on the platforms, fundamentalists have insisted that the whole struggle was for an inerrant, infallible Bible. In the past, the majority of the people were led to believe that it was the real issue, and some naive souls still think that it is. But if the authors of this book are right, it is rhetoric that has been used to gain power and control, to manipulate people, to mask personal ambition, to cover up personal insecurities, and to hide a fear of the modern world with all its complexities.

In the past, they worked hard to convince people that the controversy was about the Bible. They gathered followers who had been told that they were "shaping a new theology." But, the truth is now evident; the movement was more about a grab for power than the emergence of a new theology. It was more about imposing a "mind-set" than leading more people to experience God's freedom. It was more about excluding all who disagreed with them than finding a basis of unity in Christ. The proof of this conclusion is evident from what they did once they gained control.

There were some who were drawn into the movement and realized that they had been deceived. Their personal integrity would not allow them to pretend that the issue was the Bible when it wasn't. This was the case with Dr. Daniel Vestal, executive director of the Cooperative Baptist Fellowship. Despite his view of divine inspiration and his deep love for the Scriptures, when Vestal discovered the real agenda, he withdrew from the movement and became a spokesperson for historic Baptist principles. Richard Jackson, the retired pastor of North Phoenix Baptist Church in Phoenix, Arizona, took the same action.

But, the majority of the people who were gathered up in the movement either did not have the discernment to see what was really happening or lacked the moral courage to express their thoughts. The fact that Southern Baptists have such a love for the Scriptures makes us particularly vulnerable to those who talk about how much they believe in them. Those who have dared to disagree have been attacked, which has caused fence-sitters to avoid disapproval.

What made the fundamentalists so formidable was that the leaders of the takeover movement were allowed to define the issue. While serious study of the Scriptures will not sustain the fundamentalists' view of the Bible, when their definition of the inerrant Bible went unchallenged, they had won. Ever since the time of the Greek philosopher Aristotle, those who study the art of persuasion have agreed that those who are allowed to define the issue win the war.

The fundamentalists pictured themselves as the defenders of the Bible as God's Word—a conclusion about the Bible with which no Southern Baptist would argue. That position is reflected in our historic Articles of Faith. Then, having established the authority of the Bible, they defined its nature as an inerrant book. While their definition was questionable from many different viewpoints, not the least of which was that the Bible itself will not sustain it, people either did not understand what was wrong with the definition or were afraid to question it.

Their "argument from definition" meant that all who disagreed with them on any subject were accused of not believing in the Bible. Once they had established themselves as the defenders of the "high ground" on the issue of the Scriptures, it was just a matter of time until they created a list of issues with their "official" interpretations. In this way, they gave the same authority to their interpretations that they had given to the Bible, much like the Roman Catholics treat the teachings of the Pope. Those who question authority are given the Baptist equivalent of "excommunication."

The fatal mistake that everyone made was believing that the struggle was over the truthfulness of the Bible. It was really a struggle for the soul of a denomination, a struggle for political power, and an effort to impose a mind-set on the faithful. The battle was not fought in the classroom, where the open Bible was studied, nor in a healthy dialogue among people of good will. It was waged behind pulpits and on platforms with rhetoric, and the fundamentalists were better at it than the moderates. And those who lost were made to feel like aliens in their own denomination.

To rally so many people so quickly, fundamentalists needed an enemy, a devil to fight. They were able to get the necessary support from rank-and-file Baptists by making the seminaries the scapegoat for the ills of the denomination, ignoring completely the wide range of factors that affected the church. That their accusations about the seminaries were, for the most part, not based in fact did not seem to bother the attackers.

They were more pragmatists than purists, and the approach "worked." That was all that seemed to matter.

However, it is not entirely appropriate to credit the fundamentalists with the wholesale takeover of the SBC. They had help from the moderates. Walter Shurden describes it accurately: "Passion won; moderation lost."[1] Noted Southern Baptist pastor and past executive director of the Cooperative Baptist Fellowship (the moderate's breakaway organization), Cecil Sherman elaborates in his analysis of the situation:

> Moderates did not have enough moral energy to win. We could not bring ourselves to use moral language to describe our cause. Truth was butchered. We said nothing. Good people were defamed. We were silent. Baptist principles were mangled and Baptist history was replaced, rewritten. All the while, teachers who could have written about the problems in calling the Bible inerrant, did not. And preachers who could have called us to arms said nothing. The want of moral energy was the undoing of the Moderate movement.[2]

As painful as Sherman's statement is to many, those of us who have been close to the whole experience know that it is the truth. I myself was a witness to the key events he describes.

Today, the fundamentalists control every Board of Trustees of every Southern Baptist seminary, and they are well into the process of implementing their agenda. The fact that they were better at gaining control than they are at administering the institutions they captured should surprise no one. That they won is no longer a question, though there are still naive souls who try to pretend that this is not the case.

The authors of this book affirm what many have suspected for a long time. This controversy was always about persuading others and never about the Bible or theology. While I am not a student of communication in its classical definition, I am a communicator. I have a profound appreciation for the way the authors of this book have studied in detail the messages that were preached at conventions, Pastor's Conferences, and various Baptist meetings to document the thesis of the book.

My agreement with the thesis of this book is born of my personal experiences and observations during the past twenty years. I know personally the individuals who planned and executed the successful takeover of the Southern Baptist Convention. I know personally all of those who were in charge of the institutions under attack. I was present when many of the pivotal events took place. I also know many of the victims of the destructive conflict.

It is obvious to those who had close ties to the leaders of the fundamentalist movement that they are not all that serious about the Bible or theology. Early in the conflict, when Adrian Rogers, pastor of Bellevue Baptist Church in Memphis, was holding rallies in which he was building support by attacking the seminaries, his main target was Dr. Roy Honeycutt, then the president of Southern Baptist Theological Seminary. After Honeycutt disagreed with his attackers, they suddenly discovered he had written volume 3 of the *Broadman Bible Commentary*, which included I and II Kings. However, they seemed more interested in finding something with which to hurt Roy than to discover how he had dealt with those difficult passages.

During the early years of the controversy, behind-the-scenes stories about the loyalists were legendary. In particular, a story about Adrian Roger's attacks on Roy Honeycutt produced a biblical blunder of ironic proportions. Adrian was entertaining the crowd by poking fun at Honeycutt's interpretation of II Kings 2:23–25 in which, as punishment for calling the prophet Elisha "baldy," she-bears came from the woods and tore up the children. He assured the crowd that God had done the right thing in sending the bears, because the word that had been translated "children" was really a reference to "teenage punks" from a pagan temple who had gotten what they deserved for not showing the proper respect for the prophet.

I shared the tape and transcription of Adrian's talk with Dr. Page Kelley, a longtime Old Testament professor, and asked for his comments. He pointed out that the word that was translated "children" in the II Kings passage was the same word used in the messianic passage in Isaiah 9:6, "for unto us a child is born."

I thought to myself, "Wouldn't it be fun to be at Bellevue Baptist Church when Adrian preached his Christmas sermon on 'Unto us a teenage punk is born'?" In Dallas, at one of the conventions, I asked him how he had arrived at his interpretation, which was not supported by the text of the Bible. With a sense of pride he said, "I got that from the footnotes of the New Scofield Bible," as though that was the most responsible source of biblical scholarship.

Adrian Rogers is the man who had a major role in replacing the seminary trustees, who consulted with those new trustees as to the strategies they would use in implementing their agenda, and who, as an outspoken member of the SBC Peace Committee, spent eight hours haranguing Roy Honeycutt about what was being taught at Southern Baptist Theological Seminary. It is therefore no surprise that he gave his approval to replace Honeycutt with a thirty-three-year-old who had never taught a semester and never administered any school larger than a student church vacation Bible school. (Currently, Al Moehler is the president of Southern Baptist Theological Seminary in Louisville, Kentucky.)

While the movement tries to draw into its leadership men with doctoral degrees who will lend an air of intellectual respectability to their cause, what they often get are well-educated persons who are willing to be used in exchange for a place of honor. Adrian Rogers; Judge Paul Pressler of Houston; Paige Patterson, president of Southeastern Baptist Theological Seminary; Bailey Smith; Charles Stanley, pastor of the First Baptist Church in Atlanta; and the rest have captured the soul of a great denomination, but that speaks more to their political skills than their interest in biblical exegesis. They are more in love with their theories about the Bible than what is taught in it.

Just as I know the players in the conflict within the Southern Baptist Convention, I also know many of the victims—individuals who have been injured, institutions that are being destroyed, and Baptist principles that are being laid to rest.

The victims who touch my heart most are people whose lives have been, and still are being, damaged. What happens to people is always important. One reason the takeover movement was so successful was in how it dealt with those who dissented. Those who disagreed with the takeover leaders were attacked, labeled, isolated, and banned. There was no serious dialogue on the issues, only an effort to smear those who dared to disagree.

It would be difficult to overestimate the damage to theological education caused by the takeover group of fundamentalists. During the 1960s and early 1970s, other denominations looked at Southern Baptist theological education with envy. There was a genius in the way in which each of the seminaries was set in a cultural context. The schools had diversity in their history, their setting, and their faculty, but they were unified in their commitment to provide quality theological education to those whom God called. Their diversity was their strength, not their weakness.

Their friendly rivalries were natural, but not destructive. Often faculty members were exchanged, and students who did undergraduate work in one seminary did their doctoral work in another. Our schools were the envy of other denominations because of their enrollment, their funding, and the placement of their graduates. But now, that is not the case.

If there is anything in this book that encourages, it is the reminder that the spoken word still has great power to change people and institutions. But the clear message of the book is that the spoken word can be prostituted to lesser motives. That is what has happened in the Southern Baptist Convention. Instead of being led out of Egypt to a new and exciting promised land, we find ourselves in Babylon, in captivity.

— *Kenneth Chafin*

Notes

1. Walter B. Shurden, *The Struggle for the Soul of the SBC* (Macon, Ga.: Mercer University College, 1993), 288.

2. Shurden, *Struggle for the Soul*, 288.

Acknowledgments

We wish to express our appreciation to those colleagues whose encouragement and writing have helped us: Hal Fulmer, Steve Pullum, Dennis Bailey, Helen Sterk, Harold Mixon, Jim Clark, and Mary Evelyn Collins. We have also received valuable assistance from denominational critics such as Richard Bridges, Luther Brewer, Greg Warner, Bob Watson and Daniel Vestal. We are grateful to Bill Sumners, archivist of the Southern Baptist Convention Archives, Nashville, Tennessee, for his valuable assistance regarding the full resources of the archives.

In particular, we wish to thank Howard Dorgan of Appalachian State University, Boone, North Carolina, for confirming our perception that the rhetorics of fundamentalism, inerrancy, and exclusion are central to the analysis of the contemporary Southern Baptist Convention.

We are grateful to our mentors who have inspired us to appreciate the rigors and contributions of the historical-critical method. Moreover, because of them, we are fully appreciative of the rightful place and significance of the rhetorical perspective in the study of social and religious discourse. They have helped us understand the rhetorical anchors that are central to our everyday lives. More than they know, Ralph T. Eubanks, Eugene White, and Bob Gunderson have enriched our affinity for the power and analysis of the spoken word.

Finally, we acknowledge Kenneth Burke and Richard Weaver, whose theories have helped us understand the main objective of loyalist discourses: the purification of the membership through the use of victimage to achieve a purer denomination, regardless of the pain to the believer and the local church.

Introduction

Since the 1979 takeover of the Southern Baptist Convention (SBC) by those loyal to inerrancy and exclusion, the South has been the scene of a rhetorical civil war of enormous importance for the hearts and souls of fifteen million people. The mighty Southern Baptist Convention is the largest Protestant denomination in the United States. Once unified, it is now split, and the battle is being waged between two principal groups: those persons loyal to the exclusively male pulpit autocracy in Nashville, which is the home of the male-dominated denominational Executive Committee, and those dissidents organizationally confederated in Atlanta, Richmond, and elsewhere in the South.

Key loyalist rhetor-preachers such as former SBC presidents Adrian Rogers, Bailey Smith, and James T. Draper have three purposes in their persuasive campaign: to preserve, perhaps enhance, the autocracy of the Southern Baptist pulpit; to enforce new denominational membership requirements; and to return the South to an antebellum period of social stability. Then, females were subservient. Today, male loyalist rhetors are the exclusive arbiters of the faith, and women must again be subservient. An obedient "Southernness" purged of contamination from objectionable "isms," whether denominational or secular, is a noticeable goal of the Nashville oligarchy.

The effects of this schism have been momentous for dissenting female church pastors; denominational officers, whether female or male; and missionaries whom the male leadership has expelled or ostracized. Enormous casualties have occurred on both sides. The strife has forever altered, perhaps destroyed, the once monolithically proud denomination. Southern Baptist congregations have been ripped apart, various ministers have been exiled from their churches, and new or changed church membership allegiances are required from members. In the 1980s, while Wall Street was obsessed with mergers and conglomerates, loyalists vigorously pursued a series of hostile takeovers of seminaries, boards, and agencies from the moderates.

The purges of uncooperative, disloyal, or dissenting adherents from their church posts have been, and continue to be, common in the 1990s. Consequently, ordinary Southern Baptists in the pew are faced with new and sometimes harsh choices. Fundamentally at stake in this conflict are the loyalties of millions of members (and potential members), the overwhelming number of whom live in the South.

The denominational leadership has articulated an exclusivist rhetorical system designed to reshape the denomination in at least three ways. First, in its official communications, the leadership consistently projects a conformist, doctrinaire, and gender-explicit leadership model to its membership. Regardless of the rhetorical clarity of its messages, the leadership constantly demands that adherents should obey its dictates. Second, the deviation of individual, church, and agency membership from the conformist standards of denominational exclusivity may be penalized by the leadership autocracy. Finally, leadership rhetoric stresses that female adherents must be submissive or they will suffer pulpit dismissal, membership exile, or intimidation for their waywardness.[1]

The male hierarchy has attempted to develop a unified communication system for two purposes: to promote its message of exclusivity to gain new adherents and to promote the excision of those who disagree with their ideological objectives. Such actions are desirable to the denominational hierarchy because they both legitimize the leadership's description of the reclaimed denomination as "more pure" and validate the hierarchy's claim that it has a newly reconstructed, if not more obedient, organizational church structure.

These goals reaffirm the denomination's non-romantic quest to regain its lost role as the South's most preeminent and influential Christian denomination. To promote its goals, major SBC preacher-officers rely on interpersonal, electronic, print, and especially church pulpit communication to attract and retain members. Historically, these communication choices have been reliable and effective for Southern Baptists in securing converts. Loyalist SBC leaders will likely continue to use these approaches because they have the money and appropriate means to do so.

The SBC is not an easy denomination to understand. The tone of their official communications seems rough, causing some to view the denomination as culturally backwards, which in turn suggests why the group is often overlooked for serious study. For example, recent Messenger, or delegate, resolutions passed at the annual meetings have been severe, if not pitiless.[2] The SBC has voted to boycott the vast Walt Disney empire, to reject homosexuals, and to embrace a special evangelistic focus towards Jews as outside the redemptive work of God. Further, Mormons have been decreed to be non-Christians. The unsympathetic nature of these resolutions has not been counterbalanced by the recent official denominational apology regarding slavery.

Major SBC decisions in 1996 and 1997 have moved nonmembers to make sometimes harsh comments. The group has been satirized in newspaper cartoons, on talk shows, and on Internet joke lines. For example, one late-night talk show host recently produced his list of the top ten characteristics of Southern Baptists, all of which were unflattering. A list of the top seventeen effects of the SBC Disney boycott recently appeared on the Internet, and number five read: "Baptists now must visit Disney World in the same disguise they wear to the local liquor store." Then there was the email from a (non-Baptist) colleague at another university: "Hey, I heard that Disney just allowed the SBC to open up a new entertainment exhibit entitled 'Its a Small, Small Mind.'" The *Dallas Morning News* on June 19, 1996, devoted an entire satirical column to the Disney boycott decision:

> Now Disney has really gone off the deep end. Welcoming homosexshuls into their parks just like they was normal! Well, you won't find any more good Babatists goin' to their little fairyland. And then there's that other group we got singled out for salvation. Them Jews. I'll tell you, there's nothing that makes my blood boil quicker than to hear some smart-aleck say, "But Jesus was a Jew."[3]

Members of the denomination seem to disregard popular responses to its thinking. Rev. Tim Wilkins, a Messenger to the 1997 annual meeting, produced a successful resolution to establish a denominational ministry focused on the conversion of homosexuals into heterosexuals. This could be accomplished, he alleged, if the SBC actively endorsed programs focused on that objective. This "transformational" ministry was necessary, he argued, because the "church has been quick to condemn gays . . . but it has been extremely resistant to recognize it has an obligation to reach out and guide the homosexual toward heterosexuality."[4]

The alleged quality and value of this ministry notwithstanding, critics might well raise serious questions about the objective of the effort. Must the gift of salvation only be extended to heterosexuals? Is the ministry really focused on the objective of salvation, or is the formation of this ministry actually an attempt to satisfy the outcry of those loyalists who fully endorse the punishing spirit and law of Leviticus as a guide to appropriate human behavior?

A different perspective is also appropriate to consider. According to Rev. W. Wayne Lindsey, the "transformational" ministry is unnecessary. "I believe we are created in the image of God . . . why would God heal us of that?"[5] Lindsey's comment is instructive, for God's creations include the homosexual and the heterosexual. Furthermore, is it necessary for the human being to be heterosexual to enter the kingdom of heaven? Lindsey's concerns raise additional doubts regarding the nature or existence of Biblical proof text justifying salvation only for the heterosexual. The controversy is clear: "transformational" ministers argue that heterosexuality is a necessary criterion for salvation, while opponents argue that there is no place in the Bible that indicates you must be "straight" to be a Christian.

Although the secular press often notes that Messenger resolutions at the annual SBC meetings are not binding on the local Southern Baptist church, such an assertion is meaningless because the resolutions are still influential. Through the use of denigrative language, these resolutions justify new policies designed to intimidate the offending person, policy, or institution. Defunding and disassociation actions have been taken against denominational agencies, commissions, and organizations deemed unworthy, including the denial of personnel appointments (or reappointments) to various denominational positions of importance. The coterie of top sermonizer-leaders in Nashville preach favorably about these decisions. Their preaching might have established a rhetorical climate that favored open debate and discussion. Unfortunately, the deliberative climate today is fundamentally repressive, for it neither allows for nor encourages dissent among or within member churches.

Viewed another way, asserting that the annual Messenger resolutions are uninfluential on the policies of the local church is akin to the notion that the local Southern Baptist pulpit is no longer a central part of the denomination. No serious student of Southern Baptist discourse would defend such a wild assertion.

It is also true that the SBC is an enduring group of millions of members. They have been a denomination since 1845, which bypasses any need to argue about the longevity of their existence. They continue to grow in numbers, even as other Christian denominations decline in membership. That Southern Baptists were organized because of their affinity for slavery is dismaying, yet other white Southerners of that period would have been shocked if the denomination had done anything else. It may be paltry, and much too late, but at least this denomination has officially apologized for its previous endorsement of slavery.

Southern Baptists may be ignored by many, yet they believe that they are the moral backbone of the South. Through their sermons, publications, resolutions, and evangelism of others, the SBC appears to focus on matters of ethical permanence, virtue, and Biblical morality. This denomination argues for television and movie decency, prayer in the public schools, and the cleansing of the welfare rolls to eliminate fraud and waste. It also argues against a woman's right to an abortion, women as preachers, and homosexuality. The denomination's need for a pronounced and clear moral position in today's climate of public and private immorality has propelled Southern Baptist leaders to use their pulpits to influence others. Their messages provide the data for this study.

As critics, we have explored three SBC leadership rhetorics that have been used for the purpose of solidifying the organization's membership.

The first is the rhetoric of *fundamentalism*, which centers on three principles: Jesus Christ is the only Son of God; all believers are priests with direct access to God (although since 1988, the SBC has definitively revised this point by resolutions from the annual conventions of Messengers); and the Bible is Spirit-breathed—that is, its origin is directly from God, and humans were involved in the formation of the Bible only as inspired by the Holy Spirit. Dissident observers of Southern Baptists might well contend that these points closely resemble a rhetoric of historic Baptist conviction. Nevertheless, denominational loyalists seem to have supercharged such rhetoric with a harsh Leviticus-like edge, seeming to disallow individual believers a diversity of conscience.

The second is the rhetoric of *inerrancy*, which also centers on three principles: the inerrant Word is absolutely true, inerrant, and pure in all of its claims regarding all matters of faith, history, culture, and science; inerrancy is presentational because it emanates from the dynamics of the sermonizer in the pulpit; and inerrancy is centered on the argument from genus. By definition, there is no higher form of argument in Christendom than to claim that the Bible is literally and completely accurate.

The third type of rhetoric, the rhetoric of *exclusion*, is driven by various argument strategies developed in Southern Baptist Convention leadership discourses. Specifically, from our analysis of post-1979 presidential convention sermons, denominational decrees and resolutions, and other appropriate rhetorical artifacts, we have evaluated several key topoi that involve the use of attack, exposition, and expulsion; fear and comfort; and abominational language, which has typically focused on the themes of blame and accusation.

Current Southern Baptist loyalist leadership rhetoric springs from a focused inventional root: the demand that the denomination's membership must return to a purer Christianity, perhaps to the time of Christ itself. Not surprisingly, moderate Baptist rhetoric arises from the same inventional system. The difference between the two, however, is in their application of logos. Loyalists are intensely exclusionist in their emphasis on absolutism; dissenters are inclined to be much more inclusive about the role of reason and example. How this logos is expressed in loyalist rhetoric is the province of this investigation. Understandably then, this book has a much wider focus than describing another denominational schism, even if a major one.

The pulpit is the crucial focal point in this struggle to win the loyalty of Southern Baptist believers; indeed, the pulpit has always been at the center of this denomination since its founding in 1845. Perhaps one way of understanding the sermon as a significant matter of Baptist faith and practice is to explain it by looking back at the seventeenth-century sermon, especially in New England. According to Harry S. Stout, author of the definitive work on colonial preaching, *The New England Soul: Preaching and Religious Culture in Colonial New England*, the average churchgoer in colonial New England heard two, perhaps three sermons a week.

Based upon his analysis of unprinted and printed sermons, Stout calculated that these hardy souls endured "seven thousand sermons in a lifetime." Stout argues that "[u]nlike modern mass media, the sermon stood alone in local New England contexts as the only regular (at least weekly) medium of public communication."[6] Understandably, then, the sermon was the central source of influence in the life of a community, helping to distribute news, promote cultural values, define political purposes and, eventually, shape a national identity.

Stout's statistics about the New England sermon are revealing. A consideration of the quantity of Southern Baptist sermons heard by members today might be as rewarding. We calculate that we have listened to approximately four thousand sermons each since becoming Baptists, using the figure of one-and-a-half sermons a week as a base. Since Stout reckoned his statistics regarding each believer from birth, our statistics are conservative, especially if one considers that other Southern Baptists may attend church more often than we do.

Southern Baptists today accurately contend that the sermon is no less important to their lives, whether in church, in an outdoor stadium rally with Billy Graham or another evangelist, on the radio, or on television or videotape. Sermonizers of yesterday and today remain a highly successful source of public communication for more than exhortatory purposes. Whereas Roger Williams of Salem in 1634 called his congregation together to fight off the predatory politics of the Massachusetts Bay oligarchy, today's SBC president preaches against the liberalism of the Clinton administration's "don't ask, don't tell" decree regarding the American military. Dissidents and loyalists alike would argue together that the pulpit in Baptist life has power and influence over individuals, churches, and our culture at large.

The electronic media is omnipresent in American society. The best estimates are that by the age of seventy-five, Americans will have watched thirteen years of television. Considering the necessity for an interactive relationship between preacher and listener, and the mediated or unmediated reality of today's sermon, it is amazing that the sermon endures. Although there are other competitive sources of religious communication, Southern Baptists would nevertheless revolt en masse if the sermon were removed from the Sunday morning and evening service.

Just as reading the Sunday morning church bulletin is helpful when visiting a new church service, it is important to be able to identify the sermonizers and players in this situation. The act of naming in our language is essential to our existence, and the groups of members involved here are known by words that serve as defining identification badges. Denominational loyalists prefer the label *conservative*, but their critics have often described them as *fundamentalists*. Denominational dissidents prefer the label *moderate*, but their adversaries call them *liberals*. We have selected the labels *loyalist* and *dissident* to describe the rhetoric of these two groups because these terms are less polemical. Nevertheless, these two descriptors are in conflict with each other, for they are often regarded as opposite in meaning. It is intriguing that these labels would have been reversed before 1979, since the loyalists then in power were effectively thrown out by those dissenters who desired a total change of the denomination.

Words are important for they help shape our lives, and the clash we seek to describe is being fought with words. They emanate from the Executive Committee in Nashville, they are reinforced by resolution in the annual conventions, and they are interpreted and pronounced from the loyalist pulpit. The preached word has power because it is incorporated into an ideology of inerrancy developed from the Bible; the ultimate proof text of fundamentalism and inerrancy is the principal theme of SBC pulpit leadership rhetoric. Adherence to inerrancy is the newly prescribed litmus test for believers, and those unable to pass the test face exclusion or ostracism.

The denomination is a failed communication system. It does not encourage an open and free communication atmosphere that induces problem solving, encourages spirited dissent within its national annual meetings of Messengers, uses pulpit communication as a strategy to diminish the rifts among its followers, or offers adherents the option to adopt varying choices in their theological beliefs and yet remain within the denomination. Pulpit positions of authority are held solely by men, and the denominational leadership is exclusively male as well. In sum, we have concluded that much of the public communication of the denominational leadership is divisive, perhaps even coercive.

The philosophies of Richard Weaver and Kenneth Burke have been helpful to our analysis. As students of Weaver and Burke understand it, human language is not neutral or objective, for all language among humans is "sermonic." As Weaver describes it, "We are caught up in a great web of inter-communication and inter-influence."[7] Accordingly, sermons (whether private or public) are not merely a liturgical tradition, but a persuasive act, designed to influence hearers in some manner. We agree with Kenneth Burke that all rhetoric expresses more than intent. However, intent is appropriate for analysis in this communication crisis. Intent is an important part of the persuasive act, which necessarily requires the inclusion of ethical responsibility.

Further, Wayne Thompson, the author of *Responsible and Effective Communication*, has provided two helpful statements for our study. First, "communicators should serve the welfare of the immediate listeners and of society generally."[8] Admittedly, the rhetorical nature of this exclusionary effort is complex and controversial. Nevertheless, it is minimally reasonable to expect that those in positions of power must "serve the welfare" of others before themselves.

Second, communicators have "an ethical obligation to bring out the best in fellow participants."[9] Arguably, it is not always clear for rhetors to know how to "bring out the best" in others. At the very least, however, the language of victimage—which casts aspersions, denigrates abilities, and resorts to vindictive name-calling—does *not* accomplish Thompson's second point. When rhetors fail these two tests, it is appropriate for critics to point this out.

As for our own church affiliation, we have never been anything else but Baptists. We have lived, worked, and churched in Mississippi, North Carolina, Kentucky, Georgia, Arkansas, and Texas. We have over sixty years of combined Southern Baptist membership between us, and we have served in capacities from Sunday School teacher to chair of deacons in our local churches. We have preached from Southern Baptist pulpits, and we write as actively interested laypersons, even if moved to disbelief and sadness about Southern Baptist events since the 1979 takeover. Our journey as followers and critics of the denomination has been a long and sorrowful one, and we have found that pain and objectivity are difficult soul mates.

Both of us remain influenced by the word spoken from a Baptist pulpit. Our respect and admiration for the place of that pulpit in our lives impels us to evaluate the persuasive strategies and ethical dimensions of the new SBC pulpit leadership rhetoric. As critics, we are of the Roger Williams tradition, which holds that Baptists must be free from pulpit dictates and decrees. We are both freed or trapped by the conviction that the oral tradition is irrevocable. Nevertheless, the pulpit is at the center of Baptist life, and that tradition has helped us define our notion of church and the importance of our personal religious faith.

Now, there are new oral traditions. In the pulpit, denominational leaders require unswerving member obedience to the canon of inerrancy. In worship practice, some key pulpiteers have become actors on the church television stage. For them, and their followers, the most sacred moments in the most sacred of all locations have been converted into a soul-warming, show time extravaganza. The language of exclusion has replaced the language of evangelism. As critics of communication ethics, as rhetorical historians, and as Southern Baptists, we note that these are dramatic and discomforting changes, and they need evaluation.

Arguments and analysis require supporting evidence. Consequently, we have investigated the addresses and convention sermons of the annual meetings of the Southern Baptist Convention (1979–94). We have used videotapes and printed sermon texts of these discourses, resolutions passed by the Messengers at the national meetings, written correspondence, and previously unpublished rhetorical artifacts to complete this study. We have also assessed material from denominational newspapers, letters to and from various key sermonizers, and local church documents and minutes. Some of our research activities have been admittedly personal, such as attending various associational, state, and national meetings as observers and decision makers. We have also worked with various denominational leaders to develop a balanced understanding of the controversies evaluated in this book.

Dr. Kenneth Chafin, formerly Billy Graham Professor of Evangelism and Carl Bates Professor of Preaching at Southwestern Baptist Theological Seminary at Fort Worth, Texas, has written the foreword to the book. Because of his distinguished relationship with the major rhetors of the denomination over the last forty years, Chafin is a fully qualified observer. Unfortunately, he is now in exile from the Nashville pulpit leadership group since he was rejected by them because of his theological and homiletical waywardness.

As pastor, seminarian, theologian, writer, and historical witness to the takeover, Chafin provides a candid commentary. His bitterness about the schism in the SBC is tinged by his keen understanding of the rhetorical strengths of the loyalist leaders. Consequently, he explains how and why the loyalist faction was successful.

We begin our study with a special narrative that should be read aloud to understand the tone of the oral tradition so prominently known within the denomination. Since it is this oral tradition that distinguishes the pulpit, the church, and the culture of being Southern Baptist, chapter 1 will focus on the spiritual center of the denomination: the preacher and the pulpit.

Since 1845, Southern Baptists have celebrated the mysteries of the spoken word from the pulpit. In the last twenty years, the denomination has returned to an energetic and dynamic message from gifted and persuasive preachers. Today, the preached word about an infallible inerrant Word is the defining characteristic of the *new* Southern Baptist Convention.

1

Goin' to Church in Dixie

Do this in remembrance of me.

—I Corinthians 11:24

It is hazy and lazy on this sunny August Sabbath in Daycross, Georgia. Around the area there are thirty-five Southern Baptist churches, which by almost anybody's reckoning indicates that Baptists are the majority denomination. Today the churches are open, and the business of doing church is plainly evident: custodians, Sunday School teachers, and deacons have risen early to unlock doors, start air conditioners, turn on lights, check the bathrooms, post weekly activity notices on the hallway bulletin board, and generally prepare the Lord's House for the worship services of the day and evening.

In homes scattered throughout the area, church members have begun to stir on this Sunday morning. Breakfasts, avoided by the young, are enjoyed by their elders over coffee, cereal, juice, grits, eggs, bacon, and maybe a Sunday paper. However, everyone seems to know the objective of the morning: up and away to attend church. Along with the morning sunshine that suggests another hot day is coming, cars of all vintages meander on to worship services.

First Baptist Church in Daycross is typical of many Baptist churches in the South. The pillars are white, the stained-glass windows appear clean, and the zoysia grass has that cared-for look. The church is an old landmark in the community, resting easily in the center of downtown, although it seems to be sitting on the corner of yesterday, now bypassed by attractive, modern megachurches in Atlanta.

Sunday School is a quick activity, over before a meaningful lecture from the Bible can be properly concluded, and certainly before all the gossip and news can be carefully exchanged. Youngsters in their finest scurry down the long hallway into the cavernous sanctuary meant to hold many more than would be present today. Adults mingle in the lobby or recreation hall, while some are outside finishing a cigarette, and they soon follow the stragglers to the worship hour.

Southern Baptist families are regular in their tithe-giving and predictable in their search for their favorite and cherished location in the sanctuary. Baptists have never *purchased* their pews, of course, but most feel they *own* them because they have occupied them for so long. For them, their seats are as choice as those at a high school football game—better, for these are cushioned. The Ruth Sunday School class is seated to the left of the pulpit; the senior men's class to the right. In between those two are groups of young people, mostly near the back, of course, with the singles and younger couples sitting closer to the front. Some families always sit together, and they are the backbone of the church. At the very rear of the church, there are some new parents whose children daily prove that their human physiology requires the nearest and quickest exit to the restrooms in back of the sanctuary.

For several days, the pastor has been in his study at home, and in the tiny church library, gnawing away at scripture, pulling stories together, outlining key points, and rewriting the introduction and the conclusion to bring home the presentation of God's words for the congregation. The preparation is not easy, and as he works, he thinks of the needs and problems of his membership. They are his personal flock, not a corporate entity, and he must adapt his sermon to them. He speaks *with* them from the pulpit, not *at* them, because he is fully aware that the continuation of his ministry rests finally on his persuasive abilities when communicating with his congregation.

On Sunday morning, he has only twenty-five minutes to speak, for these days parishioners become very uncomfortable with anything longer. His sermon must be a dialogue that creates new ideas from the Holy Scripture, and it must be applicable to the "wicked" world. At times, he must spur his listeners on to new personal goals or remind them of their obligation to church and denomination. His delivery from the pulpit must be dynamic, not just loud enough so that all can hear. It must change to fit the power of his words and yet be pleasing to the ear. Effective preaching is, and has always been, a difficult task.

In this church, the gasps and breathlessness of mountain-style preaching would be out-of-place. At First Baptist, the old style of strident hell-fearing and fist-pounding is gone, save for the occasional revival speaker or annual summer encampment where speaking of this type is expected, or at least tolerated. Here, there will be no tirade. Instead, the pastor has adroitly moved through the Scriptures with skill, proving and reproving that this Book in his left hand is literally true from red-bound cover to red-bound cover. Today, listeners shall fully understand that there is no doubt at all in the inerrancy of the Holy Word. There never has been.

At the end of the sermon, a pulpit call is issued. No Baptist service worth anything has ever concluded without a pulpit call, and this one is no exception. Personal decision making is now the objective. While some walk down the aisle—an aisle that frequently seems very long—to ask for inclusion in the brotherhood of church membership, still others walk away with a quiet, personal resolve to live a corrected life in His sight. This ritual and reality of decision making is *the* defining moment in a minister's career, wherein the congregation's awareness of its oneness in Christ and his Holy Word has been realized.

At the end of this service, members amble out, some shaking hands with new members or old friends they haven't seen since vacation. As they leave, they engage in the time-honored custom of the handshake with the pastor. Some will praise him, some will say nothing, and still others will indicate they want to chat with him in the upcoming week. Together and separately, this congregation disperses, many not to be seen again until the Wednesday night prayer meeting or choir practice.

First Baptist Church, like thousands of other Southern Baptist churches, has participated in the noblest act of God's children—to speak and listen to the Word, in spirit and in truth. For many, that spoken Word has been inerrant, the Bible true in all things. The Word has been preached, although perhaps more about its nature than about its Author.

In Sundays to come, the pastor will brook the unnerving subjects of a woman's place in church leadership and in the pulpit. Not since Sherman paid an unwelcome visit to Atlanta has such an issue aroused such fervor. Added to the concern over women as church leaders is the uncertainty of a threatening and poorly understood contemporary culture of dual-career marriages, single-parent families, and the stress of the ever-changing work place. Loyalty to a company through years of work is not worth much these days. There are new requirements and standards in which to believe and by which to live, and they seem to promote family instability.

The First Baptist Church is a participating member of Southern Baptist Convention organizations, for it has long been a member of the local association, and it has sent its full quota of Messengers to state and national meetings. The pastor's sermon is a reflection of organizational loyalty, and some this particular Sunday morning are a bit disturbed by that. Nevertheless, the majority of those who listened to the sermon were warmed by the appeals to live by the Bible and the strength of the pastor's plain, Puritan language style.

The congregation has begun to understand the pastor's new role as arbiter and interpreter of biblical meanings. The Southern Baptist Convention decreed such a role, and those in the sanctuary now seem to expect him to weigh the verses for nuance, meaning, and metaphor. The pastor is the authority regarding God's breathed message in the Holy Scriptures.

He exercises that authority legitimately, for it has been mandated by resolution from the Convention.

After the service, the congregation files out into the noon air in a manner reflecting a reinvigorated relationship with the Almighty. As the members leave, the words of the pastor remain on the minds of many, and the sermon will be discussed at the local restaurant or family gathering over apple pie and ice cream. Some may discuss a particular phrase, the call to live a renewed life, or the active delivery of the sermon. For those who needed a word from the Lord's interpreter, the pastor's message has been helpful. For others, their hearts were nurtured and fed.

In the evening, the pastor might speak on more earthly crises to the faithful few who have returned: the issues of drugs, crime, and the need to restore the family to its sanctified place in yesteryear. In this pulpit, as in thousands of others, Southern Baptists revere the spoken word as much more than just a part of a respected oral tradition. This oral tradition fills an expected, but necessary need. For most Southern Baptists, church could not be church without the dynamic spoken word from the pulpit. The Baptist churchgoer has always shared a bond with the skilled and hard-driving sermon artist. After all, we were raised in this heritage. History, like ties of blood, is hard to break. The pastor has spoken, and many Southern Baptist congregations wouldn't have it any other way.

2

Uncertain Times: Trouble in Zion

God does not err
The Bible is God's Word
The Bible does not err.

—Evangelist James Robison

The pastor of the imaginary First Baptist Church, Daycross, Georgia, is only one of approximately 36,000 Southern Baptist pastors who spin scriptures and life stories into the spoken word every Sunday morning. The pulpit is clearly the source of power where the most human of the public arts—holy speech—is coproduced by congregation and pastor alike. Nowhere are there more real issues discussed and human emotions unraveled for God's forgiveness than on Sunday, when Southern Baptist pastors preach the Word.

Persuaders all, pastors are leaders in community affairs. But, they are also more than that. They are the arbiters of the Bible's message for people in need of renewal and forgiveness. As the conduit through which God speaks, pastors are more than just spokesmen; they are the source of Divine ideas.

For all of them, "In the beginning, God created . . . "[1] marks the opening stanza of Holy Scripture and the establishment of the absolute authority of God who inspired its writers and the infallible nature of their expressions. Denominations have risen and fallen over the issue of how to interpret the Bible: what it means, which passages are more important for church and personal piety, and even which denomination has the correct analysis of which church is "the church."

Across the centuries, American Protestantism has witnessed the development of several denominations that heralded the second coming of Christ and called men and women to a personal belief in a personal Lord. None have been more denominationally conscious and organizationally committed to evangelizing to a lost world than Southern Baptists.

From the brush arbors of its country churches in west Texas to the divided chancels of a major downtown church in metropolitan Charlotte, North Carolina, the Southern Baptist Convention (SBC) has established a denomination that is one of the largest and most influential church groups in the country. The history of Southern Baptists in the twentieth century is marked by the consistent growth of new churches, new "born-again" Christians, new home and foreign missions personnel, enhanced financial resources, and grand schemes for the coming century. In the same breath, however, the best laid plans of man and God have fallen on hard times.

Southern Baptists are in the struggle of their collective lives for the hearts and souls of the denomination. The national press has had a field day for twenty years as brethren have fought with brethren over an earth-shattering and life-changing issue—"What is the Bible?" From west Texas churches to the congregations of Georgia and Florida, this one question dominates the discussion of loyalists versus dissidents in the Southern Baptist Convention.

Who are these people called Southern Baptists, and why all this fuss over the Bible? A review of some statistics provides a partial answer. The SBC is a world-wide organization of over 37,400 churches and nearly sixteen million members, which includes a home and foreign mission service organization as well as a rich tradition of organizational loyalty. Since 1845, Southern Baptists have coalesced into strong local churches, area organizations, and state and national conventions, with a surprising unity of purpose.

Southern Baptists have developed from four divisions that once existed in the South and that currently mark the Convention in the 1990s. These four traditions are the Charleston tradition, the Sandy Creek tradition, the Georgia tradition, and the Landmark tradition. We have summarized Walter Shurden's remarks on these traditions as follows.

The Charleston tradition. According to Shurden, the First Baptist Church, Charleston, South Carolina, established a distinctively Calvinistic motif to worship and service. Those of the Charleston tradition were concerned with orderly worship, the value of baptism, the Lord's Supper, and personal piety and ethics. Committed to education, they founded Furman University, Wake Forest University, the University of Richmond, and the denomination's first seminary, the Southern Baptist Theological Seminary in Louisville. Many of the preachers were well educated and evangelistic in Reformed theology.

The Sandy Creek tradition. Shurden states that these separate Baptists came into the South riding the crest of the wave of the first Great Awakening. Under the leadership of Shubal Stearns and Daniel Marshall, a group of separate Baptists formed the Sandy Creek Baptist Church, Sandy Creek, North Carolina. Shurden states that these Baptists were characterized by spontaneity, enthusiasm, dramatic preaching, and spirited singing. Fearing too much education, jealous of congregational autonomy, and guardians of their own souls, these separate Baptists spread into Kentucky, Tennessee, Arkansas, Louisiana, and Texas. As the rhetorical analyses of the controversy in the Southern Baptist Convention unfold, the theological history of the Sandy Creek tradition represents the deep wellsprings of rhetorical battles over inerrancy and fundamentalism.

The Georgia tradition. Shurden holds that the third source of Southern Baptist history is the Georgia tradition. Located in Augusta and Atlanta, the Georgia tradition supported Southern sectionalism, a centralized form of denominational organization, and a concentrated missionary effort in Atlanta.

The Landmark tradition. Shurden has marked the fourth tradition as the Landmark tradition. Starting in the 1850s in Tennessee and Kentucky, Landmarkists took their name from Proverbs 22:28, "Remove not the ancient landmark, which thy Fathers have set." This group sought to purify the Convention regarding the church, baptism, the Lord's Supper, and salvation. With a sense of being the true church, Landmark Baptists alone kept the true ordinances. Anyone receiving baptism in a non-Landmark Baptist church was required to be baptized again. Moreover, the Lord's Supper could be received only by a specific congregation, a specific church family.[2]

William Leonard, a scholar of the Southern Baptists, argues that, for the Landmarkists, local churches alone constituted the true church of Christ. They suggested that a line of Baptist churches existed throughout Christian history, preserving the true New Testament doctrines. In a sense, the term "Landmarkism" was a kind of history "in the neighborhood of make-believe," constructed as a means of verifying Baptist doctrine, defining Baptist ecclesiology, and maintaining Baptist identity in competition with other religious groups. Landmarkists took great liberties with historical materials in their effort to establish their primitive credentials. The efforts of Landmarkists to impose their theology on the entire Convention led the SBC to the brink of schism on several occasions.[3]

Beyond these four traditions, which help explain the diverse strains of a people and its beliefs, there are two additional points that help us understand Southern Baptists of the 1990s. Leonard cites John Franklin Loftis's doctoral dissertation as he discusses "the evangelical denominational tradition" and what Baptist historian Leon McBeth calls the "Texas Baptist tradition."[4]

The evangelical denominational tradition featured a conservative theology and a Southern Baptist way of behaving. The Texas Baptist tradition began in the early twentieth century under the leadership of B. H. Carroll. With a state as big as "all outdoors," early Texas Baptists took on a siege mentality and a conservative theology to win Texas for the Lord.

Do Southern Baptists have any theological consensus in spite of their various traditions? Leonard asserts that there are four theological standards that best characterize Southern Baptists:

> 1. "The sacred scriptures are the sole norm for faith and practice." The Bible is the authoritative guide for faith and order in the church and in the life of the individual.
>
> 2. "The New Testament church composed of baptized believers." Each individual is called to a personal faith in Christ as a prerequisite to baptism and church membership. Baptism and the Lord's Supper are "ordinances" of the church.
>
> 3. "The priesthood of the believer and the autonomy of the local congregation." All Christians have direct access to God through Jesus Christ. Each local church governs itself under the authority of Christ. Laity and clergy cooperate together.
>
> 4. "The principle of religious liberty and the separation of church and state." Each person is responsible to God for religious choices and commitments. The state cannot compel faith from any individual.[5]

With a variety of cultural traditions, folkways, and mores, Southern Baptists developed churches and converted sinners to a Christian and a denomination's view of church and fundamentalism. Sociologist Nancy Ammerman argues that "fundamentalism began as traditionalists who perceived some challenge to their core identity, both social and personal."[6] Providing a harbor for worship and a certain belief in the Bible became a battle cry for Southern Baptists as the fundamentalist/modernist debate began heating up in the 1920s.

Central to any denomination or religious entity is the statement of their goals, visions, and positions of faith and testament. The SBC's 1925 *The Baptist Faith and Message* was a response to the various "traditions" arguing with one another over a "fundamental vs. modern" understanding of the Bible. A major revision of the statement came in 1963 after the furor caused by Ralph Elliott's 1961 *The Message of Genesis*. In the book, Elliott argued that Genesis chapters 1–11 were symbolic rather than literal, an argument that runs counter to Article 1 of *The Baptist Faith and Message*, which states that "Holy Scripture is without mixture of error for its matter." Elliott's book galvanized the loyalists in their insistence on a focused adherence to the doctrine of inerrancy, which asserts that every word of Scripture is without error in all matters.

Interestingly enough, the historical-critical method of research, long revered in the humanities, served as the tool of biblical analysis for Ralph Elliott's moderate analysis, as well as for G. Henton Davies' conservative analysis in the 1969 *Broadman Bible Commentary*. The Messengers at the SBC's 1970 annual meeting voted to recall Elliott's book and have it rewritten because it disagreed with Davies' analysis. Southern Baptist seminary professor Clyde Francisco was asked to rewrite the work even though he showed a preference for the historical-critical method as well. Leonard stated that the Convention let the matter of whether a moderate or conservative interpretation using the historical-critical method was the best approach to take because, according to Shurden, "denominational unity is more important to Southern Baptists than theological arguments about the Bible."[7] But, holding the Convention together at the expense of an inerrant Bible and bedrock truths was too much for the loyalists.

The value-rich truth for loyalists of both the Sandy Creek and the Texas traditions is a singular belief in the "truth of Scripture." These loyalists would have the Southern Baptist family offer to its people a purity of life and experience in a modern, humanistic culture.[8] However, the rhetorical truth for the loyalists is that the Convention is infected with the cancer of liberalism, which threatens the body of Christ and the Southern Baptist Convention itself.

Throughout the 1970s, loyalists forced the issue in their attack of liberals and liberalism in the Convention. The historical-critical method and those educators who used it drew special attention. In particular, Harold Lindsell's 1979 *The Bible in the Balance* and an earlier work written in 1976, *The Battle for the Bible*, developed a careful dialectic on inerrancy, noting that the institutions of both the inerrantist and the noninerrantist were filled with false doctrines and teachers.[9] A religious denomination rides the back of its pulpit-orators who, with passion and pronouncements, can carry a congregation, and, in this case, a convention to new heights. So it was, and so it remains, for the loyalists.

In Southern Baptist Convention life, the Pastor's Conference is the rhetorical "Beulah land" of a pastor's trip to the annual convention. Dressed in their best suits, pastors of all types get to watch their most skilled spokesmen teach them for an entire day or more prior to the annual meeting.[10] By 1977, the Pastor's Conference was a powerful forum for major figures like Dr. W. A. Criswell, First Church, Dallas, Texas, and Dr. Adrian Rogers, Bellevue Baptist Church, Memphis, Tennessee, to rail away at the "liberals among us."[11] The agendas for change were developing along theological and political lines as these men, especially Criswell, assailed the "false" men of the liberal persuasion. It was a Criswell-led vendetta that lashed out with the San Antonio, Texas, 1988 SBC convention's second "signal flare" sermon of the earliest hours of the controversy, "The Infallible Word of God."

In the sermon, Criswell argued at length about an errorless Bible, dazzling the pastors in attendance while providing each man with a new series of examples and stories that they could use in their home church for Sundays to come. At the conclusion of "The Infallible Word of God," Criswell intoned:

> From the beginning to ending there is not a word or a syllable or a revelation in the Word of God that has contradicted or ever will contradict any sure, substantiated scientific fact. The reason is very simply. The Lord God who inspired the Book is the Lord God who made these things from the beginning. That is why when the Lord speaks through His servants, you can base your life and your soul and your salvation on what God has said.

There is not a more familiar story in the annals of literature than the story that describes the death of the immortal Scot poet and novelist, Sir Walter Scott. As he lay dying he turned to his son-in-law, Lockhart, and said to him, "Son, bring me the Book." There was a vast library in Walter Scott's home and, bewildered, the son-in-law said, "Sir, what book? Which book?" The dying bard replied. "My son, there is just one Book. Bring me the Book." It was then that Lockhart went to the library and brought to Sir Walter Scott the Bible.

> "There's just one Book," cried the dying sage,
> "Read me the old, old story."
> And the winged words that can never age
> Wafted him home to Glory.
> There's just one Book.
> There's just one Book for the tender years,
> One Book alone for guiding
> The little feet through the joys and fears,
> The unknown days are hiding.
> There's just one Book.
> There's just one Book for the bridal hour,
> One Book of love's own coining;
> Its truths alone lend beauty and power,
> To vows that lives are joining,
> There's just one Book.
> There's just one Book for life' gladness,
> One Book for the toilsome days,
> One Book that can cure life's madness,
> One Book that can voice life's praise,
> There's just one Book.
> There's just one Book for the dying,
> One Book for the starting tears,
> And one for the soul that is going home,

For the measureless years,
There's just one Book.

—Anonymous

"For the prophecy came not . . . by the will of man; but holy men of God spake as they were moved by the Holy Ghost" (11 Peter 1:21). And this is the inerrant, infallible, holy, eternal Word of the living God. "The grass withereth, the flower fadeth; but the Word of our God shall stand forever" (Isaiah 40:8). "Heaven and earth will pass away, but my word will not pass away" (Mark 13:31). "For ever, O Lord, thy word is firmly fixed in the heavens" (Psalm 119:89, RSV). Oh, what a blessedness, what a holiness, what a foundation, eternal and immovable, is the living word of the living God! "And his name is called The Word of God" (Revelation 19:13).[12]

The pastors returned home to preach with renewed vigor, armed with a full awareness of the enemy in their midst, to fight with the sword of God and the shield of faith to ward off the liberal strain in the Southern Baptist Convention.

We're Marching on to Zion

While waving the banner of the cross, a persuasively gifted host of preachers went about condemning seminary professors and other wrong-thinking Southern Baptists. Leading them was the loyalist-driven Pastor's Conference, the first phalanx in the rhetorical war against liberalism. Speaker after speaker paraded before the 1977–79 Pastor's Conferences extolling the virtues of inerrancy across the Convention. These men spoke with passion and skill about the classic tenets of fundamentalism—an inerrant Bible, Christ's virgin birth, substitutionary atonement, the premillenial second coming, the belief that Adam and Eve were the first two human beings on earth, and the belief that Satan is a distinct, personal being. While all of these Pastor's Conferences found willing hearts and minds at the national conclaves each June, a grassroots political master plan was well underway to assure a victory in the presidential election at the 1979 SBC convention in Houston, Texas.

Paul Pressler, a Houston Appeals Court judge, and Paige Patterson, the president of the Criswell Center and Criswell College, teamed up to develop a year-long plan to travel the main streets and back roads of the Convention states in order to win the support of fellow Baptists. Their plan was to ensure the election of a series of SBC presidents who would redirect the Convention from its liberal path. They were successful because Pressler and Patterson justified the wholesale takeover with the "argument for Genus"—the highest order of argument according to the rhetorical scholar Richard Weaver.

The rhetorical high ground of the inerrantist-loyalist camp was the establishment of the Bible as inarguable and unassailable—an inerrant, perfect Word. In an imperfect world, among an imperfect people, the churches of the Convention, large or small, would be those, as argued by Adrian Rogers, who have "a pastor who believes in the inerrant, infallible Word of God."[13] Adding fire to the brimstone, Rogers quoted evangelist James Robison from Robison's sermon at the Pastor's Conference, with the appeal to cast out the "liberal rattlesnakes and termites" in the Convention.[14]

Rogers was elected on the first ballot by 51.4 percent of the vote. In a pattern that began in 1979 and continued for years to come, busloads and carloads of loyalist Messengers from churches adjacent to Dallas, Texas, poured into convention halls to vote, leaving as soon as they came. With Rogers's election, the deed was done, the agenda was set in motion, and the mission of the Pressler-Patterson plan was well underway.

The Southern Baptist Convention Presidents, 1979–1994

In succeeding years, the conservative majority elected an unbroken string of pulpit presidents to develop their agenda for the Southern Baptist Convention. They are listed in order below:

Adrian Rogers (1979), Bellevue Baptist Church, Memphis, TN (who declined an unopposed second term)

Bailey Smith (1980–81), First Baptist Church, Dell City, OK

James T. Draper (1982–83), First Baptist Church, Euliss, TX

Charles Stanley (1984–85), First Baptist Church, Atlanta, GA

Adrian Rogers (1986–87), Bellevue Baptist Church, Memphis, TN

Jerry Vines (1988–89), First Baptist Church, Jacksonville, FL

Morris Chapman (1990–91), First Baptist Church, Wichita Falls, TX

Ed Young (1992–94), Second Baptist Church, Houston, TX

From the Vines years to those of Morris Chapman, the dissenters focused their efforts and resources to counter the loyalists' army of pastors and laymen. They were led in these efforts by Dr. Daniel Vestal, who, during those years, was pastor of Dunwoody Baptist Church, Atlanta, Georgia. But their efforts were in vain, for the dissident pastors who would not join the camp of the loyalists were never able to develop a counterargument to the argument from definition. They certainly had the nerve, but never the rhetorical abilities, the passion, nor the heart to fight a war over the Bible. They were pastors, preachers, and shepherds, not soldiers or warriors in a holy cause. The war was over before it had really begun. The moderates-dissidents just did not know it.

The loyalists understood that the key to changing the national agenda for the Southern Baptist Convention was to capture the presidency, for each year the president selects the major committees, boards, trustees, and other national bodies of the Convention. The plan was to develop a decade's succession of presidents. Their leadership would ensure the full and complete takeover of the national denomination of Southern Baptists.

Elections of all kinds are known to hinge on a small percentage of the electorate located near the center. With each succeeding year after 1979, the loyalist presidents gained a slow but sure grip on the reins of power. The voting percentage of the loyalist candidates remained remarkably stable after the conservative movement emerged victorious in the 1979 annual meeting in Houston. So, too, have the dissidents' percentages.

But there has been a slight variation, and the actual percentages have oscillated back and forth from small conventions to large ones. However, the difference has been determined not by whether one side or the other "turns out to vote," but by which side controls the soft edge of what has been the yearly convention geographic area conservative voting block. Loyalists had a built-in 40–45 percent of the vote; dissidents had slightly less, 40–42 percent. The difference was not whether there were 10,000 or 100,000 Messengers but who persuaded the 8 or 10 percent in the middle. Take these years, for example:

> 1979—(15,760 Messengers). Adrian Rogers won on the first ballot, drawing 6,129 votes (51.36 percent). Five opponents drew 48.56 percent, or 4,804 votes.
>
> 1980—(13,844 Messengers). Bailey Smith won a first ballot victory, drawing 51.67 percent, or 5,739 votes against five opponents, who gained 48.38 percent, or 5,130 votes.
>
> 1981—(13,529 Messengers). Bailey Smith won a second term, drawing 6,934 votes to Abner McCall's 39.30 percent or 4,524 votes. (This was the first announced-in-advance challenge).
>
> 1982—(20,456 Messengers). James Draper and Duke McCall had a runoff, the only runoff in the presidential balloting since 1979. Draper drew 46.03 percent of the vote (8,081) on the first ballot against three other candidates, John Sullivan and Perry Sanders (both Louisiana pastors) and Duke McCall.

Sullivan got 1,625 votes (9.26 percent); Sanders got 6,124 votes (34.88 percent). In the runoff, Draper won 8,331 (56.97 percent) to McCall's 6,292 votes (43.03 percent).

1983—(13,740 Messengers). Draper reelected by acclamation.

1984—(17,101 Messengers). Charles Stanley won on the first ballot.

The inerrantists solidified their control over Convention business with each succeeding president to the present day. As noted earlier, the president names the committee on committees that, in turn, selects the Convention's boards of trustees, committee memberships, and all other Convention organizations. In due time, the loyalist agenda moved into every substructure, affirming the inerrantist agenda. The early years of the loyalist presidents were focused on biblical inerrancy and heralding the battle cry of the absolute integrity of Holy Scripture, for the authority of an error-free Bible relies on a strong pulpit-oriented rhetor figure who argues for three basic issues:

1. the conservative Christian response to social, family, and personal problems;

2. the nature of ministry—professional and personal for men only;

3. the role of women in the church as non-professional leaders and followers.

During the early years of these presidents, the rhetorical counterappeal to individual freedom served as the first line of defense and attack against the loyalists by the dissidents. Dissidents argued for the freedom of each person to decide how to interpret the Bible, the freedom of any congregation to ordain whomever they desire (male or female), and the freedom of the Southern Baptist Convention to live in harmony or disagreement.

The loyalist vision versus that of the dissident has resulted in an extraordinary battle for the hearts and minds of Southern Baptists. On the one hand, loyalists started and continued their rhetorical attacks on liberal leanings from the early 1980s to the present. On the other hand, dissidents misread the issues and missed their opportunity to rhetorically counter the loyalists in the early years.

For a variety of reasons to be examined later, the moderates failed to develop a counterrhetoric to the claims of an "error-free" Bible and the attending implications of creed, Christianity, and the new doctrinaire orientation of conservative Southern Baptists. As evangelist James Robison proudly trumpeted at the 1979 Pastor's Conference,

God does not err
The Bible is God's Word
The Bible does not err.[15]

Forced marches, whether to Zion or elsewhere, often lead to certain problems and uncertain successes. While it was often termed a "preacher boy's" fight, the rhetorical battle for this denomination was fought on the field of carpet and wood with a wide mixture of Christian soldiers, some pastors sure and many others unsure of the reason for the fight, perplexed by the prospects of victory and loss. Among rank-and-file Southern Baptists, there was really no interest in the matter. For most, it *was* a "preacher boy's" fight. But, the business of understanding the religious and church life of Southern Baptists is a complex issue at best, and understanding how Southern Baptists perceive the Bible is crucial to coming to grips with the church as an audience.

In today's Southern Baptist Church as well as in sister denominational and independent fellowships, people under the age of forty are seemingly unimpressed by any sense of denominational loyalty. Most "baby boomers," regardless of birth date, early or late in their generation, are looking for a "church family," not for a "church fight." Whether on the outside of the fold or on the inside, being invited to come in out of the cold of ruined lives or unsatisfactory material gains was the rhetorical issue of the inerrant Word.

However, an accompanying struggle for the center of a troubled Convention can and has caused many to bolt to other worship centers and has dissuaded many from getting embroiled in a crisis not of their making. For whether one is in or out, the American Southern family has been disjointed for so long that even the Bible seems lacking in its power to cement a person's place in the home. While a Convention was fighting a rhetorical war of unparalleled magnitude, its members were fighting their own wars at home and losing at almost every turn.

For the past twenty-five years, the changing nature of the American family has been a case study in cultural change. For the most part, the model of a father at work and a mother at home has been relegated to history. Census bureau data indicates that the number of households in which a married couple lived with young children was 20 percent in 1990, down from 40 percent in 1970.

The nuclear family of *Leave It to Beaver* has become *Married with Children*, with single mothers, childless couples, single fathers, and some families taking their adult children back for a period of time following marital discord or other changes in life. While it is clear that families still matter, the old patterns of family life will never be the same. There are, in fact, many kinds of families and a wide variety of needs for the state to consider—day care, family leave, middle-class tax cuts, and income tax exemptions for dependents. There is also a need for options for working parents who have children and have changing needs. If there is trouble in the workplace of the South, there is certainly trouble in Zion, the church place of the South.

While the American family has been changing, so has the American church. The stereotypical white, middle-class family of the 1950s is no longer the point of departure for discussing the church family. Nor is the 1990s model of the family sufficient to explain the changes in church attendance and denominational loyalty.

The so-called "baby boomers" rejected religion in their antiestablishment days. But, they are returning to the church in the 1990s. But with that return comes an entirely new attitude about their worship. With little sense of denominational loyalty, today's boomers are "church hopping and church shopping."

Boomers tend to gravitate to large churches where there is diversity and where there are options, as in a large shopping mall. With gymnasiums, education programs, weekday preschools, contemporary music programs, nondenominational churches, and old-line denominations, the so-called "New Age" churches are marketing their services and theology to the fragmented American family.

But, most of all, we believe that the families of the 1990s and beyond are looking for a "church family," functionally similar to the 1950s model, where warmth, love, and nurturing experiences were consistently provided. In spite of all these changes in the family and church, the world's largest Protestant denomination has responded with a corporate takeover emphasizing male-dominated leadership, obedience to doctrine, and the exclusion of those who disagree.

Despite the problems of a troubled Southern Baptist family and the larger, inclusive concerns of the American family, church membership in the Southern Baptist Convention is strong in numbers of churches, numbers of adherents, and geographic presence. A 1992 demographic study of churches and church membership reports that:

1. Southern Baptist adherents are reported in 2,514 of the 3,105 U.S. counties.

2. There are 37,922 Southern Baptist Churches, more than any other denomination.

3. Southern Baptists are most dominant in numbers of adherents in Mississippi and Alabama where about three of every ten persons are identified as Southern Baptists. Southern Baptists are identified as Southern Baptist. Southern Baptists are

> strongly dominant in Virginia, North Carolina, South Carolina, Kentucky, Tennessee, Missouri, Oklahoma, Arkansas, Louisiana, Georgia, and Texas.[16]

From troubles in the Convention to uncertainties about the future of the nuclear family, the Southern Baptists of the 1990s and those seeking a church home live in difficult times. For the decades of the latter twentieth century, Southern Baptists have been preaching that American culture is woefully decadent and fraught with problems that only the Christ of Scripture can fix. In the 1980s and 1990s, Southern Baptists looked to their preachers and to their own private needs for spiritual assistance. Some members undoubtedly found uncertain voices, even troubled voices, while others listened and followed the course-correction rhetoric provided by their own church minister. In their own particular style, these pulpit presidents have put their stamp of rhetorical flourish and cannonade to the battle hymn of an inerrant Bible.

Their story is the centerpiece of the next chapter, which examines the ethical issues of an exclusionary rhetoric that sealed off major constituencies in the church from leadership positions. Far beyond the reach of our analysis is the continuing story of excluded believers within the Southern Baptist Convention, as the chilling effect of the rhetorical successes of the loyalists continues unabated. The legacy of the loyalists' rhetorical campaign remains a painful reminder that groups who do not fight back against a perceived injustice will suffer the consequences. Southern Baptists of various persuasions outside of the loyalist hierarchy have been exiled from the Convention, proving to all that there is trouble in Zion.

The battle cry of inerrancy has served to march one and all to a seemingly uncertain future. However, the one certainty has been that the battle was worth the fight; the Word was worthy to be defended, and those who would not follow lockstep would be left behind. Based on the fundamentals of the faith, loyalists have felt justified in taking on the world in their march to Zion. As warriors for the Word one moment and pied pipers of the New Testament the next, loyalist leaders have been caught up in the grand scheme of establishing the absolute authority of the Bible as an added icon to the Holy Trinity. As the Southern Baptist Convention moves toward the twenty-first century in uncertainty, the denominational loyalists have left a once proud regional organization of churches and state conventions in near ruins, all in the name of the Father.

3

Preaching the Word: The Nature of Persuasion in the Southern Baptist Holy War

This SBC split is a "preacher boys" fight.

—Church member to one of the authors

In the early years of the takeover from 1980 to 1984, the loyalist camp of the Southern Baptist Convention gathered around the one idea against which no one, laity or pastor alike, could argue—God's word is inerrant, or literally true, in every word and line. All who dared to disagree were branded as liberals—that dangerous "word" in every sector of public and private life. But, there is an even more significant word, the "word": fundamentalism. Biblical scholar Martin E. Marty argues that loyalists abide by "rock-solid, hard binding, time-tested verities that give believers total assurance in God's Word."[1] Because they believe so earnestly in defending the sacred Scripture, loyalists have created the "other," the dissident members of the fellowship.

In the latter days of the 1970s, loyalists gathered to themselves the leaders necessary to define their rightful place in the world of Southern Baptists. Their goal was to bring the then fourteen-million- member Convention back to the right from a leftward drift created by the seminaries, which to their mind had watered down the message, its messenger Jesus Christ, and the vessel of His Word, the local pastor. By design and by definition, the loyalists understood that, as rhetorical theorist Richard Weaver argues, "one way to interpret a subject is to define its nature—to describe the fixed features of its being because definitions deal with fundamental and unchanging properties. Furthermore, the argument from genus is the highest order of appeal for it involves arguing from the nature of essence of things."[2]

In their view of God's and man's world, loyalists in the Southern Baptist Convention understood that they had to be about restoring God's Word to its rightful place. To accomplish that purpose, a time-honored tradition would be called in to marshal the laity and defend the Word that requires no defense. Through the extraordinary agency of the spoken word in the mouths of powerful spokesmen, a persuasive movement of monumental proportions was set into motion. The Southern Baptist Convention would never be the same again.

Just how did these SBC presidents, leaders, and local pastors accomplish the impossible? It is our claim that the turnaround in the Southern Baptist Convention was enacted in the pulpits of convention cities and local churches by and through the art of rhetoric. We understand the classical art of rhetoric to be the study of persuasive strategies of influence prepared for specific audiences, as well as the resulting arguments and emotional appeals. In this study, we further claim that the rhetoric of the SBC's struggle for its center was carefully developed and argued from narrative and biblical proof texts that were extraordinarily convincing in their force.

In general, we argue that there are three bodies of rhetoric to be found in the battle for the Bible in the Southern Baptist Convention. First, there is the master rhetoric of fundamentalism: a body of persuasive arguments that pits loyalist Southern Baptists against any who would act as if some part of Scripture was merely symbolic or poetic. Second, there is the rhetoric of inerrancy: a body of persuasive arguments based on various scriptures that affirm the Bible as totally accurate. Finally, stemming from these two rhetorics is yet another—the rhetoric of exclusion. The rhetoric of exclusion forges a series of arguments that expel any individual or group who is not in harmony with the dictates of Scripture, such as women who serve as leaders or ordained professional pastors, gays and lesbians, and for a time, the Masonic order. (See the table on the following page.)

It is our claim that the overarching rhetoric of fundamentalism in the Southern Baptist Convention is drawn from three principles common to the 1845 confederacy of various Baptist societies that formed the SBC:

1. Jesus Christ is the only Son of the living God who was born, lived, performed miracles, and transformed the life of many. He then died and was raised to live again, and became the atonement for the sins of all now and forever.

2. People become priests, rightly dividing the Word of truth—the Holy Bible—so that they communicate directly with their Heavenly Father, His Son, and the Holy Spirit. No church or professional leader need or should speak on their behalf. No organization can dictate the merit or fruits of their salvation. In Christ, the redeemed form the priesthood of believers.

3. The Holy Bible is Spirit-breathed. Every word of Scripture is literally true and pure in every respect.

The Rhetorics of Southern Baptist Life

I. The Rhetoric of Fundamentalism
- Rhetorical Vision Principles
  1. Jesus Christ is the Son of God.
  2. Priesthood of Believers.
  3. Bible is literally true.

II. The Rhetoric of Inerrancy
- Rhetorical Vision Principles
  1. Argument from definition.
  2. "Bully pulpit."
  3. Bible is literally true.

III. The Rhetoric of Exclusion
- Rhetorical Vision Principles
  1. Attack-expulsion paradigm.
  2. Fear-comfort argument.
  3. Attack on liberalism and dissidents.

Key Areas of Attack-Defense

Women	Homosexuals	Masons	Liberals
• denial of leadership • scriptural proof texts • defense/denial • persuasion of their proper place • attempts at harmony	• attack on fitness for life in Christ • denial of membership in SBC • expulsion of churches that openly accept them • ongoing attempts at salvation of souls and lifestyles	• attack on men who "claim" that Masons teach humanism *and* Christ as guides for life • specific attacks on masonic teachings that diminish the role of the church	• full-scale attacks on any critical review of the Scripture that denies a *fundamental* understanding of the Bible

From these rhetorical principles that have been familiar throughout the history of the SBC, a second body of principles forms the platform for the Convention seen as veering off course in the 1960s and 1970s. Simply stated, the new, yet timeless arguments for an inerrant, perfect Bible have been represented by loyalist preachers to herald a new direction in denominational life. Much like the organizational structure of modern business, the outline of this second body of principles that forms the rhetoric of inerrancy is comprised of a vision statement and a set of goals.

The rhetoric of inerrancy is forged by a vision that the Scripture is God-breathed with no error or fault in its original autographa or current versions, out of which three principles proceed:

1. The inerrant Word is absolute in its claims. By the argument from definition or genus, no one can escape a total acceptance should he or she wish to believe any of the Holy Scripture.

2. The inerrant Word is presentational in its force. The pul-

> pit becomes a bully platform to develop support and to assure the conviction of one's sins. For in no other forum can so many hear and understand the reality and power of the Word.
>
> 3. The inerrant Word is definitional in its character. At the peak of the pyramid of arguments that constitute humankind is the nature of things (genus). There are countless understandings that form the conduct of human affairs, all with proofs, emotional appeals, and a range of ethical implications. But there is only one argument to which there can be no counterpoint—the argument from genus, or the doctrine that the Bible is literally and completely true.

The essence of the rhetoric of inerrancy is the propositional claim that the true Southern Baptist is a Bible-believing, hell-fearing individual that brooks no variance in what the Bible says about itself and what the true church must be in the present time. Therefore, as a cooperating Southern Baptist, one's church must stand for the inerrant truths of Scripture, while quietly or openly staking one's claim on practices that challenge modern humanism and popular culture. To do otherwise is to abandon faith.

In a tightly-wound argumentative structure of "if 'a' is true, then 'b' is also true," the line of connection can be made between the overarching rhetorical theory of fundamentalism, the rhetoric of inerrancy, and the rhetoric of exclusion. In outline form, the rhetoric of inerrancy appears as an easy-to-follow, hard-to-practice perspective on the Bible. In order to accept Jesus Christ as Savior and to reject Satan, sinners must make basic changes in their lives. When one becomes a Christian and then a Southern Baptist, there is another devil to exorcise—the "other." Cast as having several identities, the "other," according to Dr. Jerry Vines, the pastor of the First Baptist Church in Jacksonville, Florida, is "the old thief, the Devil, Satan, destructive criticism. On the other side is the infallible Son of the Living God."[3] The "other" could also refer to dissident members of the fellowship—historical critics with so-called liberal views of Scripture and a group who would call into question points of biblical truths.

Vines and other pastors of the inerrancy movement moved quickly to attack seminaries that fostered the "destructive" nature of the historical-critical method. Ed Young, pastor of the Second Baptist Church in Houston, Texas, and president of the 1994 SBC, spoke specifically to the real threat of the historical-critical method at the 1994 convention when he asserted that:

> There are among us Absaloms at the gate. I can't tell if they are inside the gate and the wall or outside the wall and gate, but they are like Absalom of old, just waiting until something

> takes place and taking the opposition side. These Absaloms almost perform like terrorists sometimes among us. They have said to us that we as Southern Baptists no longer believe in separation of church and state. We believe in separation of church and state, and we believe it because it is taught in the Bible. We have been told that we don't believe in soul competency and a lot of these doctrines have been redefined, but I tell you we believe in soul competency because it is taught in the Bible. We have been told that we do believe in this and we do not believe in that. Let me tell you that our basic doctrines are in place.
>
> We have been told, for example, that we need to work through this and that we need to work through that, but I tell you that we believe on the authority of Bible, the basic doctrines of our faith. For example, the role of the pastor. The pastor is a servant, he is an undershepherd, he is an underroler and the pastor is a spiritual leader because he has been called, he has been set aside for the purpose of being a spiritual undershepherd and a spiritual leader. That is his role. He doesn't function as a ruler per se except as the people bestow of him that pastoral leadership as a servant, as God's servant and slave to the people. That's the role of the pastor. We believe that is the role because that is the teaching of the Bible.
>
> Now we have gone through a theological reformation, and therefore we have come to the point where we are ready for a spiritual reformation because a heresy of spirit is more deadly even than a theological heresy. Jesus says, "By this ye shall know ye are my disciples because you have love for one another."

Young went on to firmly state that "we are conservative, evangelical Southern Baptists who believe in every fundamental of the faith that is taught in the inerrant Word of God."[4]

For Ed Young and his fellow presidents, the "Absaloms at the gate" wielded the crooked, blunt instrument of historical-critical methodology. In their sermons and addresses at SBC conventions, the presidents alluded negatively to the historical-critical method as another name for satanic influence in biblical criticism. For them, it is "he" who comes to rob the Bible of its seamless perfection with any scholarly hint of imperfection. It may well be that the target of the loyalist agenda was the presence of the historical-critical method in seminary instruction.

The third type of rhetoric we will explore, the rhetoric of exclusion, affirms the internal, Bible-based requirements for membership, participation, and leadership in the Southern Baptist Convention. As rhetorical theorist Ernest Bormann argues: "Rhetorical Communities bound together by a common vision and sustained by a common communication style generally have to deal with the social reality of evil."[5]

Similarly, sociologist Nancy Ammerman states that "fundamentalists began as traditionalists who perceived some challenge to their core identity, both social and personal. . . . They fight for and fight with real conditions and concepts, fight against insiders and fight under God."[6] Accordingly, the loyalist rhetoric results in an "attack-defend" structure that is mandated so as to rid Christ's church of those who will not follow its demands.

The rhetorical goal of the exclusionist's persuasion is comprised of three rhetorical strategies:

> 1. The inerrancy of Scripture requires an attack-expulsion paradigm. The case against groups not sanctioned by Scripture for membership or leadership must be vigorously pursued in the mass media and preached about from the pulpit. In short, the pastor-speaker uses Scripture to attack those who don't comply with Scripture, effectively expelling them in word and deed, and then defending such rhetoric by the very Scripture used to call the "dissident" out for rebuke.
>
> 2. A dual argument of fear and comfort that says woe to those who would argue against the Bible on certain points, such as the denial of the biblical injunction that declares homosexuals, like all sinners, can be saved, and gives comfort to those who accept and defend Scripture.
>
> 3. A reliance on abominational language that focuses on blame, accusation, and moral judgment.

In sum, these three modes of persuasion rest on differing rhetorical ideas. The rhetoric of fundamentalism is a reassuring and reliable grouping of scriptural references that affirm the literal and accurate nature of the Bible. The rhetoric of inerrancy builds on these bedrock principles of the Bible that empower the pastor to "bully" his congregation with the argument from definition, which claims that the Bible is what it says it is. Evolving out of these two rhetorics is the ultimate weapon of the loyalist—the justification to exclude people or groups because the Bible says they are unfit to participate.

The key groups this rhetoric targets are liberals, women, homosexuals, and Masons. Although some of these four groups have received more criticism than others, the one "group" that is singled out is the liberal, or "dissident," Southern Baptist. Throughout the twenty years of the controversy, it was the Southern Baptist who questioned even one idea of the loyalists who was branded as a dissident.

On the other hand, while women serving as ordained pastors are clearly at odds with an inerrantist's view of Scripture, the loyalists spent a great deal of time and energy in "repairing" their own rhetoric to include women in the everyday affairs of church business and in the raising of money for missions. As we will argue in subsequent chapters, women are useful in a male-dominated loyalist church hierarchy, but not as senior pastors and not as congregational leaders of men.

As for homosexuality, "words too terrible to utter" fill the mouths of loyalist preachers as they defend their right to exclude gays and lesbians from church membership (if they know who they are). Later in the book, we will document the stories of churches expelled from their conventions, both state and national, because of open acceptance and support for the homosexual lifestyle. They are "unfit," "unclean," and at odds with God's plan, according to the loyalists. These open or closeted people can still be "won to Christ" if they will only repent and revoke their current "lifestyle," say the loyalists. If only life were that simple.

For a brief period, the order of Free and Accepted Masons came under attack for leading men away from Christ by teaching that humanism and Christianity were compatible lifestyles. But, it is one thing to deny women an equal place with men in positions of service and leadership. It is quite another thing to assault good Christian and Southern Baptist men concerning their private lives as Masons and cast doubt on their public lives as Southern Baptists.

The essence of the rhetoric of exclusion is the claim that there are a variety of sanctioned, scriptural texts that any loyalist might use to ferret out and rid the body (congregation) of any person or group who does not follow the Bible literally and does not mind saying so. The rhetorical righteousness of Southern Baptist loyalists who castigate non-scriptural acts, such as women as leaders or homosexuals as church members, will claim to his peers that it is a necessary and appropriate way to write or speak. Rhetorical responses against such disaffected people, justified by appropriate biblical texts, are badges of honor for today's loyalist Southern Baptist leader or congregation.

To understand the struggle for the soul of the Southern Baptist Convention is to understand the rhetorical history of the nation's largest Protestant denomination. For it is in this struggle that the master rhetors of the Convention's most powerful churches became catalysts for the development of the present oral tradition of fundamentalism, inerrancy, and exclusion. With power and effectiveness, the presidents of the SBC in the 1980s and 1990s delivered fiery sermons that defined the simple, basic language of the rhetoric of fundamentalism, as well as the case for inerrancy and exclusion. To a man, these presidents have repeatedly affirmed that all scripture is given by the inspiration of God and a God of truth cannot inspire error.[7]

In any communication situation such as a church service, the rhetorical purpose of the pastor is to bring about change. When the sermon or written material is preserved on videotape, audiotape, or in printed form, the item becomes an artifact, an existing instance of rhetoric that can be reviewed, studied, and evaluated. If the pastor or writer is explaining, clarifying, or justifying a position, then he is presenting an "apologia." When a pastor or writer presents a persuasive case that calls attention to evil, provokes fear for the future if things do not change, or presents a "righteous" prophecy of future events, then he or she is delivering a "jeremiad." The characterization of such "gloom and doom" originated with the voice of judgment who brought retribution down upon the children of Israel—the prophet Jeremiah.

Another key term for the study of rhetoric is "identification." This concept refers to the ability of a speaker or writer to form a psychological bond with the audience, as in the sacramental belief that the bread and wine become the Body and blood of Christ. In more earthly terms, identification occurs when pastor and laity bond during the sermonic experience or other public and interpersonal experiences—where speaker and audience share a common set of beliefs or when a member of the audience says to him or herself, "I know where you're coming from." This is the concept of identification in the real world.

It is clear that the political objective of the loyalists was the full and complete capture of the once proud Southern Baptist Convention. In effecting this capture, the preservation of the faithful and the expulsion of the dissidents could only be achieved by rhetorically persuasive strategies and parliamentary decisions rendered in the Convention pulpit and at the Convention ballot box. The historic principles of Southern Baptists are, by design, far removed from political agendas. Southern Baptists have practiced "church" by sturdy, independent, private, democratic congregational means and by doing what they please as a local church. Throughout their storied history, Southern Baptists have known who they are, what has been their great commission, and why they remain the nation's largest Protestant denomination. To be told otherwise was unheard of!

Times change, but the proud SBC of the 1980s would never have thought that it would be fighting to save its Bible nor its membership from those who would disagree. Even more shocking would have been the need to develop a Christian agenda to champion the Bible among a people who would dare to question any word of its text. For some, the defense of the obvious, the Bible, would be an uneasy, embarrassing experience. For others, filled with the zeal of the refiner's fire—the inerrant Word—they were in for the time of their religious lives in the last years of the twentieth century.

Persuasive communication from the pulpit is often strengthened by printed communication, and that is the case with Dr. James Draper's book on inerrancy that we consider in the next chapter. Draper, a fervent apologist for inerrancy, served as president of the Convention from 1982 to 1984. He is now the president of the Southern Baptist Sunday School Board in Nashville, Tennessee. Draper's work added greatly to the denominational membership's understanding of inerrancy, particularly towards establishing inerrancy as a rhetorical icon.

4

All Scripture Is Given by Inspiration of God: An Apologia for Inerrancy

Every Scripture is God-breathed—given by his inspiration.

—II Timothy 3:16 Amplified Translation

All Scripture is given by inspiration of God.

—II Timothy 3:16 AV, as quoted by Adrian Rogers, 1987

Traditionally, critics of the evangelistic oral tradition have evaluated the individual sermons of God's warriors to assess their worth and impact upon laypersons. Critics have studied these spoken discourses by analyzing their appeals to listeners, their message strategies and language, and the attractive qualities of vocal delivery from the pulpit artist. Undoubtedly, these studies have helped us to understand the dynamic interaction of preachers and preaching. Furthermore, it is advantageous to study oral sermons (and the sermon givers) for they have greatly influenced the growth of the denomination.

Baptist laypersons, past and present, have fully sympathized with the rhetoric of personal change for better Christian living regardless of their theology. They have become accustomed to the sermonizers' attempt to change the ways of those in the pew. The rhetorical strategies of scriptural exegesis, religious instruction, and moral imperative are traditional and welcomed.

It is equally rewarding to analyze the *written* apologia of the leadership hierarchy as a helpful guide to current denominational rhetorical ideology and the leadership's implementation of that ideology within their communication. From this perspective, an apologia is not merely an explanation of an idea or a description of behavior, but rather a chart of that idea or behavior. Knowing the features of the chart may be helpful for laypersons as they plan their journey through the mine fields of denominational justifications and explanations on inerrancy. Additionally, such knowledge may help laypersons hypothesize about future inerrantist rhetoric, a key feature of fundamentalism.

Consequently, in this chapter, we have analyzed the written inerrancy apologia of Dr. James T. Draper. His 1984 book, *Authority: The Critical Issue for Southern Baptists* can be fairly regarded as an official doctrinal statement on inerrancy since it was written while he was president of the Southern Baptist Convention, and it has been generally available to laypersons through SBC bookstores.[1] He has been president of the Southern Baptist Sunday School Board, was once the pastor of the First Baptist Church of Euliss, Texas, and he is the author of more than a dozen books including: *The Church Christ Approves*, *Foundations of Biblical Faith*, and *Hebrews: The Life That Pleases God*. In his writing, he has consistently upheld an inerrantist interpretation of the Holy Scriptures.

It is not our intent to critique Draper's theology. Instead, we have focused on his suasory methods of written discourse. Draper is an ardent advocate of inerrancy, and he is prominently known in the denomination because of his pulpit effectiveness and his extensive writings. Most importantly, from an evaluation of his argumentation, we can better understand Draper's exegesis on inerrancy and thus better understand him as a denominational apologist.

Inerrantists have generally positioned themselves as loyalists to the denomination, its resolutions, and its actions. At the same time, since 1979, noninerrantist moderates and liberals have just as frequently positioned themselves as dissenters from various denominational dictates and actions. To dissenters, two offensive actions include the SBC's 1987 redefinition of the priesthood of the believer, and the firings or nonappointments of otherwise qualified persons to denominational positions because of their beliefs on inerrancy. While denominational loyalists frequently espouse inerrancy, denominational dissenters may also describe themselves as inerrantists. But, the two groups frequently disagree on the matter of requiring inerrancy as a litmus test of ideology within the denomination. In an organizational sense, denominational loyalists have placed only inerrantists who belong to SBC congregations onto SBC committees, boards, and commissions. This exclusivity has infuriated the dissenters, even though they are typically members of break-away Baptist groups, such as the Cooperative Baptist Fellowship.

Both loyalists and dissenters view themselves as evangelical and both are ardent supporters of missions' endeavors locally and around the world. Loyalists tend to endorse and support creedal uniformity as well as a communitarian spirit of obedience to the teachings, resolutions, and decisions of the denomination. On the other hand, dissenters are more likely to affirm the diversity of individual freedom, often disagreeing with the necessity for a creed of uniformity, and they fail to accept or may actively disagree with the denomination's decisions as a binding act either upon themselves or upon individual churches.

Inerrancy has been a controversial issue among theologians for many years, and perhaps equally so with pulpit artists such as Jerry Vines, W. A. Criswell, Adrian Rogers, and Bailey Smith. Draper's book is, therefore, a timely source of discourse on the advocacy of inerrancy, and it deserves careful attention by rhetorical critics and believers alike. Just as peeling off the layers of an onion reveals its center, so is it important to strip away Draper's arguments to reveal the essence of his defense of inerrancy. The philosopher Kenneth Burke offers laypersons an approach to the problem of understanding Draper's suasory technique of argumentation with unseen others. Sociologist Joseph R. Gusfield, an interpreter of Kenneth Burke, has observed, "One can picture [Burke's] work as an attempt to rid us of the view of appearances as understandably ordered and to go beyond the disorder of appearances to perceive the forms which are constant."[2] For Burke, the problem of securing order in a society is central, and according to Gusfield, "it is the fact of authority, i.e., hierarchy, that is the source of order and rejection of society."[3]

The concept of order is evident in the official discourses of the Southern Baptist Convention. For example, in 1988, Resolution 5 was passed by the Messengers assembled in San Antonio. In this resolution, the Messengers authorized the individual church minister to supply sanctioned interpretations of biblical doctrine, thus legitimizing the church pastor as the official rhetor of doctrinal matters on the local level. Some Messengers dissented from the decision, marched out of the convention hall, and publicly burned a copy of the resolution in front of the Alamo and a number of surprised tourists. The SBC decision was denounced as a reversal of the priesthood of believers, which asserts that believers need not have an earthly mediator between themselves and God.

In addition, these dissenters challenged the spirit of the resolution when they claimed it was typical of a denominational episcopacy and was an encroachment upon laypersons' personal freedom to define the doctrine for themselves, and therefore the historical opposite of Baptist ideology. Yet, since 1988, Draper and his colleagues have urged their followers to agree with such a major doctrinal change in interpretive authority. It is clear that the opponents of this change will not accept such an interpretation, thus helping to define a conflict that now seems neither bridgeable nor mendable.

Currently, there are at least four commonly held beliefs in the denominational communication system that together constitute a rhetorical ideology with one unifying principle: Christianity can be described as the center from which all other forms of human motivation have gradually diverged. Thus, God is the central point of explanation for creation, life, and death. God is the ultimate evaluator of all human action. The commonly held beliefs that emerge from this are as follows:

1. Southern Baptists commonly affirm the Trinity. God the Father is understood to be the Creator. The Holy Spirit is the vehicle for communication between God and humankind, and Jesus Christ is viewed as the incarnation of God in human form who died, was resurrected, and ensures human salvation in life after death.

2. Denominational leaders refuse to allow Christianity to be integrated into other religious faiths (such as Hinduism or Buddhism), believing that such separateness, or distinctiveness, is appropriate and indispensable to maintain a sense of denominational purity. There is a strong motivation by the SBC leadership to promote this ideology of separateness in their worldwide missionary efforts to attract others of all religious faiths.

3. Prayer is interpreted as a method of communicating with God through the Holy Spirit and Jesus Christ, without the need for an intercessory to the act.

4. Denominational loyalists accept the Holy Scripture as divinely inspired and believe that the Bible furnishes knowledge for guidance about personal morality and religious activity, as well as being a historical record of believer activity. Consequently, the Bible is more than a collection of proverbs. It is also more than a mere group of stories with moralistic conclusions or narratives about miracles written many years ago by individuals whose names may or may not have been recorded within secular or biblical history. The Bible is the written expression of God's words for all humankind.

A rhetorical ideology that places Christianity at the center for all human motivation is a vital unifying principle. Equally significant is the form and tone of argumentation concerning inerrancy in Draper's work. Consequently, as a study of his approach, we have synthesized two relevant premises:

Premise 1. The Bible is the Word of God; it is framed from the original autographa of biblical documents; the copies of the autographa were penned by various authors; the autographa contained absolutely no mistakes, no matter how minor and such a law is applicable to science, history, politics, and so on, indeed for all biblical knowledge.

Premise 2. If the Bible is inerrant, then it is also infallible. The term *infallible* focuses on the claim that the handwritten copies of the original autographa and the copies of that original, throughout the centuries, are not prone to mislead or cause error in anyone. Consequently, if there are minor errors, in either factual detail or grammar, for example, then the copies only reproduce the truth of the original.

The sermonic argument for inerrancy and its corollary—infallibility—seem to turn on an "if, then" statement: if God and his Word are to be believed without equivocation, then the believer cannot entertain any doubt about the Author of the Bible. To accept the notion that the Bible contains errors but still remains the sacred word of God is to acknowledge doubt. Allowing doubt to enter within the layperson's understanding of these doctrinal matters does not emanate from God. The Bible is clear, and all you need to do is read it. Understandably then, the rhetorical centerpiece of inerrancy is the Bible as God's truthful, written, and authoritative Word.

Thus, Draper approaches the Bible as the ultimate source of textual authority. To him, the Bible is without error in its original manuscripts in science, faith, history, and revelation. While scholars of hermeneutics have often contended that inerrancy is multidefinitional, Draper's position is congruent with the decision of the 1978 International Council of Biblical Inerrancy:

> We affirm the propriety of using inerrancy as a theological term concerning the complete truthfulness of Scripture. We deny that it is proper to evaluate Scripture according to standards of truth and error that are alien to its usage or purpose.
>
> We further deny that inerrancy is negated by biblical phenomena such as a lack of modern technical precision, irregularities of grammar or spelling, observational descriptions of nature, the reporting of falsehoods, the use of hyperbole and round numbers, the topical arrangement of material, variant selections of material in parallel account or the use of free citations.[4]

In Burkean terms, rhetor-leaders such as Draper tend to define inerrancy scientistically, that is, terms such as *verbal inspiration*, *plenary inspiration*, *infallible*, or *inerrant* "essentially say the same thing."[5] There is little need for the reader to have definitional clarity since "in the original autographs, every word is inspired of God." Thus, contends Draper, "those who criticize conservative Christians for using all of this terminology should consider the reason why we have to keep coining new terms to describe our position. It is because unnamed others keep usurping the old terms and twisting them into something totally different from their original meaning" (90).

The quality of Draper's assertion aside, laypersons desirous of assessing the inerrancy conflict for themselves should investigate his position. Helpfully, Draper provides several laws that govern his definition of inerrancy to help laypersons understand his apologia. These laws are bound together by his one unifying rhetorical principle that states "the doctrine of inspiration simply says that God the Holy Spirit superintended [and] overruled men's imperfections, and did not allow those imperfections to intrude into the Scripture which they wrote" (80). Furthermore, "by inspiration we mean that the Bible is *accurate* in all that it says and that it will not deceive its readers theologically, historically, chronologically, geographically or scientifically . . . whatever it says, the Bible says it accurately" (89; emphasis added).

Draper's first law states that, regardless of the meaning of inerrancy, "*it does not mean mechanical dictation*," that is, God did not dictate the Scriptures to the writers "as a businessman would to his secretary" (80; emphasis in original). Thus, God did not waive the "human intelligence, literary style or personal feeling" of the writers, yet God "supernaturally prepared the penman" and the "complete and coherent message to man was recorded with perfect accuracy" (81). Draper's position is presumably acceptable to those adherents who are convinced that "perfect accuracy" was entirely recordable by God's chosen receivers whether or not the messages were dictated or recorded verbatim.

Secondly, Draper alleges that "biblical inspiration does not mean that the translations or editions are inspired—only the original manuscripts, the autographa" (82). Despite the intriguing quality of his assertion, Draper neither discloses the locations of all the original manuscripts nor does he cite those that are extant. Such disclosures might be very helpful for adherents, although he discounts the survival of all original manuscripts. According to Draper, "perhaps God allowed the autographa to perish because, if they had survived, they might have fallen into unscrupulous hands and be altered so as to produce heresy; then there would be no way to restore the original readings" (84). Nevertheless, Draper's reasoning is entirely consistent with the unifying rhetorical principle that God is the ultimate evaluator of all human action.

Draper's argumentation presents interested laypersons with a dilemma. Believers might evaluate and find helpful the original error-free manuscripts if we had them available to us, but we do not. On the other hand, if we had them, such an evaluation would be difficult for us to undertake because the manuscripts might contain errors, thus promoting confusion at best and misleading adherents into heresy at worst. In any case, from Draper's reasoning, the matter appears unworthy of believers' concern because adherents may suitably trust loyalist apologists for interpretations of scriptural purity and doctrinal clarity. Thus, Draper (and other denominational apologists) will provide laypersons with authoritative evaluations, regardless of their origin or quality.

Draper's third law concerning inerrancy contends that "biblical inspiration does not eliminate the human element" in Scripture because "God superintended the process so that no error intruded into the text" (85). What is the "human element"? Draper provides neither a clarifying example of his assertion nor a definition of an "intrud[ing]" error that might help believers understand this presumed development of an error-free manuscript. Consequently, his assertion is difficult for laypersons to evaluate. On the other hand, had Draper explained in his exegesis how the "human element" had helped in the process of biblical textual development, he might have been forced to admit the possibility of human error. Such an admission would have been contradictory, since the originals are presumably without human error and therefore uncontaminated by human frailties. His analysis fails to include any illustratively correct clarifications of errors, perhaps because such illustrations could be construed as potentially heretical.

With his fourth law, Draper argues that "biblical inspiration does not eliminate figures of speech . . . when we talk about literal interpretation, some people take that to mean that we believe all the Bible is to be interpreted in a very plastic, literalistic fashion, ruling out all figures of speech. This is absurd." Furthermore, "we need to emphasize that it is just as destructive of biblical truth to take a figurative passage literally as it is to take a literal passage figuratively or allegorically. Either will destroy the intended meaning of Scripture" (86). Draper amplified his assertion by attacking the doctrine of transubstantiation, which states that the "elements in the Lord's Supper literally become the body of Christ and the blood of Christ." Thus, Roman Catholics are guilty of a "grossly literal misunderstanding" for "by taking literally what was intended to be metaphorical we find great misinterpretation and misuse of a simple truth" (86).

But, Draper's fourth law is inconsistent. The reader is admonished to literally understand the Scriptures, but when confronted with an example of literalism, the example is dismissed because literalism cannot be interpreted as "metaphorical." His viewpoint is confusing at best, and tautological at worst, although that need not be worrisome to believers. Presumably, when the problem is the interpretation of a passage that can be defined as anything else other than literal, it is safer for members to rely on those meanings given by a denominational authority, such as Draper. In such instances, a believer's failure to trust denominational authority for sanctioned interpretations might risk the consequent destruction of the intended meaning of the Holy Scriptures, which, the author warns, is heretical, even if unknowable.

Draper's fifth law states that "biblical inspiration does not eliminate approximations and loose quotations" (87). Because this dictum is but an expansion of the previous point, our queries above still apply. Draper fails to provide a definition of a "loose quotation." Are Bible paraphrase translations from the non-original manuscripts sanctioned for the believer to use? Furthermore, should John 3:16 be interpreted literally? Not so, asserts Draper, for an "approximation" interpretation is an acceptable deviation from inerrancy. Unfortunately, a sanctioned list of acceptable scriptural deviations from inerrancy is not available within Draper's book, thus depriving followers of potentially valuable assistance.

In his sixth law, Draper argues that "inspiration does not demand exact duplication in parallel passages—such as in the Gospel accounts" (87). Arguably, if there are scriptural "discrepancies," they can be attributable to "incomplete understanding," and that "when all the facts are known to us eventually, we will find that they are perfectly compatible and simply give different aspects of the event" (88). Perhaps, but such an explanation is remarkably blasé. Who has the "incomplete understanding," the writer or the believer as receiver of the idea? If there is only one accurate account of the original texts, then what is it? For example, we have two genealogies for Jesus (Matt. 1 and Luke 3); two versions of the Beatitudes (Matt. 5 or Luke 6); and two versions of the death of Judas (Matt. 27:5 or Acts 1:18).

Draper's final law holds that "inspiration does not mean grammatical and syntactical conformity" (88). Perhaps this is so, although it is not the meaningful issue. Inerrantists could help laypersons support their discourse with the use of the autographa that they claim are indisputably true, but that we have not seen. Furthermore, the burden of argument rests upon the apologist of inerrancy to outline the nature of inspiration and why readers should disavow any other interpretation. According to Draper, "grammar simply describes how a society has spoken and written in a particular generation and thus communicated effectively" (88). His comment elevates grammar and syntax beyond a linguistic record into a successful system of persuasion. Critical believers might well question such an assertion, and without supportive material, they would likely reject it.

Draper readily admits, however, that "individual idiosyncrasies" in biblical texts exist, but they are nevertheless not errors. Instead, these "idiosyncrasies" are only "peculiarities" of the individual biblical writer. Perhaps this is the unintrusive "human element" at work in the text. Believers may or may not agree, but they may nevertheless wonder how Draper can label these "peculiarities" as "idiosyncrasies" and yet conclude that the Scriptures are without taint by human beings, and therefore perfect.

Using Draper's book as an authoritative apologia for inerrancy, what conclusions should laypersons draw from his rhetorical ideology and his strategy of argumentation for inerrancy? Draper and his loyalist colleagues may be correct that the Bible is without error or imperfection; proving or disproving that point is not our objective. Furthermore, in his favor, SBC dissidents are not unanimously in disagreement with Draper's perspective on inerrancy, nor are all loyalists necessarily in agreement with him.

However, two points are fundamental. First of all, to develop his inerrancy apologia, Draper failed to link his arguments to a larger, more expansive denominational ideology. If readers were able to fit Draper's laws into that ideology, with illustrative examples and appropriate biblical citations, it would furnish loyalists with a helpful defense of Scripture. Such an apologia would be clarifying for Draper's followers and valuable to those denominationalists whose beliefs on inerrancy are undecided. Draper has consequently written a book for loyalists who do not require such a linkage, whose needs are focused only on the necessity for his explanation of how the Bible is God's inerrant, pure Word.

Secondly, Draper's argumentation centers on the use of a straw man technique, for he furnishes rebuttals to unstated premises from unnamed opponents. Ironically, his method of argument is the same one that he claims "liberal thinkers" have used against inerrancy doctrine—"it is necessary to destroy some of these 'straw men' that have been unjustly set up and frequently used" (90). His rebuttals therefore avoid the burden of proof usually assumed by those arguing in favor of a cause.

We conclude that Draper's argumentation strategy forces those who disagree with him to prove that his negatively stated laws are not true. Even if that could be done, however, readers still might fail to understand the nature of inerrancy. Consequently, readers can determine what inerrancy *isn't* from Draper's exposition, although we are left with the author's assertions as to the positive qualities of inerrancy. Therefore, the concerned Christian wishing to accept Draper's thinking must do so without encountering the equivalent of an affirmative proposal or supportive evidence that proves or clarifies his case. Given the importance of developing a personal belief about inerrancy, such an unquestioning acceptance may be asking too much for most inquiring laypersons.

It would also be beneficial if Draper had demonstrated more concern for the use of original Scripture manuscripts to clarify or illuminate his points. This lack of concern undermines the quality of his claim. Furthermore, he did not seem to consider that his method of negative argumentation with its inconsistencies and tautologies could be a potential vehicle of confusion or even heresy for believers.

Readers may also find that his negative argumentation methods are confusing because of the author's interpretation of the word "inerrant"—namely that there are acceptable deviations from inerrant truth although inerrancy is absolutely accurate. If Draper wishes to argue that biblical history is totally accurate, then one cannot sanction deviations from that history and still claim that it is reliable *without exception*.

Nevertheless, these disputes about the ultimate source of inerrantist authority, the Bible, reinforce the applicability of Kenneth Burke's claim that, in religion, order is central. Furthermore, as Gusfield pointed out above, Burke asserts that "hierarchy . . . is the source of order and rejection of society." Draper, and those denominational leaders and pulpit artists who sympathize with his views on inerrancy, apparently find the need for personal interpretations on inerrancy unnecessary. For those leaders, such problems are not a part of their rhetorical map. The Bible is the destination rather than a stop along the way on a believer's journey.

Dissenters skeptical of inerrantism might well argue that Draper's position is equivalent to idolatry, or more specifically, bibliolatry. Inerrantist advocates sidestep that claim, for they contend that their opponents are guilty of idolatry when they substitute human reason for divine revelation. The consequences of such sin are evident, Draper asserts, because it has caused a decline in the evangelical missionary fervor to convert the world to Christianity. Accordingly, Draper alleges that when the human acceptance of biblical authority declines, "missions and evangelism also decline very quickly" (95–96). Draper supports his assertion with statistics documenting the alleged decline of Protestant foreign missionary placements in the 1960–80 period: Episcopalian foreign missionary deployment, down 79 percent; Lutheran foreign missionary deployment, down 70 percent; United Presbyterian Church foreign missionary deployment, down 70 percent; the United Church of Christ missionary deployment, down 68 percent; the Christian Church missionary deployment, down 66 percent; and the United Methodist Church missionary deployment, down 46 percent. Critics may question whether this attempt at causal-effect reasoning is accurate or simply another example of religious double-talk, something Jesus warned about when he told his detractors, "Woe unto you, scribes and Pharisees, you hypocrites."[6]

For laypersons, the Southern Baptist Convention's strategic plan for the future appears to be a journey into a territory guided by an authority that demands unquestioned obedience of its followers. For loyalist members, the map will require reliance upon the law of ministerial authority, a leadership demand for member obedience, and attention to appeals for greater centrality of authority within the denomination. Faced with potential denominational disintegration, such an organizational communication system mimics an episcopacy model that is present within Draper's rhetoric.

Southern Baptists who become confused or uncertain about the authority of biblical text as a part of their Christian journey, need not be concerned, for the way is smooth. Draper's inerrantist interpretations of biblical text will be authoritative beyond the need for member exploration. Under his religious autocracy, doctrinal pollution will be absent, the believers world will be understandable, and the denomination will be far more single-minded in its pursuit of the unifying rhetorical principle that God is the central point of all human motivation. Just as our Puritan forefathers sought to establish a city of light upon a hill for all to see, loyalist apologists promise a denomination much closer to the purity of Christ's disciples.

Today, the redesigned denomination relies upon a persuasive strategy of enforcing the concept of biblical authority and order. Membership submission to this ideology will reinforce that order. Arguably, this system is advantageous for the loyalist hierarchy, since they are safe and secure within a stable autocracy. Denominational loyalists are advantaged because they presumably receive clear scriptural meanings and doctrine from the pulpit. Ideally, such clarity substantially reduces believer confusion, a desirable conclusion to any communication situation.

Since 1979, there has been a clear theme of concern from the presidential pulpit at various national meetings. According to these rhetors, the denomination is under attack from the enemies of inerrancy, whose Darth Vader–like presence is omnipresent and omniscient. Such a rhetorical strategy from the pulpit may be effective. It is appealing to those rhetors who fear a denomination without the security and stability of an imposed and consistent policy of inerrancy for its adherents. The power of the spoken word to change our lives has been the strength of evangelical pulpit rhetoric, and it has always been so in the Southern Baptist Convention. Understandably, the presidential pulpit's campaign against unnamed enemies of inerrancy will continue until their persuasive goals are reached.

Nevertheless, discovering how Draper and other SBC presidents argue for inerrancy is not easy. The philosopher Richard Weaver offers an approach to resolving the problem of understanding how SBC presidents argue for inerrancy. Weaver suggests that in some organizations, members sometimes employ the argument from genus, that is, the argument from definition, to achieve their persuasive goals. For example, denominational loyalists contend that members must subscribe to inerrancy. If the believer cannot or will not accept such a belief, then by definition, the believer is unqualified or unfit to be a member and exclusion is justifiable.

From the pulpit hierarchy's perspective, then, *choosing* an acceptable or appropriate definition for a word such as inerrancy may not necessarily be the *receiver's* option. A key aspect of this justification for exclusion is power. This basis for exclusion from membership is entirely legitimate because they determine—and enforce—the appropriate definitions of admission to the denomination. Furthermore, whether popular or sanctioned meanings of inerrancy are similar to each other may be irrelevant to these official rhetors of the denomination. An expression of the loyalist argument strategy for inerrancy reminds us of the following passage in Lewis Carroll's *Through the Looking Glass*:

> Humpty-Dumpty said: "There's glory for you." "I don't know what you mean by 'glory,'" Alice said. Humpty-Dumpty smiled contemptuously. "Of course you don't till I tell you. I meant, 'There's a nice knock-down argument for you.'" "But 'glory' doesn't mean a 'nice knock-down argument,'" Alice objected. "When I use a word," Humpty-Dumpty said in a rather scornful tone, "*it means just what I choose it to mean, neither more nor less.*"[7]

It is curious that dissenting Southern Baptists have not yet developed a rationale of counterargumentation to the definitional claims of inerrancy, preferring instead to abandon the field of arguments that might provoke inquiry about inerrancy. Of course, as early as 1980, no self-respecting Southern Baptist would have believed that one brother in the Lord would reject another brother with the threat of exclusion from the denomination over the test oath of inerrancy. How could any Southern Baptist dare dream of disagreement with President Adrian Rogers in 1979 when, with his dramatically pleasing and powerful baritone voice, he preached: "Every Word of God is pure. Every Word of God is God-given. The Word of God is eternal. It is not a matter of going back to the autographs. It was settled in Heaven."[8]

In the early years of the division, dissenting Southern Baptists failed to develop an appealing pulpit alternative to inerrancy in order to counter the advocacy of such renowned preachers as President Draper, President Rogers, and their colleagues. The dissenters tacitly conceded the grounds of argumentation by default, perhaps because they saw little reason not to do so. More likely, however, they conceded because most dissenters were unwilling to develop an apologia around a strategy of arguing with unseen "others," then invoking the argument from definition as a justification. Arguments developed out of open dialogue and consensus have always been more important to the dissenting laity. This group has long been accustomed to relying on arguments developed from the membership forum rather than on decrees imposed by an ecclesiastical hierarchy.

Regardless, the battle for control of the Southern Baptist Convention has occurred on the inerrantist's terms, and the pulpit artists who use them have a shared vision of inerrancy that urges correctness and obedience from those in the pew. To SBC presidents, the rhetorical concept of order has become so important that it allows for little deviation in definition for the layperson.

Since the 1980s and early 1990s, Southern Baptist Convention presidents Draper, Rogers, Vines, Smith, and Stanley have thundered out the theme of inerrancy to Messengers. Whether W. A. Criswell of First Baptist Church in Dallas—elected president of the SBC in 1968—furnished the match to light the inerrancy fire from the pulpit depends upon whom you ask. Nevertheless, these adept sermon givers have authorized the doctrine of inerrancy with their imprimatur for use by other Southern Baptist preachers. In the late 1990s, inerrancy is a sanctioned sermon topic for congregations. Furthermore, as a tool of sermon exposition, the use of the appeal to authority, whether from biblical proof text or from a ecclesiastical hierarchy, reinforces the rhetorical concept of order.

There is one constant in this dispute from the pulpit for the will and heart of Southern Baptists. Over the span of nearly four hundred years of stern independence, ordinary Baptists in the pew have typically been questioners and challengers of order and pulpit authority, especially outside of the local church. In particular, submission to external ecclesiastical authority has been ahistorical for Baptists. We were formed from the best of the dissenting tradition to refuse autocracies and imposed doctrines. Baptists have never bowed to a patron saint. Instead, we have always respected the independent spirit of John Smyth, John Murton, Thomas Helwys, and Roger Williams. The denomination's preachers who seek to impose inerrancy on laypersons appear blissfully ignorant of the lengthy record of Baptist dissent.

Yet, from the earliest days of the takeover in 1979, the new SBC pulpit presidents have provided their loyal flock with comfort. In their annual meeting sermons, they have hammered out the rhetoric of inerrancy upon the anvil of God's Holy Word, the ultimate and sacrosanct proof text of all proof texts. Sure of their crusade to reinvigorate the denomination to its rightful place in history, they have also placed their persuasive stamp on the doctrine of inerrancy. In addition, they have demonized liberalism and all other "isms," a point that is explored later.

The new SBC presidents—all men—have set the persuasive tone for hundreds of sermons, Sunday School lessons, and conversations among the membership. Following each annual meeting since 1979, thousands of clergy have typically returned to their congregations each June to explain, rephrase, summarize, and preach inerrancy. Ordinary church members also came to the meetings to read, study, listen, converse, and hear, for these were not usual convention proceedings; they were occasions to hear God's Word preached with tremendous vigor.

Messengers at these meetings often used their programs for sermon notes. Following the sermons, they augmented their notes by purchasing print and audio copies of the sermons as well. Later in the day, they purchased video copies. The book expositions also provided Messengers with additional assistance: books written by their presidents, sometimes autographed. Certainly, Draper's *Authority: The Critical Issue for Southern Baptists* provided a clear interpretation of inerrancy for loyal laypersons. Over the last quarter century, the saliency and strength of inerrancy has been a principal characteristic of Southern Baptist presidential rhetoric.

Perhaps these pulpit sermonizers have taken their cue from the past. During the American pre–Civil War period, South Carolina's nullification controversy was developed by John C. Calhoun. In turn, his followers traveled the roads of the state to spread disunity regarding burdensome national tariffs and the alleged remedy for a central government gone wild: nullification. These "fire eaters," as their opponents called them, stomped the upcountry and lowcountry for states rights. Yet, it was the kingmaker, John C. Calhoun, who maneuvered his young rhetors to be persuasive agents with the common folk.

In the Bible, the Day of Pentecost was climaxed by "tongues of fire" on each man's head so that all could hear God in their own tongue. Today, the SBC presidents have developed their own tongues of fire about inerrancy to all those who would listen. The Holy Scriptures note that "those who have ears, let them hear." For those Southern Baptists who could not or would not hear and follow the dictates of the new post-takeover presidents, the message was stinging. They were called *liberals*, the ultimate devil word of today's loyalist sermonic rhetoric.

The South may have lost its cause in the nineteenth century, but the region itself has grown to be the leader in politics and population growth. Its politicians are prominent in Congress and the White House. The SBC has deliberately sought to have a prominent place in this renewal, yet it is intriguing to speculate about the Convention's success or lack of success. The SBC's presidents appear to have focused inward in order to retain and reinforce the membership against the sinful ways of corporate and secular America. The successful preaching of those like Chapman, Draper, Smith, Rogers, and Vines notwithstanding, the denomination's influence upon secular society is arguable.

These presidents were instrumental as pulpit sermonizers, for their communication redirected the denomination's path, influenced fellow believers, and served as a major force for social and political change in the South. Furthermore, dissenting Southern Baptists are now in exile, having been turned away from their churches in one way or another. Refusing to bow to the dictates of the SBC, they are now members of splinter groups befitting their conscience. It is significant, however, that they have no dynamic pulpit rhetors to lead them out of their disunity. On that point, dissidents have been bested by the SBC pulpit presidents since 1979.

5

Tongues of Fire: The Inerrancy Rhetoric of Southern Baptist Presidents

> We accept the scriptures as an all-sufficient and infallible rule of faith and practice and insist upon the absolute inerrancy and sole authority of the Word of God.
>
> —James M. Frost, first corresponding secretary of the Baptist Sunday School Board

This statement by Frost served as a historical source for several SBC presidents and untold numbers of pastors making a case for inerrancy in their home churches. It is worth noting that an extended Frost citation, highlighting this quote, is set in a frame outside of the executive offices of Dr. James T. Draper, Southern Baptist Convention Headquarters, Nashville, Tennessee.

Understanding the theoretical constructs of the rhetoric of inerrancy is an ideological and theological experience. Preparing and delivering the theory of the inerrant Word of God from the pulpit is quite another matter. In the uncertain arena of denominational politics, there is a rhetorical certainty. The presidents and other leaders of the SBC have brought the tenets of inerrancy to life with a verve and unique platform style that captured the right and most of the center of the Convention. Delivered annually at SBC conventions, the messages of these leaders were a clarion call to the thousands in attendance and the millions scattered across the nation. As if in harmony, these men raised their voices and their Bibles to affirm the complete, perfect truth of God's Word.

Dr. Kenneth Chafin was right when he stated in the foreword to this book that the rhetoric of inerrancy is more about a battle for the soul of a denomination than finely crafted sermons concerning the nature of the

Bible. From a rhetorical perspective, the victory of the battle was won on national rostrums in the sermons of the presidents, namely Adrian Rogers, Morris Chapman, Jerry Vines, and W. A. Criswell. These men spoke brilliantly, urging their listeners, near and far, to take up the Sword of the Lord.

These leaders, one and all, were excellent speakers. In their sermons, they alternately roared, coaxed, pleaded, joked, sang, rhapsodized, and, at times, whispered the unfathomable riches of the Bible. For them, the Scripture served as its own footnote when argued from the nature of things—the argument from genus. In a twenty-year line of succession from the early years of the controversy, the presidents knew all too well the power of the spoken word. For each man, the art of rhetoric has always been a welcome guest in the house of God.

Throughout history, the art of persuasion has had its diverse voices whether in social, political, or religious environments. The artful rhetoric of inerrancy found the voices of victory in these men. This chapter documents the significant messages of these presidents, at once simple and eloquent. Taken together, their rhetorical moments stretch across time to establish a prima facie case for inerrancy.

There are three phases of rhetorical activity in the takeover story. Part one of the story spans from 1980 to 1984, which were the stormy years for the inerrancy movement. Beginning with Dr. Adrian Roger's "The Decade of Decision and the Doors of Destiny" to Dr. Russell Dilday's "On Higher Ground," these are the best expression of the two sides of the inerrancy issue.

The second phase of rhetorical activity spans the years 1985 to 1990 and was marked by the finest display of loyalist rhetoric on the inerrancy theme. We feature one sermon in the appendixes from among the thirty-two sermons cited and evaluated for the study—Dr. Jerry Vines's "A Baptist and His Bible."

Part three of the story of the loyalists' sermons spans from 1991 to 1994. We begin this chapter with the defining sermon—the victory speech of the loyalists—by Dr. Morris Chapman, then pastor of the First Baptist Church in Wichita Falls—"Faith Is the Victory." For it was the end of the fledgling dissident counterresponse with the electoral defeats of Dr. Daniel Vestal at the Las Vegas convention (1989) and at the New Orleans convention (1990). The "fat lady sang" in 1990, assuring the remnant in the Superdome and the millions at home that true Southern Baptists were in charge of the convention.

Sure of the goals and certain of their success in gaining control of SBC boards and agencies, the Chapman-led Convention counted its gains and savored its electoral victory over Baptist dissidents. Morris Chapman is an archetypal, modern appearing and sounding major Southern Baptist minister and loyalist statesman. Of moderate height, handsome, coiffured, and physically fit, Chapman would not be out of place or uncomfortable in the board room or in the company of captains of industry. In the third and final phase of the rhetorical history of the controversy, Chapman seemed to be the Convention's best representative to lead Southern Baptists into the twenty-first century.

On a particularly steamy New Orleans morning, June 4, 1991, Morris Chapman moved briskly to the rostrum's center stage—a plexiglass podium—to claim his office and to claim the unsearchable riches of God's kingdom for his audience of over twenty thousand. Extending his arms as if to embrace the thousands of assembled Messengers, he complimented them: "We thank God you have stayed steadfast and true in your belief that the Bible is the inspired, inerrant Word of God." Turning to his left, Chapman lashed out: "The Bible neither claims nor reveals inerrancy as a Christian teaching. Bible claims must be based on the Bible, not on human interpretations of the Bible."[1]

To argue on behalf of loyal Southern Baptists and to chastise the breakaway dissidents because of their different views of Scripture, Chapman sounded the central theme of the presidents of the Southern Baptist Convention for years to come—"When you refuse to believe the Bible to be God's perfect Word, you have stripped away God's authority. All you have is human interpretation. . . . What someone called 'the dalmatian theory,' a spot of truth here and a spot of error there."[2]

Deepening his resolve and his voice, Chapman went on to defend the Bible and Southern Baptists by stating that

> for those who suggest that belief in an inerrant Bible is not a part of our Southern Baptist heritage, please listen to the words of James M. Frost. He was the first Corresponding Secretary of the Baptist Sunday School Board. In the year 1900, he wrote these words: "We accept the scriptures as an all-sufficient and infallible rule of faith and practice and insist upon the absolute inerrancy and sole authority of the Word of God."[3]

In a rhetorical moment reflective of all of the views of these presidents during the 1980s and 1990s, Morris Chapman maintained the simple truth of inerrant ideology—"if you believe all of the Word, you're in. If you believe less than all of the Word, you're out." In the sermons and speeches reviewed for this book, the speakers have all seemed to agree on this summary view of the rhetoric of inerrancy: The Bible is God's road map leading directly to Jesus Christ. The Bible "AAA route" is direct, though narrow. If you doubt the route or try to make up one of your own, you won't get there. If you delay making the trip, you will have to choose which way to go sooner or later. If you doubt the guidebook, then you have committed the greatest error of all. Jesus Christ waits at the beginning of life's journey; he is our constant, faithful companion during our journey and he will be with us at the end of and beyond life's journey. But, to have him as companion, as Lord and Savior, you must believe his Word. All of it.

A Rhetorical Vision for Southern Baptists

Rhetorical scholar Ernest Bormann's concepts of shared group meanings have particular relevance for these new Southern Baptists. Bormann argues that people and/or groups "chain" out critical ideas that become values and attitudes among their communities. Appropriately, these ideas-to-values-to-attitudes become social dramas where one can find heroes, villains, and common causes to support or defect.[4] And so it was for Southern Baptists in the 1980s and 1990s.

We argue that the loyalists' rhetorical vision, as developed in part by the Convention's presidents, centers on five premises. Morris Chapman's remarks reflect only the first two premises of the five in his 1989 Convention Sermon, which we summarize as follows:

> 1. The purpose of the Bible (and of its adherents) is to lead men to Christ. If there is any perceived imperfection in the Bible, there is an equally damaging imperfection in the Christ of the Bible.
>
> 2. The reason that there is a weak resolve in the modern Southern Baptist Church is because of a "defective attitude toward the Bible."[5]
>
> 3. Additionally, we argue that the third premise rests on popular American disbelief in the fundamentals of the faith. There are significant minorities outside the church who do not hold the basic tenets of the Christian faith. In an Associated Baptist Press report on the matter:
>
> > A significant minority of American Christians do not hold to tenets of their faith such as the virgin birth, the devil, or hell, according to a Harris Poll released September 12.
> >
> > The poll found that almost all American adults subscribed to basic religious beliefs including the existence of God (95 percent) and heaven (90 percent).
> >
> > Four in five Americans describe themselves as

> Christians, the poll said. Almost all Christians say they believe in God (99 percent), heaven (96 percent), and the resurrection of Christ (96 percent).
>
> However, those percentages drop off when they relate to other tenets, said Humphrey Taylor of Louis Harris and Associates in New York. Only 77 percent of Christians believe in hell, compared to 71 percent of all Americans. Among Christians, 78 percent profess belief in the devil, 85 percent in the virgin birth of Jesus, 87 percent in the miracles, and 89 percent in the soul's survival after death.
>
> More surprising, said Taylor, is that 49 percent of non-Christians accept Jesus' virgin birth and 52 percent believe Christ rose from the dead.
>
> Belief in other supernatural phenomena is less widespread, the study found. Only 37 percent of Americans say they believe in astrology and 36 percent in ghosts. Among Christians, belief in astrology is 35 percent and in ghosts 36 percent.
>
> Seventy-nine percent of adults describe themselves as Christians. But, while the United States statistically is a Christian nation, it apparently is becoming less so, said Taylor.
>
> Ninety percent of Americans over 50 say they are Christians, compared to only 59 percent of those age 18–24 and 70 percent of those 25–29. Taylor predicts that as large numbers of non-Christian immigrants continue to pour into the country, the percentage of Christian citizens will fall.
>
> The poll of 1,249 was conducted by telephone in July. The sample's margin of error is 3 percent, Taylor said. Other possible sources of error in any poll survey, however, such as question wording or interviewer bias, cannot be quantified, he added.[6]

4. We argue that the fourth principle stresses the inherent struggle, within and outside the church, with the claims of an inerrant Word. The loyalists will meet this problem head-on with the rock-solid and time-tested truths that provide all with total assurance.

5. By defining and defending these sacred truths, loyalists create "the others"—the excluded ones who do not belong because they cannot accept everything by faith. As if throw-

> ing down a gauntlet, the new Southern Baptist Convention presidents have proclaimed the Bible as the inerrant standard for inclusion and exclusion.

Set to the rhetorical rhythms of these new presidents, these five premises provide an outline of the rhetoric of inerrancy and the resulting rhetoric of exclusion. During the turbulent years of the controversy, former president Morris Chapman set a standard for correctness on the first two premises about the inerrant, infallible word.

Further, his 1989 Convention Sermon echoed the words of past SBC presidents when he exhorted his audience:

> Dear folks, the Bible is the inspired Word of God, the very breath of God. The Bible is the infallible Word of God for God cannot lie and the Bible never misleads or deceives. The Bible is the inerrant Word of God because God breathed out His perfect Word. The Bible says, "The law of the Lord is perfect" (Ps. 19:7). All scripture is given by inspiration of God. Just as our Lord Jesus was conceived without sin, God's written Word, the Bible, was breathed upon this earth without error. When God decided to breathe out the Word without error, He breathed out the substance of scripture. Whether or not we allow it to function in our hearts, God gave us the Bible without error and make no mistake about it, when He inspired the holy Word of God, He inspired not only the men, He inspired the very message.[7]

Later in the sermon, Chapman struck out at the "others"—those professors in Southern Baptist schools, colleges, and seminaries who separate students from their faith. Chapman called upon an external source to buttress his sermonic argument as he noted:

> In 1987, during the annual meeting of the Association of Southern Baptist Colleges and Schools in Kansas City, Missouri, Dr. Denton Lotz, Deputy General of the Baptist World Alliance delivered the H. I. Hester Lectures. He said, "I believe the existence of a Christian or Baptist college has as its only reason for being to reclaim the minds of our country for Christ. The West will never be converted until the college is converted. And the college will never be converted until there is a radical rediscovery of the unity of all truth in Jesus Christ. A Baptist college has no right to exist as an institution of Christian education if it is not a servant of and responsible to the community of faith that nurtured and founded it."[8]

While fifteen years (1979–1994) of SBC convention preaching has provided hours of Scripture-reading and argumentation for the development of the inerrancy case, no preacher has said it better than Jerry Vines. Long a favorite of the new inner circle of loyalists, Vines played a number of prominent roles in earlier 1980s conventions. When he was asked to preach the 1987 Convention Sermon, Vines accepted and placed his indelible mark on the record of SBC sermons concerning inerrancy.

Vines's sermon "A Baptist and His Bible" is the finest national statement on biblical inerrancy we found during our research for this study. A gifted orator of the New South School of Southern Baptist preachers, Vines was the perfect combination of country preacher and gifted scholar of the Bible. Adrian Rogers, president of the SBC in 1987 and regarded as the quintessential orator of Southern Baptist life, introduced Vines. In all of the hours of videotape and transcript involving Adrian Rogers, he was never so humbled nor excited when referring to others on the podium. Vines was, for Rogers, "the best combination of scholar and country preacher in Southern Baptist life today."[9]

Jerry Vines did not disappoint, as he has always been a gifted speaker and an ardent student of the Bible's native languages—Hebrew and Greek. In the words of southern folklore, "If you don't want to believe the man, don't listen to him." In a firm, memorized textual speaking style, Vines riveted the audience to their seats for nearly forty minutes. In his sermon, Vines established the Apostle Paul as the Scripture's finest apologist, its prime defender, and its best teacher. Furthermore, Vines reinforced the long-held concept that the Bible is its own best footnote.

Early in the sermon, Vines affirmed that the "purpose of the Bible is to lead men to Jesus Christ." Because of the Bible's internal purpose, Vines claimed that "Baptists get concerned when there is any hint of attack upon it. We get upset when there is any undermining of its authority, questioning of its reliability or denying of its accuracy."[10]

Setting a tone heard in national convention sermons of the early 1980s and heard down through the years in SBC presidential preaching, Vines proposed, "How can anyone say we must trust our soul to Christ for eternity, then turn around and try to obliterate the very document which tells us about Him?"[11] Vines moved quickly to warn his listeners regarding his particular brand of the "other"—destructive criticism. For the better part of the middle section of the sermon, Vines hammered away at the historical-critical method that "destroys the scripture piece by piece."[12] For the remainder of the sermon, Vines urged his hearers to reject the criticisms of the Bible and, in turn, believe it in regard to all of life's needs. It is the "Bible . . . and It will get you home."[13]

The assembled thousands rose to acclaim the great sermon and its humble voice. The power of a literate, prepared text and clear purpose, combined with Jerry Vines's folksy rhetorical style, provided a defining moment in raising Southern Baptist preaching to a new level. The Messengers roared their approval of this finely crafted sermon, delivered by a gifted speaker to an audience eager for a fresh breath of God's Word. This sermon was a high rhetorical watermark in Southern Baptist preaching.

The Southern Baptist Convention has had its great rhetorical events in recent years, but when Vines strode to the plexiglass pulpit, acknowledged his audience, paused, and then spoke his memorized line to the gallery—"In beautiful human language resplendent with divine revelation Paul sets before us the Bible's doctrine concerning itself"[14]—everyone present knew this sermon was special.

In 1980, the first president of the Southern Baptist Convention's new leadership, Adrian Rogers, preached the first President's Address of the inerrantist movement, "The Decade of Decision and the Doors of Destiny." Setting the tone for years to come, Rogers's rich baritone voice soared when he spoke of "What the Bible says for itself":

> 1. It is the Word of God. . . . It is so called over 4,000 times in the Old Testament alone (1 Thess. 2:13)
>
> 2. It is God-breathed (II Tim. 3:16)
>
> 3. It is unbreakable (John 10:35)
>
> 4. It is invocable (Matt. 5:19)
>
> 6. Every word, not just the thoughts, are God Given (Matt. 4:4)
>
> 7. It is eternal (Psa. 119:89)
>
> 8. It is therefore perfect (Psa. 19:7)

In maintaining the total accuracy of the Bible, Rogers affirmed the key of inerrancy, namely, "So when we speak of the Bible as 'truth, without any mixture of error,' we are referring to the original manuscripts. The Holy Spirit guarded the original writers from error."[15]

Rogers and Vines preached as if they had been to the same sermon writer, disregarding the fact that the sermons cited here were preached seven years apart. Each went to the Bible to find internal evidence for proving the truth and accuracy of the Bible, even using many of the same scriptures with near identical explanations. In his 1981 President's Address, Rev. Bailey E. Smith reaffirmed the point on inerrancy: "If the Bible is the Word of God at all, it is the perfect Word of God, because God will not give a word of flaws and mistakes."[16] From year to year, these Convention presidents have promoted the greatest circular argument of all time to the level of bedrock truth, which now serves as the foundation for the rhetoric of inerrancy.

With a firm commitment to the Bible as the final authority, President James T. Draper took the next step in the defense of Scripture in 1983 when he stated that: "If the Word of God is reliable, then the Southern Baptist Convention must renew its commitment to the scripture if it is to survive." In this address, Draper told the Messengers what to do: "We will be absolutely loyal to our Lord Jesus Christ. We will recognize that by his shed blood we have been reconciled to God . . . We who declare our strong commitment to God's Word must become people who read it, memorize it, study it, appropriate it, and Live it."[17]

The following year, President Draper again emphasized the same theme by asserting that "the key to our commitment to sharing the Good News and proclaiming the Gospel . . . that is our responsibility as Southern Baptists."[18] In 1988, W. A. Criswell of the First Baptist Church in Dallas, the Convention's most renowned preacher, spoke about "The Infallible Word of God" to thousands of Messengers. Covering all the bases, Criswell's booming rhetorical style celebrated the Bible as a book of science, history, and anthropology. But for what purpose? Criswell intoned that "the reason is very simple. The Lord God who inspired the *Book is the Lord God who made these things from the beginning*."[19]

The inerrancy movement was gaining strength in the early 1990s, buoyed by the long string of victories in the presidential elections and the gradual takeover of the Convention's committee and board memberships. Taking a cue from these successes, President Morris Chapman challenged the 1992 convention attendees, telling them that "It's Time to Move." Chapman stated, "We can do no less today." Furthermore,

> For the greater part of the twentieth century, Southern Baptists have struggled to state clearly the doctrinal commitments which have formed us and which we share. Belief in the Almighty Creator of the Universe, absolute in His holiness and rich in grace; of Jesus Christ the divine God-man, the incarnate Word who dwelt among us; of His substitutionary work of redemption of Calvary's cross; of his physical resurrection from the grave; of His coming again to consummate the age; of the work of God in bringing men and women to salvation and everlasting life; of believer's baptism as the soul's confession of new life in Jesus Christ.
>
> When Southern Baptists have spoken, they have spoken clearly, they have spoken corporately, and they have spoken convictionally. We have also spoken cooperatively. In that spirit, we now offer a new fraternal message, addressed to the denomination within and the world without. It is a call to go up and over the mountain toward the promised land.[20]

The rhetoric of inerrancy has always seemed to invigorate a listening audience of Messengers. Down through the years of the sermons and speeches of the Southern Baptist Convention, it is abundantly clear that the Messengers to these national meetings from 1979 to 1994 came to hear a new claim that the Bible makes for itself, to cheer the admonitions directly from the presidents, and to loudly affirm the person of the Word—Jesus Christ. In 1993, President Ed Young proclaimed that "Jesus is the answer." For "when the main thing, evangelism, becomes the main thing again, the Southern Baptist Convention will no longer be on side streets."[21]

It is interesting to note that President Young delivered the 1980 SBC Convention Sermon entitled "Side Streets," and in 1994 he delivered the President's Address on the same theme—the "side streets" that Southern Baptists have taken and need to avoid. His 1994 sermon was reminiscent of his 1980 sermon. In both years, his theological position was identical. President Young proclaimed that the denominational battle was over, and those supporting inerrancy had won. He spoke fervently and personally to his audience:

> Over 14 years ago, the Southern Baptist Convention, as all you know, came to see that by and large we had a theological cancer. There was tremendous concern [among] a lot of people as to what was taking place in our denomination, and we know that some of our seminaries and some of our institutions of higher education were basically committed by their faculties to a neo-orthodox understanding of the Bible—to a Bultmanian approach to scripture. I tell you, for example, in the seminary I attended, three out of the four professors of New Testament did not believe in the bodily resurrection of Jesus Christ. Now that is not second-hand information. I was there. I think everybody who is Southern Baptist needs to understand we have not been in some kind of debate over a certain rigid, dogmatic, creedalizing interpretation of scripture. We have been in a battle over the Bible, and the issue is one thing. The issue in this theological reformation has been what the Bible is, and we have decided in associations, state conventions, in Southern Baptist conventions. We have decided through the report of the Peace Committee, in a document you have been handed today as you entered here that in purpose what we mean by truth without mixture of error in our Baptist Faith and Message. We have decided that the Bible is the infallible, authoritative, inerrant Word of God.[22]

However, some leaders speak to high issues such as human rights and the free conduct of life among a free people. For example, in 1984, Russell Dilday, then the president of Southwestern Baptist Theological Seminary, asked his audience to retain an attitude of inquiry regarding the issue of followership. Dilday described Southern Baptists who are

> fearful of standing alone, surrender[ing] that sacred privilege of individualism. They go along with the crowd, accepting the canned thinking of the majority. Swayed by public opinion, and glibly mouthing the popular clichés of the party in power, they are quick to espouse those causes that are in vogue. They cater to the powerful, play to the gallery, and flow with the tide.[23]

Alternately barking and shouting at his audience, Dilday not only criticized Southern Baptists as "fearful of standing alone," he pushed and prodded his hearers to "stay on [a] higher ground of spiritual persuasion, autonomous individualism, [with] the Christ-like humility where you belong."[24]

Dilday went on to argue that the real truth of the matter was the shrewdness of the brokers of presidential power in the Convention. These persons possessed selfish ambition, self-promotion, and a desire for power that thrived on a forced uniformity and an incipient Orwellian mentality through adeptly selected scriptural texts of an inerrant Bible. Dilday did not accept the loyalist rhetoric, and his dissent was clear.

It may be argued that Dilday and his sermon were impassioned targets four years later at the SBC's 1988 Pastor's Conference. It was here that W. A. Criswell highlighted and received a roaring ovation when he issued a fiery indictment of his own against "the curse of liberalism." Speaking to an estimated audience of sixteen thousand at the conference, Criswell railed at the curse of liberalism, grouping "liberals" with "moderates," saying, "A skunk by any other name still stinks."[25] Denying that the ongoing controversy in the Convention had been the cause of a declining number of Southern Baptist baptisms, Criswell called for "a resurgence, a recommitment, a regeneration" among Southern Baptists.[26] The following day, President Jerry Vines affirmed that only inerrantists would be appointed to the committees and boards of the Convention when he said "I just could not look Southern Baptists in the face and appoint people who believe there are errors in the Bible."[27]

Two years later, Vines delivered the President's Address, "The Glory of God," at the 1990 SBC convention and spoke on the same issue. Vines stated that "those denominations that affirm the inspiration, inerrancy and infallibility of scripture have a bright future. But those that do not are destined for the garbage dump of denominations. It is better for Southern Baptists to debate and settle the issue of Scriptural inerrancy today than to someday argue whether homosexuals are suitable in our pulpits."[28] No self-respecting Southern Baptist loyalist could argue with these annual arguments and claims about an error-free Bible.

Yet, some Southern Baptists are unwilling to accept the rhetoric of inerrancy. In the 1980s and 1990s, Southern Baptists have splintered into new organizations such as the Cooperative Baptist Fellowship and the Alliance of Baptists. Countless others have remained quiet soldiers in the onward march of Christians called the Southern Baptist Convention.

In the period from 1990 to 1994, a variety of personal confrontations and tactical embroilments plagued the Convention, causing some to stand, to fight, to regroup to fight again, or to leave the field of rhetorical combat. These new battles are not merely local skirmishes. They are about women in leadership and the pastorate, different meanings of Scripture, homosexuals in the church, and the proper obligations of being both a Southern Baptist and a Mason. There is no reason to believe that the resolution of these battles will heal the denomination now or in the foreseeable future.

For fifteen years (1979–1994), the leaders of the Southern Baptist Convention produced the finest defense of pulpit sermons on a single theme that had ever been seen or heard in the 150-year history of the denomination. These preachers and their rhetoric have undoubtedly influenced the direction of the Convention. Certainly, these men have helped redesign America's largest Protestant denomination. Their argumentative and emotional appeals, scriptural texts, and powerfully personalized pulpit language are attractive to audiences longing for an evangelistic style of power and a certain understanding of the Bible. Understandably, this group of pulpit artists are likely to be heard from again and again.

It is intriguing that this very small group of preachers, skilled in persuasion, have set this Convention ablaze with the sheer energy of their spoken word. They achieved it with skillful interpretations of Scripture designed for their audiences and their spiritual needs. Their achievements cannot be chalked up to tradition or a changing Southern culture. These preachers persuaded a multimillion-member convention of Southern Baptists from Virginia to Texas to return to the Bible and the Rock of Ages.

These SBC leaders spoke in harmony that all could hear, with words all could understand. Pastors, their families, and the hundreds of church Messengers returned home each year with months of ideas, conversation pieces, sermon notes, and hearts on fire for God. The rhetoric of inerrancy "chained out" to the local church, regional church associations, and eventually, the state's elected leadership, as well as to numerous sermons, Sunday School classes, and deacon's meetings.

Like the Day of Pentecost, the tongues of fire set the Convention ablaze for God and the inerrant, infallible word. The fire became "a refiner's fire," burning away the dross, consuming those who could not stand the heat of exclusion, particularly the objectionable, anti-biblical groupings—women as senior pastors, homosexuals, and Masons. Seen as objectionable believers, these persons are victims of the rhetoric of exclusion. To be excluded is to understand the dictates of an inerrant Bible. Some cannot be in the fold unless they repent and accept. "Women as leaders of men" have become a killing field in this rhetorical Holy War, for they are "objectionable believers."

Adrian Rogers. Courtesy Southern Baptist Historical Library and Archives.

Jerry Vines. Courtesy Southern Baptist Historical Library and Archives.

Morris Chapman. Courtesy Southern Baptist Historical Library and Archives.

James Draper. Courtesy Southern Baptist Historical Library and Archives.

W. A. Criswell. Courtesy Southern Baptist Historical Library and Archives.

6

Objectionable Believers, Roger Williams, and the Southern Baptist Oligarchy

> You *women* have a problem. I tell you what—you go home and raise a family and you may just see God.
>
> —Rev. Mark Coppenger, president of Midwestern Baptist Seminary

> Rise Up, *Men* of God, The Church for *you* doth wait . . .
>
> —*The Broadman Hymnal* (emphasis added)

Observers of Southern life have recently seen Southern Baptists become newsmakers in the secular realm. The front pages of any number of national, metropolitan, and local newspapers have printed stories that focused on the boycott of the Walt Disney corporation.[1] Recent stories have described the denomination's selection of Jews and Mormons as special targets for public evangelism.[2] The press has noted that SBC Messengers have voted for restrictive policies against gays, lesbians, women leaders, and political liberals. These decisions, and others, raise questions about this denomination's advocacy in general, its rhetorical ethics in particular, and its impact upon Southern culture.

The SBC has been split since loyalist Baptists assumed control of the Southern Baptist Convention in 1979 and ejected dissenters from office.[3] Twenty years later, the triumphant loyalists continue to solidify their control over the denomination although now with demonstrable impact on the local church level. In the South today, this struggle continues for the hearts, minds, and souls of SBC members.

Enormous casualties have occurred, especially for those dissenting female church pulpit ministers, allegedly disloyal denominational officers, and missionaries whom the leadership has expelled or ostracized for failing to meet the new requirements of denominational acceptance. Various seminary professors have also been fired or forced into retirement.[4] Ordinary church members in the pew have had to make new and sometimes difficult choices about their church and pulpit minister.

In this chapter, we emphasize the nature of loyalist discourse regarding women as denominational leaders and how victimage rhetoric is used by loyalist rhetors to justify the expulsion of women as objectionable believers. Victimage language—a justificatory form of language often used by rhetors in closed communication systems to legitimize their authorial decisions—casts aspersions, denigrates abilities, or uses name calling. Such masculine language focused on the objectives of power, dominance, and control in sermonic discourse is unethical.[5] It is unethical because it flagrantly disregards a conceptualization of communication that stresses relational responsibility and its enabling consequences for all believers.

In addition, we will shortly compare SBC exclusionist rhetoric to that of the Massachusetts Bay's banishment decree in 1635 against Roger Williams, who championed religious liberty for all persons as an exile in Rhode Island. Such an analogy is appropriate because the decree text and SBC presidential sermons are exclusionary, and they have similar contexts and arguments. As outlined in chapter 3, from our larger study of the denomination, we have concluded that official SBC discourses can be identified by three characteristics: fundamentalism, inerrancy, and exclusion. The importance of the Southern Baptist pulpit is central to an explanation of its rhetoric and to an understanding of the historical uniqueness of the denomination itself, which was founded in 1845. Since the takeover, all SBC presidents have been pulpit artists of denominational significance.

According to Richard Weaver, human language is not neutral or objective; rather it is "sermonic." Weaver asserts, "we are all of us preachers in private or public capacities," and "we speak as rhetoricians affecting one another for good or ill."[6] To evangelicals, sermons, whether public or private, are not merely a liturgical exercise, but a persuasive act, designed to leave hearers better off for the experience, especially regarding personal choices about one's soul. To be ethical "our language should preserve our fundamental human capacity to choose."[7] This advice necessarily requires the inclusion of ethical responsibility in making discourse choices for and with audiences.[8]

In his introduction to *On Symbols and Society* by Kenneth Burke, editor Joseph R. Gusfield advises critics to ask the question, what are the "forms [of discourse] which are constant?" to determine what is orderly and disorderly about rhetoric.[9] Such a question seems particularly valuable, since orderliness has been deified in the Southern Baptist Convention presidential sermons, and we should expect that characteristic to be prominent in SBC institutional rhetoric.

Gusfield further interprets Burke to say that the problem of order in any society is central. According to Gusfield, when a society is faced with a dynamic struggle, perhaps for its own existence, then it often proceeds through several steps in its effort to succeed: "If drama, then conflict [will follow]. If conflict, then hierarchy [will follow]. If hierarchy, then guilt [will follow]. If guilt, then redemption [will follow]. If redemption, then victimage [will follow]."[10]

Consequently, victimage is inferred from drama that produces conflict. In turn, conflict produces adversaries whose tendency is to classify and describe the objects or persons selected for victimization. The language used to justify victimization is especially important to opponents, and in this conflict, advocacy terminologies of acceptance and rejection reflect a projection of undesirable characteristics that nonmembers might avoid using.

Victimage requires sacrifice, or as Burke asserts, "In the sacrifice there is a kill; in the kill there is a sacrifice."[11] In primitive societies, purification was assigned by ceremony to the sacrifice of an animal such as a lamb or goat. Sacrifices have been ritualistically assigned social characteristics. For example, Jesus at the crucifixion was designated "King of the Jews." Simon of Cyrene carried his master's cross to Golgotha, symbolizing his willingness to carry those unwanted evils ascribed to Jesus by the Scribes and Pharisees for his alleged violations of Jewish law. According to Caiphas, the high priest, there had to be a scapegoat, and Judas was selected; a sacrifice was mandated, and Jesus was chosen.

Ideally, the model sacrifice must be worthy of the kill, so as to thereby justify the act of killing. According to Burke, three criteria apply to the determination of such worthiness.[12] First, the scapegoat may be worthy because his or her offense against moral justice, legality, truth, or correctness was so great that the offender's punishment was required to expose the heinous qualities of the offender's actions as beyond that acceptable to a hierarchy.

Second, the scapegoat may be deserving of sacrifice "fatalistically," as in a prophecy, for example, which foreshadows the deed by informing receivers of the impending event.[13] A scriptural text that exemplifies this point is from the authorized King James version of the Bible, the book of Exodus, chapter 12:21–23:

> Then Moses called for all the elders of Israel, and said unto them, draw out and take you a lamb according to your families, and kill the passover. And ye shall take a bunch of hyssop, and dip it into the blood that is in the basin, and strike the lintel and the two side posts with the blood that is in the basin, and none of you shall go out at the door of his house until the morning. For the Lord will pass through to smite the Egyptians; and when he seeth the blood upon the lintel, and

> on the two side posts, the Lord will pass over the door, and will not suffer the destroyer to come in unto your houses to smite you.

In this passage, believers are preconditioned to think of the victim as doomed and will therefore presumably understand, and perhaps be prepared, for the sacrifice. In Exodus, the slaying of the Egyptians was made known to the Hebrews in advance by the warning that they were to mark their lintel and doorposts with blood from the sacrificial lamb. Such action therefore excluded their eligibility for death, but preidentified those marked as sacrificial victims.

Third, scapegoats may be worthy of sacrifice because of their perfectness; they are virtually above the usual standards of excellence and virtue. As we shall argue shortly, Roger Williams's advocacy against Massachusetts Bay meets all three of these criteria, and the same is true regarding various contemporary female dissidents in the Southern Baptist Convention today.

It is instructive to evaluate Roger Williams's conflict with the Massachusetts Bay oligarchy in the 1630s and compare it to the present rhetorical dispute in the SBC. A suitable text for analysis is Williams's banishment sentence pronounced in the fall of 1635 by the General Court of the Massachusetts Bay Colony. The Williams expulsion decree is a clarifying and illuminating analogy of exclusionary rhetoric, because much of it focuses on victimage. Williams was convicted of sedition; the banishment text was brief:

> Whereas Mr. Roger Williams . . . hath broached and divulged dyvers and dangerous opinions, against the authoritie of magistrates, [h]as also writt letters of defamacon, both of the magistrates and churches here, and that before any [court?] conviccon, and yet maintaineth the same without retracon, it is therefore ordered, that the said Mr. Williams shall departe out of his jurisdiction.[14]

The Bay oligarchy was angered by Williams's dissidence and his persuasive skill in attracting nonconformists to the Salem church. Consequently, they wished to expel him. Unwilling to test Williams's ethos against theirs within the community of Bay churches, they instead placed restrictions on his church's freedom within the association. Williams quickly recognized this attempt at "superintendency" over his church and warned others of the dangers of such an action. According to Williams, a "presbytery" of churches would ultimately "prejudice" an individual "church's liberties" because of the Bay's disposition and power to impose unwanted rules on the church membership.

The Bay authorities, rather like the mother church in England, were wont to interfere with individual liberties, from Williams's view. Consequently, Williams wanted John Cotton to recognize that point and urge his fellow ministers in England and New England to allow more believer independence:

> Might it please God to perswade the mother to permit
> the inhabitants of New England her daughter to enjoy
> their conscience to God, after a particular Congregational way?[15]

Such an allowance was not then acceptable, at least in public discourse, and Cotton refused Williams's challenge. To Cotton, Williams was guilty of "schisme, heresie, [and] obstinacie" even for proposing such a change.[16]

Thus, Williams and his followers urged changes in church governance and practice that would have severely diminished the power of the Massachusetts Bay autocracy. When he publicly urged his followers to seek an open dialogue with the Boston divines on his proposals, he (and they) were spurned by the oligarchy. Williams's letters of defense to the individual Bay churches were denounced as "antichristian pollution." In addition, Williams could not be "reduce[d]" from his errors by Thomas Hooker.[17]

Williams's banishment was authorized by a unified secular and church alliance determined to cleanse the colony from any minister guilty of preaching nonconformity (or any member publicly supporting it). Because ministers were sanctioned rhetors in early New England, they were visibly important to the success of the oligarchy's "experiment on a hill." Whether from the pulpit, in home-based prayer meetings, or in outdoor sermons to the traders, trappers, explorers, farmers, itinerant teachers, and the Narragansett Indians whose language he spoke, Williams was a persistently powerful persuader who would not surrender his convictions.

In essence, the Boston ministers could not tolerate a dissenter who was as skilled and persuasive as they were in their communications about church polity issues. From their point of view, there was little to discuss anyway. Public debate on the issue of nonconformity would have been construed as a concession to arguing the unnecessary. Worse, it would have legitimized nonconformist discourse in the colony. It would also have authorized Williams's status as an equal in the climate of public discourse, something that John Winthrop and his associates were loathe to do. Today, however, Southern Baptist dissidents visualize Williams's ethos and discourse against the Bay as prophetic and instructive.

In the Massachusetts Bay of 1631, Williams was likely a marked man upon his arrival in Boston. He was better educated than anyone else in the colony, including John Winthrop. He was politically astute because of his tutelage from Sir Edward Coke, the developer of English common law. He was an adversary of King James I and a strong advocate for free speech in Parliament. Because of Williams's experience in Star Chamber as Coke's protégé, and his disputation experience at Charterhouse and Cambridge, Williams was a skilled public arguer in both legal and scholastic environments.[18] His previous chaplaincy to Sir William Masham in County Essex identified him as a Parliamentarian, a political affiliation that Boston ministers were not eager to publicly embrace within the promised land. Williams was thus eminently worthy of "departure" from the colony when he stepped off the boat from Bristol, England.

When Williams formally requested in writing that his Salem church be allowed to withdraw from the Massachusetts Bay church alliance, his proposal was denounced by the Boston divines as "lewd."[19] Williams, who never accepted the tyranny of the bishops in England, was equally unwilling to accept the hierarchy of the divines in Boston. Consequently, he rejected the Massachusetts Bay's attempt to stifle layperson advocacy in local churches, for that smacked of ruling "presbyteries," and he would have none of it.

Adversary John Cotton never publicly acknowledged that Williams's banishment for sedition was an edict emanating from the Massachusetts Bay oligarchy. According to him, Williams had left of his own volition from "the society of churches," and banishment was only a matter of civil, not religious, law. But, Cotton's position was disingenuous. Williams had indeed exited the Salem church when his congregation was ordered to remove him, but only grudgingly. In addition, the court had unequivocally ordered him to "depart" from the Bay in the official pronouncement of sentence. Had Williams not chosen to leave his Salem pulpit, the church's continued banishment from the Bay association of member churches would have effectively denied its influence in the colony, whether in church polity or civil law. The Boston ministers clearly wanted to rid their colony of this preacher of "dangerous opinions" and thus retain a conformist public discourse. Williams never lived to see his banishment sentence rescinded, for that action occurred three hundred years later. Undeniably, the Commonwealth of Massachusetts was not guilty of a rush to judgment, a point that is debatable regarding the SBC's exclusion of objectionable believers.

The exclusion of Baptist dissidents today seems to involve a pattern of justifications similar to that of the Boston oligarchy's. Once the dissident's discourse is labeled unacceptable by the SBC, the dissident immediately becomes a candidate for expulsion. The justification for exclusion is framed around the notion that the "scapegoat" is removable because his or her rhetoric is egregiously unsanctionable and therefore outside the realm of toleration by the SBC Executive Committee. In such cases, the dissident's exile from the community of believers is ostensibly not caused by the Nashville hierarchy, but by his or her own hand. In Williams's case, for example, his expulsion was totally justified because he had publicly promulgated his "dangerous opinions" from the pulpit. According to the Bay oligarchy, such an action constituted an abuse of the pulpit in Boston. Therefore, Williams had made himself a candidate for expulsion. Above all, however, scapegoats are worthy candidates for removal because their "lewd" opinions might infect believers, thereby causing harm to the greater community of adherents. In mid-seventeenth-century Boston, as in the Southern Baptist Convention, these justifications were and still are entirely usable.

Since 1979, this rationale has served as a justification for various implementation actions regarding dissidence. First, the deviation of an individual, church, or agency membership from the approved standards of denominational exclusivity may be penalized by the leadership. Second, annual convention sermons (and Messenger resolutions) stress that pulpit ministers should utilize a theology of inerrancy or face dismissal, pulpit exile, or intimidation for their waywardness. Third, the leadership consistently projects a conformist, doctrinaire, and gender-explicit leadership model to the membership. This closed but unified communication system likely enhances the excision of those who disagree. Enhancing this exclusion is desirable because it legitimizes the leadership's description of the reclaimed denomination as more pure and bolsters its claim that the denomination is a reconstructed, if not more obedient, organizational church structure.

The denomination has centered much of its scapegoat rhetoric towards Baptist women pulpit ministers, who in 1982 numbered approximately 175. In 1995, Rev. Molly Marshall, a professor at Southern Baptist Theological Seminary, resigned rather than face dismissal charges. In 1996, Trustee Barrett Hyman of Southwestern Baptist Theological Seminary justified such actions regarding female seminary faculty: "If you believe that pastors can be women, then you need to go somewhere else. . . . if professors believe that [women should be pulpit ministers] then it's our job to get them out of here."[20]

The 1987 case of Rev. Nancy Hastings Sehested, a prominently known advocate for various social rights ministries, is illustrative of the denominations's method of exclusion.[21] The Prescott Memorial Baptist Church of Memphis, Tennessee, called her as its pulpit minister. Later, the Shelby County (Tennessee) Baptist Association ejected the church from associational membership, thus denying it the right of membership within a body of sister SBC churches. Such an action did more than deny the church voting rights, for, like Williams's Salem church, it effectively denied it influence with its sister churches as well.

At the associational hearing called to consider the expulsion action, Sehested spoke in her own defense, and her rhetoric was devoid of recrimination. Instead, in a Williams-like spirit of dialogue with her disagreeing listeners, she raised questions for her companion believers to consider: "While we are in this place debating about who can or cannot stand behind a piece of wood, there's a world out there . . . are we going to say to that world that not all things are possible with God? Are we going to say to that world, no, not all things are possible. A woman cannot preach!"[22]

Effectively, the Shelby County Association's resolution also legitimized the banishment of Prescott Memorial from a denominational relationship with all SBC churches. Consequently, the church was transformed into a pariah, if not an untouchable. The association's actions were a clarion signal *not* to hire women as pulpit ministers, and a confirmation of the binding action of the 1984 Resolution 3, which forbade women to be pulpit ministers in the denomination.

The Shelby County Association did not deny or remove Sehested from her pulpit. Its effect upon Sehested was nevertheless momentous, for it ostracized her from other Southern Baptist Convention ministers. This forced "disfellowshipping" from other ministers was neither specifically ordered in the association's expulsion nor in Resolution 3; but it was a result nevertheless.

In another case in 1988, the Foreign Mission Board (FMB) failed to return longtime missionary Doris Walters to Japan. Allegedly, she declined to divulge the number of persons she had led to Christ during her stay. Walters was, of course, thrust into a double jeopardy situation. Had she admitted any number of converts, she would have faced dismissal, since her disclosure might have been interpreted as confirmation of her authority over men. Nevertheless, her unwillingness (or inability) to provide a number to the FMB also effectively secured her dismissal on the presumed basis of pastoral ineffectiveness.

In 1989, the Home Mission Board (HMB) adopted a policy of financial non-support to any church that chose a woman as its pulpit minister. It has also refused to disburse funds to those SBC churches who have hired females to preach. Consequently, after an inspection visit by the HMB of the Jeff Street Mission in Louisville, Kentucky, funding for the mission was discontinued because Rev. Cindy Weber's preaching may have encouraged several street residents to join the mission church.

In 1993, the Women's Missionary Union (WMU) was threatened with "disassociation" by the SBC leadership. Such an action is the same as expulsion. Over 105 years old, the WMU is an independent auxiliary of SBC women church members across the denomination. It has been an important fund-raising agency for denominational missions, both foreign and domestic. In 1992, it had raised over $115 million exclusively for missions through its support for the annual Lottie Moon and Annie Armstrong offerings. These funds then provided for half of the Foreign Mission Board and Home Mission Board budgets.

On January 12, 1993, the WMU Executive Board voted to support mission programs of "other Southern Baptist groups such as the [breakaway] Cooperative Baptist Fellowship [CBF], [to] forge relationships with evangelical missions organizations outside the SBC," and "become active in social issues." Dellanna O'Brien, then the WMU's executive secretary, indicated the organization wanted to be active on such issues as race, hunger, and homelessness. The WMU, she asserted, was simply "responding to the changing needs of women."[23] But John Jackson, the chair of trustees to the SBC Foreign Mission Board, asserted that the WMU's actions were "like committing adultery." Jackson linked the WMU's decision to enter into a relationship with the dissident CBF to marriage infidelity: "[Their action is] similar . . . to a woman having been married to a man for many, many years and all of a sudden she says, 'I have another man that I want to be married to. . . . I know that you won't mind if I bring him into our bed.'"[24] WMU leader O'Brien declared Jackson's use of the adultery analogy as "unfortunate."[25] In 1995, at the annual convention, the denomination's Messengers terminated their 105-year-long relationship with the WMU.

Thus, a significant division between dissident and loyalist leaders exists regarding the equality of female Southern Baptists. Indeed, when analyzed from a loyalist view, female SBC members are at the virtual center of the schism for two reasons. First of all, loyalists argue that women are explicitly disallowed by scriptural authorization to assume hierarchical roles superior to men, for that prohibition is textually clear within I Corinthians, as is the implicit disallowance of any pulpit-leadership function from any ordained woman. Second, the loyalists have further marked women for removal from leadership because of their "Edenic fall"; that is, it was a woman who committed the first sin on earth in the Garden of Eden.

Both of these points are developed in Resolution 3, which legalized the continued exclusion of women from SBC pulpits as preachers. The excerpted resolution below, entitled "On Ordination and the Role of Women in Ministry," contains supporting scriptural clauses:

> Whereas, The scriptures attest to God's delegated order of authority (God the head of Christ, Christ the head of man, man the head of woman, man and woman dependent one upon the other to the glory of God) distinguishing the roles of men and women in public prayer and prophecy (1 Cor. 11:2–5.)
>
> Whereas, The scriptures teach that women are not in public worship to assume a role of authority over men lest confusion reign in the local church (1 Cor. 14:33–36).

> Whereas, while Paul commends women and men alike in other roles of ministry and service (Titus 2:1–10), he excludes women from pastoral leadership (1 Tim. 2:12) to preserve a submission God requires because the man was first in creation and the woman was first in the Edenic fall (1 Tim. 2:13).
>
> Therefore, be it resolved, That we not decide concerns of Christian doctrine and practice by modern cultural, sociological and ecclesiastical trends or by emotional factors . . . and that we encourage the service of women in all aspects of church life and work other than pastoral functions and leadership roles entailing ordination.[26]

The text of Resolution 3 provides scriptural justification for the claim that women are appropriately and eternally marked for subservience in two ways. First of all, female adult adherents have historically served in submissive roles, an argument that is developed in the resolution. Thus, women have frequently filled the role of servants in private prayer and prophecy and in service-ministries. Priscilla was a teacher of the Christian leader Apollos; Phoebe received special thanks from Paul for her service to the church at Cenchrea. Second, loyalists have acknowledged their gratitude to the apostle Paul for outlining the delegated order of authority, namely, of male hierarchy. Accordingly, the book of Corinthians specifies that man is the head of woman. Her submission is therefore authorized by the ultimate source of loyalist textual authority, the Holy Bible.

The employment of exclusionary rhetoric by the male denominational hierarchy suggests more than just a cosmetic redesign of the denomination; it offers a total reordering of society, for it places humankind's sinful waywardness on the backs of women. Redemption from this sin is impossible. Women have a womb that forever disallows their absolution, regardless of their submission to men. Indeed, the possession of a womb ensures continued watchfulness or suspicion by the hierarchy. Specifically, for female and male advocates who oppose these expulsion justifications, the immediate future can be portended by the near past. Since 1979, women leaders have been the negative object of Messenger resolutions at annual conventions, and they have also been subjected to ostracism, denominational humiliation, and removal, or at the least they have been refused consideration for various denominational leadership posts.

For loyalists, Paul's letter of I Timothy is therefore *the* important justificatory text for their advocacy. In 1996, Rev. Mark Coppenger, president of the Midwestern Baptist Seminary, reaffirmed Resolution 3 by asserting that women should "learn in quietness and full submission."[27] In any case, since a woman's sin in the Garden of Eden has forever insured her submission to males, female adherents are the scapegoats who must carry the unwanted sins of humankind.

According to Carolyn Miller, a former president of the WMU, the 1984 resolution is the textual basis for change in reordering, if not significantly altering, the denomination's perspective towards female adherents.[28] Although the resolution is not *constitutionally* binding upon an individual congregation, it is important that the 1988 Messengers passed a resolution giving authority for all scriptural interpretations to individual church pulpit ministers. At the very least, such an action effectively allows these ministers to endorse and support the 1984 resolution from the pulpit. Accordingly, discourse critics of the SBC should expect to encounter future exclusionary rhetoric, since it is the basis of the hierarchy's rationale for denominational control.

But Miller has publicly disagreed with the denomination's treatment of women. According to her, the 1984 resolution represented a "major step backward," for SBC women "lost the partnership image that God gave us from creation." At the denomination's training center in Ridgecrest, North Carolina, she denied that evangelization tasks were gender specific. "All men and women," she contended, "are ordained by God at the point of salvation to preach and teach the Great Commission." Furthermore, women are "historically . . . far ahead of men in terms of starting social revolutions."[29] She also noted that Jesus was denied by a man, betrayed by a man, and condemned to death and executed by men. She specifically disavowed the value of such negative gender-specific accounts, indicating that such an exercise missed the central point: "Woman is not independent of man, and man is not independent of woman," and furthermore, "the original idea when God first created men and women was that of partnership."[30]

Miller's rhetoric strikes against the pulpit leadership's ideology. She rejects the demeaning constraint of denominational exclusivity and repudiates the sexist ideology of hierarchy that denies an equal partnership for both sexes. In addition, Miller argues for full denominational equality for all female adherents. Her discourse is a clarion call for independence, and it formulates the basis for a different rhetoric—one that promotes women as persuasive agents for change.

Interestingly, Miller's advocacy is developed around the same justification as that of the loyalists, who believe their followers must also return to a purer era of Christianity. The denomination's leadership articulates an ideology developed from the writings of Paul, whereas Miller envisages a denomination as articulated by the New Testament discourse of Jesus Christ. According to her, "Jesus involved women in all that he did, and he gave perfect models for how women are to be treated [and] he overruled the traditional culture which made women second class."[31]

From a Burkean perspective, Miller has reframed official SBC leadership discourse as at least heretical, if not unbiblical, for two reasons: first, because it ignores Jesus as the ultimate example of gender partnership, and second, on the basis that the male dominated hierarchy is guilty of avoiding Christ's rhetoric, which urges partnership equality between the sexes. Her advocacy stresses that the male loyalist hierarchy should be disavowed because they have rejected the supreme model of gender discourse and behavior—that of Jesus Christ, the Savior of humankind. Whether disaffected SBC adherents will ever want to consolidate around Miller (or former WMU executive secretary Dellanna O'Brien) in order to recapture the denomination is arguable; nevertheless, a rhetorical basis for change is clear. If denominational dissidents choose to formulate their own countermanifesto of rhetorical ideology in this civil war, they now have the outline for it.

Regardless, it is important to assess the rhetorical ethics of those rhetors who have legitimized and ordered the expulsion of objectionable believers. First of all, it is intriguing that neither the General Court of the Massachusetts Bay Colony banishment decree nor the SBC presidential sermons and Messenger resolutions ever use the word *expulsion* to describe these sanctioned ejections. The word expulsion is secular, and a secular word is imprecise in this rhetorical controversy. Hence, the Massachusetts Bay and the SBC have their own sanctioned vocabulary to describe member ejections, such as departed, disfellowship, and disassociate. The Amish use the word "shunning"; Roman Catholics use the word "excommunicate." These words are important, not only because they define and exclude, but because they label as well. To loyalist adherents, the meanings are clear: such words are used principally to describe the ejections of objectionable believers from the communication system. To exiled or expelled dissidents, the meanings are equally clear, for expulsion does more than place one outside the organization; it defines, or more precisely, identifies the expulsion as a consequence of "repulsive" behavior. Literally, "depart," "disfellowship," and "dissociate" are devil words, and they constitute the language of victimage.[32]

Furthermore, these devil words are the language of power and a traditional conceptualization of communication that negatively treats the objective of relational responsibility to an audience. Since 1979, male SBC presidents have directed their annual convention sermons and other official discourses towards the consolidation of power within this communication system. They have successfully urged their fellow decision makers to authorize the ejection, ostracism, and exile of objectionable believers. Men have been the principal agents of persuasion, and they have been the most desired decision makers in this denominational cleansing.

Perhaps these leaders are unconcerned about establishing an inclusionary view of relational communication because they simply don't have to. After all, they have successfully repelled attempts by dissidents to replace them for the last twenty years. This view is facile, however, since female denominational leaders such as Nancy Hastings Sehested and those in the Women's Missionary Union are a persuasive threat, judging by the actions taken against them by the Nashville hierarchy. Just as the Massachusetts Bay could not allow the dissent of skilled persuaders such as Roger Williams, SBC presidents have preferred to expel Sehested and other female leaders from the denominational communication system. Loyalist leaders apparently view dissidents as potential persuasion agents who might attempt to lure members away from the security and stability of an autocratic communication system where a male pulpit rhetor is the authorized denominational judge of communication meanings.[33]

There is another compelling explanation of why this all-male group of leaders has articulated a conceptualization of communication devoid of an enabling co-active and relational responsibility to audience, and it centers on culture, audience, and communication. We have concluded that the Southern Baptist Convention, through its pulpit leadership rhetoric, desires to regain its lost role as the South's, and perhaps the nation's, most influential religious denomination. In their sermons, SBC presidents have advocated a devoutly Christian nation for all, a morally pure society, and a Pauline theology of believer obedience. In the absence of undesirable "isms," society will presumably be uniform, and interpersonal roles and gender relationships will be as clear as they were years ago before the Civil War. These changes are necessary because the leadership holds that our country is in moral chaos and that believers have lost their theological moorings. Consequently, the denomination's presidents are dedicated to the purgation of theological and doctrinal contamination from its membership, schools, and seminaries. The correctives offered by the key pulpit leaders are intended to stabilize our culture, reinvigorate the denomination, and return both to a former period of security.

Consequently, SBC presidential pulpit artists and Resolution 3 have formulated a dronelike state of inequality, along with a demeaning communication system for women adherents, by stressing the necessary return of women to a subservience of antebellum Southernness—a time when life was allegedly much simpler and more orderly.[34] Such a new world envisages a return to a serenity sanitized from the pollution of the social gospel, liberalism, homosexuality, and feminism.[35] To loyalists and their sympathizers, the clarity of such a communication system is appealing, for it seems to offer security against undesirable changes. Consequently, from a loyalist viewpoint, a transcendent understanding of discourse as one that includes both influence and relational requirements for all believers is unnecessary.

As rhetorical historians know, however, this conceptualization of communication is not new to American religion; it was tried by our Boston forefathers in the middle of the seventeenth century. The three most prominent rhetors of the Massachusetts Bay—John Cotton, John Winthrop, and Thomas Hooker—attempted to enforce a similar coercive communication definition upon all believers in Boston. They failed, and we predict the same thing will eventually happen with the Southern Baptist Convention.

Whether right or wrong, Southern Baptists today seem to have problems with others different than themselves. They negatively regard two of their most prominent members, President Bill Clinton and Vice President Al Gore. They have angrily distanced themselves from various forms of humanistic legislation in Congress. They castigate secular humanists, gays and lesbians, political liberals, atheists, lotteries, gambling, alcohol, and any male who welcomes women in positions of leadership.

7

By Scripture and Argument: An Apologia for the Ordination of Women

> But, I would have you know, that the head of every man is Christ; and the head of the woman is the man; and the head of Christ is God.
>
> —I Corinthians 11:3

> But I suffer not a woman to teach, nor to usurp authority over the man, but to be in silence.
>
> —I Timothy 2:12

> And your sons and daughters shall prophesy . . .
>
> —Acts 2:17

> There is neither Jew nor Greek, there is neither bond nor free, there is neither male nor female: For ye are all one in Jesus Christ.
>
> —Galatians 3:28

In this chapter, the study examines the apologia rhetoric of the Baptist Women in Ministry (BWIM), the new name adopted in 1994 for the former Southern Baptist Women in Ministry, as they seek to respond to the loyalist-governed Southern Baptist Convention with an affirming rhetoric of their own, which concerns women as leaders and as ordained ministers. Resolution 3 denounces the ordination of women, clearly excluding women from pastoral leadership to preserve a submission God allegedly requires because "man was first in creation and woman was first in the Edenic fall."

Since the beginning of the 1990s, it has been clear that the loyalist conquest of the Southern Baptist Convention has worn out its followers on all sides of the church aisle. Larry McSwain has marked the 1990 Morris Chapman election for president as "the end of the most intense schismatic struggle for institutional control in the history of the denomination and the beginning of a new era in the shaping of the character and structure of the Southern Baptist Convention."[1] Among the certainties that were carried over from the furor of the 1980s was the SBC's 1984 Resolution 3, which passed with 58 percent of the vote. Although this resolution has already been discussed elsewhere, the full text concerning the ordination of women is particularly helpful here because it is the central theme of the takeover plan and its rhetorical genesis:

> Whereas, We, the messengers to the Southern Baptist Convention meeting in Kansas City, June 12–14, 1984, recognize the authority of Scripture in all matters of faith and practice including the autonomy of the local church; and
>
> Whereas, The New Testament enjoins all Christians to proclaim the Gospel; and
>
> Whereas, The New Testament churches as a community of faith recognized God's ordination and anointing of some believers for special ministries (e.g., I Timothy 2:7; Titus 1:15) and in consequence of their demonstrated loyalty to the Gospel, conferred public blessing and engaged in public dedicatory prayer setting them apart for service, and
>
> Whereas, The New Testament does not mandate that all who are divinely called to ministry be ordained; and
>
> Whereas, in The New Testament, ordination symbolizes spiritual succession to the world task of proclaiming and extending the Gospel of Christ, and not a sacramental transfer of proclaiming and extending the Gospel of Christ, and not a sacramental transfer of unique divine grace that perpetuates apostolic authority; and
>
> Whereas, The New Testament emphasizes the equal dignity of men and women (Galatians 3:28) and that the Holy Spirit was at Pentecost divinely outpoured on men and women alike (Acts 2:17); and
>
> Whereas, Women as well as men prayed and prophesied in public worship services (I Corinthians 11:2–16), and Priscilla joined her husband in teaching Apollos (Acts 18:26), and women fulfilled special church service ministries as exemplified by Phoebe whose work Paul tributes as that of servant of the church (Romans 16:1), and
>
> Whereas, the Scriptures attest to God's delegated order of authority (God the head of Christ, Christ the head of man, man the head of woman, man and woman dependent one upon the other to the glory of God) distinguishing the roles

> of men and women in public prayer and prophecy (I Corinthians 11:2–5); and
>
> Whereas, while Paul commends women and men alike in other roles of ministry and service (Titus 2:1–10), he excludes women from pastoral leadership (I Timothy 2:12) to preserve a submission God requires because the man was first in creation and the woman was the first in the Edenic fall (I Timothy 2:13 ff); and
>
> Whereas, these Scriptures are not intended to stifle the creative contribution of men and women as co-workers in many roles of church service, both on distant mission fields and in domestic ministries, but imply that women and men are nonetheless divinely gifted for distinctive areas of evangelical engagement; and
>
> Whereas, Women are held in high honor for their unique and significant contribution to the advancement of Christ's kingdom, and the building of godly homes should be esteemed for its vital contribution of developing personal Christian character and Christlike concern for others.
>
> Therefore, be it resolved, that we do not decide concerns of Christian doctrine and practice by modern cultural, sociological and ecclesiastical trends or by emotional factors; that we remind ourselves of the dearly bought Baptist principle of the final authority of Scripture in matter of faith and conduct; and that we encourage the service of women in all aspects of church life and work other than pastoral functions and leadership roles entailing ordination.[2]

The 1984 Southern Baptist Convention affirmed a variety of positions about the value of women. As noted in chapter 6, the Convention argued its case against ordaining women from scriptural texts: the Divine Order of Authority (Gen. 1:27; 2:21–22) and Paul's exclusion of women from pastoral leadership (I Tim. 2:12; 3:2–13). A rhetoric based on an inerrant Bible that teaches that women cannot exercise authority over men (I Cor. 14:33–35) seems appropriate considering the beliefs of the denominational decision makers. Since the denomination's position has not changed since 1984, we assume that gender exclusiveness will remain for the foreseeable future.

Historian William Leonard explains that "many fundamentalists saw any action to ordain women as a direct contradiction of the biblical teaching regarding the subordinate role of women": Like every other creature, women have a particular "place" in the scheme of things; "Ordination . . . violates the teaching of Holy Scripture and upsets the order of creation."[3] As stated in I Timothy 3:2, a pastor is to be "the husband of one wife." Therefore, women are unqualified to be ordained ministers, and there would seem to be no room for argument from any side of the denomination. However, as we will see, that is not the case.

A careful reading of the 1984 SBC resolution reveals a Pauline perspective, especially from the Epistles. The first Epistle to Timothy was written during the last years of Paul's life. As with II Timothy and Titus, I Timothy is known as a pastoral epistle. As churches in the first century increased in number, questions of church order and discipline arose. There was a requisite, even necessary, authoritative teaching required concerning faith and order during this period, including, but not limited to the place of women in the church and the qualifications for deacons in the church. While encouraging all other varieties of Christian service, the Southern Baptist Convention's 1984 Resolution 3 forbids pastoral functions and leadership roles entailing the ordination of women.

The core of the loyalists' argument centers on six major scriptural passages.

Acts 6:6

Acts 14–23

I Timothy 2:7

I Timothy 3:4–14

I Timothy 5:22

II Timothy 2:2

Titus 1:15[4]

With these scriptures as proof texts and Resolution 3 as a national mandate for Baptist polity, the die was cast. What could this community of ordained or soon to be ordained women do to respond to this exclusionary policy, which effectively exiled hundreds of persons?

When attacked or sealed off from desirable progress, humans often stop, turn, and defend themselves. Usually that defense takes a rhetorical form, namely, speeches, sermons, tracts, articles, conferences, or other mediated communication forms. The organized group among Southern Baptists for women's ministry and service, BWIM, had been working to make its mark prior to the acceptance of Resolution 3, and they were not totally unprepared for what happened in 1984. Apologists all, these women had been serving in the ministry for years, at great personal cost. The resolution against them would not terminate their service, since nothing before had done so.

The first meeting of the Southern Baptist Women in Ministry, as it was then called, was held in Pittsburgh prior to the 1983 annual meeting of the Southern Baptist Convention. Agreeing to be independent, the group affirmed its support for ordained and unordained women in the ministry, as well as their supporters. In 1998, Baptist Women in Ministry—the group deleted "Southern" from its name in protest in 1994—continues to defend its calling in an increasingly hostile denomination.

BWIM has adopted a political and scriptural agenda in response to Resolution 3. First, it must be noted that the 1984 resolution did little to discourage the ordination of women. On the contrary, BWIM was energized by the resolution, demonstrated by the fact that 55 percent of ordained women in the SBC received their ordination after 1984.[5] Today, approximately 1,225 women serve as Southern Baptist clergy, mostly as chaplains and counselors, either on a church staff or in an agency position.[6] There are approximately four hundred women and men who belong to BWIM, with hundreds of other female nonmembers serving in church staff positions.[7] The growth of this organization is not necessarily a reaction only to the Southern Baptist Convention. Pastor Fred Wolfe of Cottage Hill Baptist Church in Mobile, Alabama argued that "women's ordination is not a moral issue . . . it's a matter of . . . conviction."[8]

An understanding of the rhetorical battle regarding the ordination of women requires a pairing of arguments and supporting proof texts. It is equally helpful to know that the 1984 Kansas City convention established a denominational precedent. Although the population of ordained women is growing, two-thirds of these female ministers have considered joining another denomination. Most have not left, in fact, their numbers continue to grow faster than in any other denomination.[9] While a "chilling effect" on ordination from exclusionist actions may have been expected from the 1984 decision, the reverse is true.

To frame the apologic rhetoric for the ordination of women as BWIM would perceive it, we have referred to a special report, "The Role of Women in the Church" by the Special Study Committee, November 9, 1983, First Baptist Church, Columbia, South Carolina. This church adopted a motion in December, 1982, to appoint a committee to study barriers to the election of women to the diaconate so that they could serve as deacons, ushers, and associate deacons and to report its findings to the church on April, 1983.[10] The report was submitted and then adopted by the church in November 1984.

The study is instructive for two reasons: First, it offers a balanced review of the Bible's teaching concerning women and the church and was produced by laypersons prior to the 1984 SBC annual meeting. Second, we offer our explanation of what we think serves as the rhetorical foundation for an understanding of BWIM's stand concerning the ordination of women.

Following this extended excerpt from the final report, we will outline the apologic rhetoric that argues for the ordination of women. We have analyzed unpublished documents of BWIM in the Dargan-Carver Library at the Southern Baptist Convention Historical Commission in Nashville, Tennessee. While we concede that this excerpt is lengthy, the report is an extraordinarily clear, coherent, and unified apologia for the ordination of women, and it provides a rare opportunity to examine how one local church addressed the issue of the role of women as leaders.

> *Special Report, "The Role of Women in the Church," Special Study Committee, November 9, 1993, First Baptist Church, Columbia, South Carolina.*

Biblical Teaching—Part I

There are three basic principles found in the Bible upon which this report has been developed. A statement of each with some explanation follows:

> And God said, Let us make man in our image, after our likeness; and let them have dominion over the fish of the sea, and over the fowl of the air, and over the cattle, and over all the earth, and over every creeping thing that creepeth upon the earth. So God created man in his own image, in the image of God created he him; male and female created he them. (Genesis 1:26–27) (KJV)

1. The first principle is that human beings—male and female—were "both and equally created by God and in His Image." Both received the blessings of God and both were charged to have dominion over the earth in "unity and partnership." The Scriptures express the ideal of God for mutual equality as the perfect relationship, and Jesus repeats this intent in Matthew 10:6:

> "But from the beginning of the creation, 'God made them male and female.'"(KJV)

Paul declared and applied this ideal for all believers of all times in his statement of Christian liberty found in Galatians 3:28.

> "There is neither Jew nor Greek, there is neither slave nor free, there is neither male nor female; for ye are all one in Christ Jesus." (KJV)

2. The second principle, really a corollary to the first, is that male and female are both equal in "personhood" and directly responsible to and under the authority of their creator—God—

with neither male nor female exercising authority over nor requiring submission from the other. Within a fellowship of believers which makes up a New Testament church, this principle is seen as the concept of the "priesthood of the believer." The Baptist Faith and Message reads:

> "The church is an autonomous body, operating through democratic processes under the Lordship of Christ. In such a congregation, members are equally responsible."
>
> "Such a definition places all members of a fellowship on the same high plane. No one is placed in a position of inferiority for reasons of age, sex, or any other difference. It is at this point that we begin any study of the roles of members of the body of Christ. Each person is responsible for being one's own priest, completely accountable to God without the necessary intermediary role of any other except Christ. This is the basis of equality, unity, and congregational Baptist policy."

3. The third principle is an extension of the second and affirms the autonomy of each New Testament church where decisions are made and action taken within and by the fellowship and not by any outside person, group, association or convention. This principle means that the members of this congregation decide what offices are needed and what officers shall serve the Lord through this fellowship.

Biblical Teachings—Part II

The Report goes on to argue there are three areas of Scripture that need to be examined. First, what does the Old Testament show about women in the religious structure of these times? Second, what do the Gospels record that Jesus taught and did concerning women? Third, what do New Testament writers tell about women in the churches of the first century?

Old Testament

God's ideal that men and women whom he created as equal in his image to live in unity and partnership was altered when the newly created persons sinned. The subordination of the physically smaller and weaker female to the larger and stronger male becomes the order in a fallen society. The Old Testament shows the inferior state in which women existed, almost as chattel at all levels of life—social, legal, religious, etc.—in Israel under the patriarchal structure of family life which was formed by the descendants of Abraham. However, Old Testament writers give vivid accounts of specific women God called to special service—Miriam, Deborah, Huldah, Esther, and Ruth—and in Proverbs 31, the ideal woman is described. Also, the Law allowed women to take the vow of the Nazarite with the men, and women were included in the renewal of the Covenant under Nehemiah and Ezra. Women, however, were not given an education and were not allowed to participate in the synagogue teaching.

The Gospels

The Gospel writers provide an examination not only of the life, death and resurrection of Jesus, but also of his teachings and ministry as well. The most significant fact derived from these four books is that Jesus uttered no specific teaching directed to or for women. This is irrefutable evidence that his words and work were equally applicable to both men and women. He came to set at liberty all persons—male and female. By speaking with women, by healing them, and by praising their fidelity, Jesus challenged the status quo and gave worth and personhood to women. "But when the time has fully come, God sent forth His Son, born of a woman . . . " (Galatians 4:4) (RSV).

Thus, Mary, a woman, was used by God to bring salvation through Christ to the world.

Women were a visible and significant part of Jesus' ministry, and women responded gratefully and wholeheartedly to Him, traveling in the band of disciples and providing financial support.

> "Soon afterward he went on through cities and villages preaching and bringing the good news of the kingdom of God. And the twelve were with Him, and also some of the women who had been healed of evil spirits and infirmities: Mary, called Magdalene from whom seven demons had gone out, and Joanna, the wife of Chuza, Herod's steward, and Suzanna, and many others, who provided from them out of their means." (Luke 8:1–3 RSV)

> "(Who also, when He was in Galilee, followed Him, and ministered unto Him;) and many other women which came up with Him unto Jerusalem." (Mark 15:41 KJV)
>
> "And many women were there beholding afar off, which followed Jesus from Galilee, ministering unto Him. Among which was Mary Magdalene, and Mary the mother of James and John, and the mother of Zebedee's children." (Matthew 27:55–56 KJV)

The woman of Samaria became an evangelist and a missionary when she encountered Jesus. The depth of spiritual understanding and devotion of Mary when she "anointed Him for his burial" went beyond that of his closest disciples. Women were the last at the cross and the first at the tomb. No woman went to sleep in the garden. No woman denied Him, and no woman betrayed Him.

Jesus appeared to the women at the tomb and commissioned them to go and give the first report to the disciples of the miracle of the Resurrection, the greatest event the Christian world has ever known. Matthew 28:1 names the women who shared in this great event, Mary Magdalene and Mary the mother of James and Joseph. These women were the first to be a witness to Christ's conquest over death and the first to be sent to go forth and tell others that they had seen the risen Lord.

Women waited in the upper room with the eleven disciples, and the first Christian congregation before Pentecost included not only the eleven apostles but also the women. On the day of Pentecost, Peter proclaimed the significance of the Holy Spirit's coming using the words of the prophet Joel: "Your sons and your daughters shall prophesy . . . and on my servants and handmaidens I will pour out in those days of my spirit; and they shall prophesy" (Acts 2:17–8) (KJV).

New Testament Writers

The "church" as it is identified in the twentieth century experience did not exist until the last sixty years of the first century. During the nearly 2,000 years preceding the birth of Jesus, the Hebrew people had worshipped Jehovah according to his revelation and according to the writings of Moses and the prophets first at designated altars, then in the Tabernacle, and finally in the Temple at Jerusalem. During and after the

Captivity, small local units called synagogues were established among the Hebrew people for worship and instruction. Some synagogues remained small while others were quite large. After the Temple was rebuilt, the theocracy of the Jewish people was again structured with the synagogues as important units. This was the religious system into which Jesus Christ came to build His church.

Recognizing that the church of Jesus Christ includes all believers of all times, the organizational unit to which Southern Baptist believers relate is the independent, autonomous, local New Testament church, modeled after the ones of the first century which had, in turn, followed the structure and pattern of existing local synagogues.

However, and most importantly, the functions of the New Testament church went beyond worship and instruction. To share the good news of Jesus Christ—evangelism—became the focus. Closely linked was the commitment of members of this "body of Christ" to the teaching of the Savior and to a life of service or ministry under this Lordship.

New Testament writers directed their writings to situations in these first century churches and to the people who made up their membership. Most of Paul's epistles were written to particular churches, in particular locations, faced with various particular problems. He was writing within the context of first century culture. Not all of His background was changed by His conversion. He was a Jew and a Pharisee. He was the product of His immediate environment and of a long past. In orthodox Jewish synagogues, the male would pray thankfully to God "who hath not made me a Gentile, a slave or a woman."

Some of the writings of the Apostle Paul have contributed more than any other to the subordinate role of women through the centuries. Paul said that women must keep their heads covered in church (1 Cor. 11:3–10). Women's hair was not to be shaven because this was considered disgraceful. Paul asserted that women must keep silent in the church and should ask their husbands at home whatever they desire to know. (1 Cor. 14:33–35). Here Paul was dealing with a problem of disorder in public worship. Paul contended that women must be silent and submissive and must not teach or have authority over men (1 Tim. 2:11–14). Nonetheless, Paul in his writings involved women in the work of the church. He considered women to be his co-workers on an equal basis with men, and he applied the truth that all persons are one in Christ Jesus. Examples include the following:

> Lydia, a woman from Thyatira, who lived at Philippi, was a business woman, a "seller of purple." In Acts 16, Paul relates how Lydia listened and the Lord opened her heart of understanding; she became Europe's first convert. Soon afterwards, she was baptized and then her household. She did not think of how this decision might affect her business. "Her customers of the purple cloth or dye would probably have scoffed at the Gospel of Christ, but Lydia did not wait to see." She put Christ first and was baptized as were members of her household. We are not told whether those who were baptized were members of her family or those connected with her business. In any case, they respected the good judgment of Lydia and were willing to follow her lead. She was one of many to help spread the Gospel of Christ through Europe.
>
> One of the most influential women in the New Testament church was Priscilla, a Jewess, who came out of Italy with her husband, Aquila. They left home at the time when Claudius had expelled all Jews. Acts 18:1–2. When Paul first met them, they lived in Corinth; they were tentmakers and so was Paul. He stayed with them, but later they went with Paul to Ephesus. When Paul left for Syria, he committed the work in Ephesus to Priscilla and Aquila. About a year later, he returned and found that they had established a well-organized congregation in Ephesus. Later, Paul wrote his first letter to the Corinthians from Ephesus and sent greetings from Aquila and Priscilla "with the church that is in their house." (1 Cor. 16:19) In Acts 18:26, we read that Priscilla and Aquila introduced Apollos, who was a very learned man, one who had received the baptism of John to the true Christian faith. They recognized that he had only a superficial knowledge of the new Christian faith.
>
> In Romans 16:1–2, Paul introduces Phoebe, a

> "deaconess" (RSV) as the bearer of his epistle to the Romans. In choosing Phoebe to carry his epistle, Paul conferred a great honor upon her.
>
> Paul describes Phoebe in a few brief words, but gives a vivid picture of the type person she was. First, he calls her "our sister." Second, he calls her "a servant of the church." The word "servant" comes from the Greek word, diaconos, from which the word "deacon" is derived. Dr. Lee Anna Starr, in The Bible Status of Women has conjectured that Phoebe was a minister, even as were Paul, Timothy and others.
>
> Paul also describes Phoebe as "a helper of many." This suggests that she was one who had come to the aid of converts in need and one who had fought the battles of those who were oppressed. In addition, Paul records that Phoebe had helped him also. In the same Roman letter, Paul greets by name at lest seven women who were part of the church at Rome (Romans 16). He further instructs the Roman congregation to help Phoebe "in whatever she may require from you." Indeed, Paul acknowledged women to be his co-workers on an equal basis with men.[11]

The principles in this report serve as the linchpin of pro-women's ordination arguments around which every argumentative appeal and figure of speech leans for support in BWIM materials. What was developed in 1983 by the First Baptist Church in Columbia, South Carolina, stands as a contemporary testament to the views of dissident Southern Baptists who see their world as an equitable balance of ordained men and women in the denomination.

With this statement as a biblical analysis, we argue that the rhetorical historian can extract a rhetoric of apology from Scripture as well as contemporary Christian experience. There are four arguments by definition, one prime argument from circumstance, and two arguments from consequence that constitute the rhetoric of defense used by BWIM.

An Apologic Rhetoric for Ordaining Women in the Ministry—BWIM

An example of an argument by definition—an argument evolved from the use of scripture and the original autographa as to what the Bible really means—is found in the claim that men and women equally reflect the image of God with no priority or inferiority of gender expressed or implied.[12] By use of counterarguing the opposite effect, any argument for the subordination of women based on the order of creation logically leads to the subordination of man to plants and animals, which were created before him.[13] Consequently, it follows that, by means of an argument from circumstance, it can be inferred that men and women are equal in "personhood." Neither gender can exercise authority or require submission from the other.

The positive argumentative appeal of the claim for the equality of personhood is that, rather than claiming that woman comes from man, it holds that the main emphasis of Genesis 2:21–23 is the mutual, equal relationship of woman and man.[14] From this we can infer that, because of the "priesthood of each believer," each church should understand that God's calling is gender free. It follows that the local Southern Baptist/New Testament church decides what is required to conduct its own policy and practice, as well as who shall be entrusted to carry them out (an argument by definition).

Southern Baptists can read for themselves, the appeal holds, that there is abundant evidence concerning how women took a prominent place in Christ's ministry from the time of His birth until the time of His death. William Hull argues that male dominance and female subjection belong to fallen humanity, not to God's good creation.[15] So, a "stasis," or a clash of opposite arguments, seems to exist. Scripture seems to argue against scripture when one passage states "should only men be ordained," and other passages seem to argue for the inclusion of women as ordained members of the community of denominations.

Another argument by definition, the empowering scripture for gender equity in Christian service, claims that "[y]our sons and daughters shall prophesy" (Acts 2:17; Joel 2:28). At a crucial nexus of argument and counterargument, William Leonard notes that the loyalists counter the question of ordination for women incontrovertibly with I Timothy 3:2 or whatever scripture helps to prove their point. Since a woman cannot meet the qualification of being a man, women could only presume God "called" them. God would not violate His inerrant and infallible Word.[16] As a counterpoint response, the arguments for women's ordination evolve out of Acts 2:17 and Joel 2:28 and, as such, seek to establish the rightness of the defense for the "Gifts" argument, which is to follow, the trump card in the "no, you can't"—"yes, we can" debate on women's ordination.

Gifts of the Holy Spirit for Women

In their strongest voice, the BWIM argues by definition that the Holy Spirit gives gifts for the ministry, or Xapiouaia, without regard to gender, which each recipient must use fully. Molly T. Marshall-Green states that the primary teachings in the Scripture concerning gifts for the ministry are presented in Romans 12:1–8, I Corinthians 12:1–11, and Ephesians 4:7–13. Especially in I Corinthians 12:1, the Greek word is plural, indicating that no one, male or female, lacks a gift. Christian service is the use of the gift or gifts one may have received. In particular, I Corinthians 14:1 renders prophecy as the superior gift, and as already noted, men and women may receive that gift.[17] By the use of scripture, the rhetorical claims of the BWIM aim to define a parity between men and women for God's call to religious service. By defining the nature of how both men and women receive the divine call to serve God, women can become equipped to do all of the work in the church, including ordination for professional service.

Additional scripture used by BWIM to support the "gifts of the Holy Spirit" and "equal call" appeal are:

> Romans 16:1—Phoebe is a servant of the church.
>
> Philippians 4:3—Paul speaks of those women who labor with him in the Gospel.
>
> Luke 2:36—Luke records the testimony of Anna, a prophetess.
>
> Luke 10:38–42—Luke describes Martha's and Mary's contrasting, but dedicated, service to Christ.
>
> Luke 23:49, 55—The women who served Jesus at the burial are noted.
>
> Romans 12:1–8—Paul writes here about Christian life and service, particularly about service through gifts of the Spirit.
>
> I Corinthians 12:1–11 is a supportive set of scriptures.

The results or consequences of following a "Divine Call" renders a new understanding of "inerrancy," that is, God's private call to anyone, male or female, is perfect, infallible, and true.

The first argument from consequence, which is a natural extension of the argument from definition, is that women have always had a constitutive and a prominent place in Christ's ministry from the time of His birth. Jann Aldredge Clanton states that "not only did Simeon confirm the baby Jesus as the long-awaited Messiah, but also the prophetess Anna declared the redemption that would come through Jesus."[18] Shirley Stevens argues that Jewish oral tradition may have declared that, while the testimony of one hundred women was not equal to that of one man, it was Jesus who trusted the Samaritan woman to communicate the news about His identity.[19] As a consequence of Christ's view of women, it is appropriate to contend that all three synoptic Gospels use a form of the Greek verb *diakoneo* to describe what women did in His service. The noun cognate of this verb may be translated "minister" or "deacon."[20]

A second consequential argument concerning the mutual ministry of women and men concerns the balance of gender in His teaching illustrations. Clanton argues that

> Jesus portrays God not only as a shepherd seeking one lost sheep, but also as a woman seeking one lost coin (Luke 15:3–10). Jesus compares the kingdom of heaven not only to a grain of mustard seed which a man sows in the field, but also to leaven which woman mixes into flour (Matthew 13:31–33). By His teachings and actions, Christ leads us to affirm the equality of men and women in every sphere of life, including the ordained ministry.[21]

Finally, in Galatians 3:28, Paul proclaimed that there is neither "male nor female" in Christ Jesus. The rhetorical appeals used to defend the calling of women to the ministry can also be used for a variety of soul-saving purposes. Appropriately, the Word does go out "to seek and to save."

The Southern Baptist Convention stands alone among every other mainline Protestant denomination in not recognizing the contributions and full value of women in all areas of its ministry. The denomination's isolationism might seem inconsequential in the larger picture of Baptist policy, with over 1,500 confirmed clergywomen representing scarcely 2 percent of the total Baptist clergy.[22] But, the rhetorical fallout from the SBC's 1984 Resolution 3 has had an impact that has reached much farther than its intended target audience.

On the level of laity, the local Southern Baptist church has always depended on the loyal majority of its members—women—to teach, serve, greet, assist, and prepare the church for its service. Women also take up the offering, serve on major committees, become deacons, and chair major staff search committees.[23] However, the effect of the creed-like rhetoric coming out of Resolution 3 is instrumental within the denomination. The impact of its exclusionary paragraphs is profound as it stretches out its enveloping net to stifle all women who might respond to God's call for service.

We have argued that inerrancy was and remains the potboiler on the front burner of the loyalists' fight. It is equally clear that the exclusionary language of inerrancy justifies and legitimizes the denomination's expulsion and exile of its own female leaders, for the rhetoric of Resolution 3 exemplifies the spirit of purgation. The role of women as leaders in the church has been and will continue to be central to an understanding of the claim of the inerrant and infallible Word of God.

The BWIM's 1984 report, "The Status of Women in the Southern Baptist Convention," is clear regarding the role of women in a male-dominated denomination. Betty McGary Pearce states:

> Over half the members of churches that constitute the Southern Baptist Convention are women but women currently hold only 13 percent of the leadership positions in agencies, institutions and churches of the convention. Women hold a statistically insignificant percentage of pastoral positions and 22 percent of church staff positions. There has been a 1 percent decrease overall in the percentage of leadership positions held by women since 1952. These were the findings in a recent study which compared the percentage of positions held by women in 1952, 1967, and 1982 in the Southern Baptist Convention.
>
> [An] analysis of selected Sunday School literature for the same years reveals that males are portrayed as possessing a wide range of personality characteristics (i.e., analytical, inquisitive, courageous, compassionate, impulsive, perceptive, great, etc.). Females were portrayed as possessing fewer characteristics (i.e., loving, caring, patient, loyal, lover of children, sympathetic or unfaithful, deceptive, promiscuous, etc.). With a few exceptions females were portrayed as either all "good" or all "bad" while males were portrayed as having both strengths and weaknesses. Over twice as many characteristics were attributed to males as were attributed to females. Females are portrayed as limited. Males are portrayed as unlimited, expansive.[24]

Issued in the same time frame as Resolution 3, this study anticipated a clear, supportive response from the Southern Baptist Sunday School Board, which is the publishing division of the SBC. But, such a response was not forthcoming. Since 1984, more women have been ordained, but there are no increases in female pulpit leadership.

Is the apologic rhetoric to ordain women that we have outlined a reasonable logical, scriptural, and persuasive body of argument and appeals? Is the case for ordaining women developed by the leadership of BWIM in their journal *Folio* and their sermons a prima facie case, standing as acceptable on its own merits? As in any rhetorical situation where influence, argument, self-promotion, and a faithful adherence to the biblical proof text is present, a proactive response by the local church to hire women as preachers has not occurred. In the council chamber, sanctuary, and private residence, the ordination issue remains hot to the touch.

What is clear is that the rhetorics of fundamentalism, inerrancy, and exclusion are blasting caps, igniting rhetorical controversies concerning the direction of the Southern Baptist Convention. The arguments used to justify the expulsion of groups from membership and leadership, such as lesbians, homosexuals, Masons, and ordained women who would stain the shirt and creedal collar of a male-dominated, Bible-worshipping hierarchy, are pivotal in understanding the controversy. Kathy Manis Findley of Providence Baptist Church in Little Rock, the only female senior pastor in Arkansas and a past BWIM president, argues that the SBC excludes what it cannot explain or understand.

In addition, based upon the loyalists' inerrant reading of the Apostle Paul, the Convention leadership seems to feel it has made its case against ordaining women and has sought no other counsel on the matter. But perhaps the same may be said of those who support ordaining women, particularly BWIM. Dissidents and loyalists alike appear convinced that they are right and that their positions are attractive to their followers. What has occurred in the Southern Baptist Convention over the past two decades is that a skilled team of loyalist pastors and SBC presidents, along with a region-wide army of laymen, have flamed the fires of fundamentalism bent on countering the claims women make for gender equity in Christian service.

What all of these rhetors on each side of the aisle may not have realized is that the rhetorics of fundamentalism, inerrancy, and exclusion are combustible. Such a major implosion of people moving out from the circle of the church who could not accept His Word as inerrant and infallible, did not and will not go quietly. These loyalist leaders, preachers, and laypersons whom we have chronicled, have calculated the results of their persuasive effectiveness, and therefore they have a special burden on their shoulders. They have challenged gender equity in Christ's service as a litmus test for the rhetoric of inerrancy. Furthermore, the effects of their persuasion can be measured by the expulsions and exiles of persons dedicated to advancing Christianity rather than to just defending the Word and following its precepts.

The ultimate argument from definition, even higher than the argument from definition concerning an inerrant, infallible Bible, is the unmistakable call to personal Christian service. Neither loyalists, dissidents, nor even the rhetorical champions of the denomination can deny the will of God in a gender-free call to ministry. It is the call to God's service, the call to speak, to address the assembled believers that make up the "church," that seems to be the center of the apologic rhetoric of BWIM and those who support its cause. Sara Frances Andrews pinpoints this claim when she argues that "most women feel . . . ordination is not a biblical issue; it is an ecclesiastical issue. . . . it's a church problem, not a Bible problem. Many of them are not trying to prove anything. They are simply service-oriented. They feel like the best recognition of their position is ordination."[25]

The matter of ordination is not, however, without its perils, especially from denominationalists who contend that the matter is not ecclesiastical at all, but a biblical and culturally binding issue. Recently, a Texas female Southern Baptist minister filed a lawsuit against the Baptist General Convention because she was ordained but unrecognized by the local or state convention. In an article from Associated Baptist Press and reprinted in *Folio* (fall 1995), it was reported that

> Raye Nell Dyer was employed at [the University of] Texas Medical Branch in Galveston, TX as campus minister when she sought to be ordained. [The] controversy came during this process and some ministers within the association favored her termination.
>
> Although she had served faithfully as a minister in the Baptist General Convention for ten years she was fired based on the issues surrounding her ordination. Her insurance coverage was discontinued in March by the Baptist General Convention of Texas. However, she was not informed of this insurance termination until April. The state convention does not offer the COBRA insurance plan to its employees.
>
> The suit was filed July 17, 1995 in Galveston District Court, naming as defendants the Baptist General Convention of Texas, Galveston Baptist Association, and Jack Greever, recently resigned director of student work in Texas.
>
> The suit alleges that Dyer's removal from her director's position at UTMB and subsequent termination by the Texas convention were based on gender and that she was paid at a rate "substantially lower than [a] male counterpart," both in violation of the Texas Labor Code.
>
> The Reverend Dyer was ordained into the gospel ministry by South Main Baptist Church in Houston, Texas in November, 1993. She is a board member of BWIM.[26]

The major published rebuttal to "Gender and Image" came from Dorothy Kelley Patterson, an apologist for denominational loyalists, in *Baptist History and Heritage* in 1988. In a ringing conclusion, Patterson argues against the BWIM rhetoric of the past and present by arguing how the real issue at hand is not ordination itself but the authority of the Bible:

> Nothing in Scripture infers that godly women assumed positions or authority over men in either the church or the home. Scripture does not permit a woman to be ordained as a ruling or teaching elder. Concerning the diaconate, the Scripture does not support ordination, but neither does it clearly prohibit a woman's serving in the diaconate, if following the New

> Testament pattern of this office. Subordination in the home, church, school, or marketplace has never abolished equality any more than equality has abolished subordination . . . Even a lie, if told often enough, will soon be believed. A partial truth or truth taken out of context is even more dangerous (note Adam and Eve with Satan in the garden). Nowhere in Baptist history, except perhaps in this generation, has religious freedom come to mean that one can be a Baptist and believe and teach anything he personally desire . . .
>
> The church has never sought to suppress gifts God has given but rather strives to ensure full and proper use of those gifts in a divinely given framework based upon natural order of creation and appropriateness of function within a master plan. One cannot accept the Bible as authoritative while rejecting its authority concerning home and church order. One cannot negate truths concerning the structure of church and home, such as the image of the relationship between God and Israel and between Christ and the church, just to satisfy cultural whim or to accommodate higher plateaus of education and opportunity. One cannot lift outward manifestations, such as a man's prayer posture or a woman's head covering (1 Cor. 11), and use them to ridicule or belittle the timeless directives given to protect and edify men and women within the Kingdom.
>
> Without doubt, women did have a variety of positions of service, influence, and even leadership and teaching in the early church. The text of Scripture, however, bears witness that the functions they assumed were done with modesty and order (1 Cor. 11:2–16; 14:40), and that they did not teach or exercise authority over men (1 Tim. 2:11–15; 1 Cor. 14:33–35).[27]

The underpinning of the apologic rhetoric of BWIM is buttressed by the inerrant, infallible Bible, which speaks more eloquently than any president of the Southern Baptist Convention or speaker at the annual Pastors Conference. BWIM apologists have rallied around a verse in Revelations: "Behold I have set before you an open door, which no one can shut . . . " (Rev. 3:8). It is not a matter of personal conviction, as Southern Baptist Convention dissidents would argue. BWIM argues that the ordination of women is a response to God's calling through His Spirit and not obedience to historical tradition or the dictates of men.

The apologic rhetoric of the women of BWIM to defend their call to the ministry rests on a variety of strategies. It remains a rhetorical quest for appropriate language, argument, and effective appeals, as we have outlined here using BWIM materials. Speaking to the rhetorical character of the issue, J. P. Ford cites Jann Aldredge Clanton's book *In Whose Image? God and Gender* commenting that the greater variety of images we use, the greater depth of the concept of personhood we get. The inclusion, use, and empowerment of all members and their unique gifts bring the church closer to its potential as peacemaker, as reconciler, and as agent of change.[28]

In the historical understanding of the speech of apologia, the requirement is to defend one's self, family, or business, implying some error committed or damage done to others. The apologia is a recognized classical form of spoken or written defense required by consequence or situation. It would appear that BWIM has developed an apologic rhetoric to defend and persuade others to understand and accept its case in any appropriate denominational forum.

As the 1990s come to a close, the Southern Baptist Convention stands alone in American organized religion on this matter. It appears that the SBC's 1984 Resolution 3 has the weight and force of a papal encyclical, and there is no hint of retreat from the male-dominated Southern Baptist Convention hierarchy.

Nevertheless, the BWIM apologic rhetoric of defense and the opportunities for persuasion are present in many Southern Baptist churches. Denominational advocates may assume that they have silenced dissident rhetors on the ordination of women to the pulpit. BWIM apologists disagree, and their increase in numbers, their growth of influence in dissident Baptist circles, and their persuasive skills in presenting their case lead to a different conclusion.

8

The Rhetorics of Silence and Abomination: The Troublesome Issue of Homosexuality

> If a man also lieth with mankind, as he lieth with a woman, both of them have committed an abomination.
>
> —Leviticus 20:13a

> This is my commandment, That ye love one another, as I have loved you.
>
> —John 15:12

In this chapter we focus on two rhetorics—silence and abomination—especially as they involve official SBC pronouncements and decisions regarding homosexuality and the non-inclusion of homosexuals as church members. This approach will allow for a greater understanding of the negative character of SBC exclusionary communication, and its damaging qualities to individual persons. We further argue that such communication contributes to a repressive social climate, thus harming the opportunity for therapeutic communication to occur.

Given the opposite and historical nature of silence and abominational rhetorics, it is reasonable to discuss them within the national social setting in which they have occurred, especially since the 1990s have been a time of social contradiction. For example, the entertainment media seems to glorify violence against the person at the same time that the movie industry is trying to explain a new ratings system for viewers. Yet, citizens appear to be demanding a return to movies similar to the golden-oldies of the 1950s, which allegedly were devoid of harmful actions to others. Questions should be raised about whether depictions of violence against women in the media are exalted by Hollywood. Four recent movies adequately raise the issue. In *Rob Roy*, *Showgirls*, *Strange Days*, and

Leaving Las Vegas, rapes of women are graphically and savagely portrayed. As one movie reviewer has noted, "it is impossible not to notice this wave of chic, [and] few people have protested against it."[1]

Furthermore, while the U.S. Constitution promotes both happiness and equality, unresolved ethnic, gender, and racial divisions are present throughout the nation. Crime is a profitable occupation, murder is commonplace, and rapes are often unreported. Citizens have responded by arming themselves with legal and illegal hand guns and assault weapons to assuage their fears of the known and unknown. Yet, killing a family member with one's own gun is more common than killing a criminal in self-defense.

The family structure of today is dramatically different than it used to be. The number of persons living together out of wedlock now exceeds four million.[2] Nationally, divorce rates appear to be high, suggesting that the traditional marriage is greatly troubled. Yet, the institution of marriage is certainly not dead.[3] It is intriguing that Southern Baptists have yet to sort through their understanding of what constitutes a family. At the 1998 Salt Lake convention, the Messengers voted down a statement that defined single adults, childless couples, widows, and widowers as "legitimate expressions of family."[4] Yet, according to a 1991 denominational study of membership, over one-third of SBC members are single.[5]

How these social contradictions have affected the national discourse is unclear. From a Southern Baptist perspective, however, the world is a dangerous place, full of evil waiting to displace the good, and the faithful must be militantly encouraged to protect themselves against the forces of Satan. To avoid surrendering to wicked temptations, converting others from their sinful nature is therefore an appropriate goal for Southern Baptists. That point is likely nowhere more pointed than in their discourses regarding homosexuality and its attendant issues, such as church membership and same gender marriage. It is our contention that the official SBC use of silence and abomination is harmful and conflicting, especially to those SBC families who have homosexual members.[6]

At their 1997 convention, and in a very limited sense, Southern Baptists considered the issue of homosexuality. Messenger Tim Wilkins proposed that the denomination study and analyze the topic. He also favored the establishment of a "transformational" ministry—one that was aimed at getting homosexuals to change their sexual orientation. Although Messengers endorsed his proposals, his "transformational" ministry posed a double-sided problem: to receive Christ one must be heterosexual; yet, if one is created by God why is such a change necessary? This latter position was the basis for Rev. Wayne Lindsey's claim that there is no need for homosexuals to be transformed. If we are "created in the image of God," he questions, "why would God heal us of that?"[7]

In contrast, the Tim Wilkins resolution seeks to assist homosexuals in changing their sexual orientation. To effect this change, an organization called "Homosexuals Anonymous" has developed a "fourteen-step" method. The alleged generosity of this approach may seem similar to the Alcoholics Anonymous method, yet closer study suggests otherwise. Both groups emphasize avoidance behaviors. However, while AA groups accept the person along with their problems, Homosexuals Anonymous stresses that the person is guilty of the sin of homosexuality, must admit it, renounce it, and then accept heterosexuality as a necessary condition to becoming a Christian.[8]

Three reasons justify an analysis of this topic. Firstly, Southern Baptists make up the largest Protestant denomination in the country, having over fifteen million members. Understandably, what this powerful denomination says in its official proposals and statements impacts others, whether they are Baptist or not. Secondly, homosexuality is a hot topic of discussion, and is salient to the general public. Few topics arouse discussion in the SBC more than the inclusion of gays and lesbians in church life. Finally, there are communication problems with Baptist families containing homosexuals. Unfortunately, loyalist preacher-rhetors have failed to provide a therapeutic model of denominational communication on the issue of families with members who are homosexual. In this chapter, we evaluate these matters and their negative impact.

Homosexuality is also a heterosexual issue, and the denomination seems unaware of that, judging by the topic's absence from official and pulpit communications. Opportunities exist for the SBC presidents to raise and answer key questions affecting the membership from the pulpit. How will Christian heterosexual parents, siblings, and friends of homosexuals *privately* (and publicly) communicate with each other? How can these families talk and respond to their homosexual relatives who may receive verbal and physical abuse in a society that is increasingly hostile? How might family members respond when they become objects of ridicule and ostracism? How do these parents, brothers, sisters, and other relatives cope and communicate among themselves? Family members of homosexuals have often become victims in a society that seems increasingly violent. These questions, and others that arise from them, make this an issue requiring rational inquiry.

The climate for open discussion on the topic of homosexuality in Southern Baptist churches is at best indifferent, at its worst, unhealthy. This negative climate, which cannot be blamed totally upon secular forces, has been assisted, implicitly or explicitly, by the rhetorics of silence and abomination that prevent public deliberation, foster divisiveness, and punish those Christian families seeking help from the church. It is appropriate to explore how these rhetorics have been negatively employed and then to present a corrective that would seek to establish a healthier communicative atmosphere regarding the incorporation of Christian homosexuals into church life.

Official denominational communications that characterize gay and lesbian Christians with frigid silence or with Leviticus-like labels are persuasively negative forces, for they are powerful obstacles to discussion and inquiry, and they consequently encourage an atmosphere of ignorance and mistrust. Such communications are an inhibiting force to those who try to engage in a dialogue to resolve differences, regardless of their sexual orientation. Unfortunately, denominational loyalists offer little consolation to those Christians who regard the phrase "love one another" from John 15:12 as a call to action and seek to develop a rhetoric of reconciliation.

There are additional questions that the denomination has failed to answer. Can *congregations* of laypersons, discouraged by the absence of official denominational communication favoring a dialogue of inquiry, deliberate about inclusion in spite of an indifferent, perhaps hostile *secular* opinion climate? Is the conflict over the inclusion of gays and lesbians in church life merely scriptural? Or is it perceptional, because being a homosexual is seen as too terrible for heterosexual believers in the pew to contemplate? Is the "H word" too awful to say aloud? Do Southern Baptists really want to hear about the topic at all, whether in or out of the sanctuary? Is there room for exploration and inquiry, or is this kind of questioning too sensitive for congregational discussion?

SBC congregations are microcosms of a larger secular community, often reflecting a larger sense of public opinion. If that is so, the climate beyond SBC churches is likely supportive of exclusionary discourse. Cobb County, Georgia, recently became the "nation's first county to adopt an official condemnation of homosexuality as a lifestyle." In fact, the county commissioners labeled homosexuality as "incompatible with standards to which this community subscribes."[9] Reportedly, various Southern Baptists in the area, including Rev. Nelson Price, formerly the first vice president of the SBC and one-time president of the Convention Pastor's Conference, were supporters of the action.

In the state of California, the California Southern Baptist Convention executive board opposed a law that forbade employment discrimination based on sexual orientation. The state of Colorado has repealed all laws protecting gays and lesbians from discrimination. However, in April 1993, *Baptists Today* reported that Colorado had lost more than $25 million dollars in convention revenue, perhaps because of economic boycotts stemming from the repeal. Construction projects have been canceled, and various municipalities such as Los Angeles, New York, Baltimore, and Atlanta have refused to engage in contracts with Colorado companies.

In the fall 1994 elections, a number of state referenda regarding homosexuality were placed before the voters.[10] In Idaho, Proposition 1 prohibited state agencies and public colleges from granting "minority status" to people who engage in homosexual sex. It also limited the reading of library materials on homosexuality and allowed state agencies to consider the sexual practices of job applicants in hiring decisions. In Oregon, Measure 13 sought to bar state and local governments, including public colleges, from spending funds in a manner that expressed approval of homosexuality. Maine legislators have also considered similar measures.

The politicization of AIDS is also a related public opinion issue, because AIDS is still commonly regarded as a disease originating with and perpetuated only by homosexuals. The facts seem to indicate otherwise.[11] In the United States and in the rest of the world, AIDS and HIV-positive cases are increasing dramatically across various age groups, particularly among heterosexuals, much to the concern of world health specialists and economists.

The inclusion of homosexuals as church members has also deeply troubled other religious groups. Some, such as the Moravians, Episcopalians, Unitarians, and the United Church of Christ, have taken positions that seem to recognize that gays and lesbians should be welcomed as children of God. The United Church of Christ, for example, has deplored the use of Scripture to generate hatred against gays. But the Vatican, expressing a lukewarm attitude, has labeled homosexuality an "objective disorder" and has decided that "there are areas in which it is not unjust discrimination to take sexual orientation into account, for example, in the consignment of children to adoption or foster care, in employment of teachers or coaches and in military recruitment."[12]

In 1992, the National Council of Churches failed to act upon an application for membership from Cleveland's thirty-thousand-member Metropolitan Community Churches, which includes gays and lesbians. In 1993, Methodists debated the eligibility of homosexuals for clergy membership and appointment. The world's largest gay and lesbian church in the world, the Cathedral of Hope Metropolitan Community Church in Dallas, Texas, has just moved into a new $3 million facility.[13] On the other hand, Christian ethics professor Paul Simmons was apparently forced into early retirement from the Southern Baptist Theological Seminary in Louisville, Kentucky, partly because he allegedly held views supporting homosexuality.[14]

How rhetors assemble their advocacy case for and against the inclusion of homosexuals in church life is intriguing. For SBC rhetors, that development may begin with a biblical proof text. Both Baptist dissidents and loyalists have heard sermons developed from Paul in I Corinthians 13:1, "If I speak in the tongues of men and of angels, but have not love, I am a noisy gong or a clanging cymbal." Paul's advice is buttressed by the all-encompassing order from Jesus in John 15:12, "This is my commandment, that ye love one another, as I have loved you." On the other hand, loyalists will cite their biblical justifications from the Old Testament, especially Leviticus 18:22: "Thou shalt not lie with mankind, as with womankind: it is abomination." The penalty to avoid following the legalistic injunction of Leviticus is clear, for such persons "shall surely be put to death; their blood shall be upon them" (Leviticus 20:13b).

The book of Leviticus describes a milder penalty for those who disobey Leviticus 18:22. If homosexuals are unclean, perhaps diseased, because of their abominational behavior, then perhaps they are the equivalent of the Old Testament leper. Leviticus authorizes the banishment of lepers from the community of believers. According to Leviticus 13:46b, "The leper is unclean: he shall dwell alone; without the camp shall his habitation be." Thus, the question occurs: are homosexuals today's untouchable lepers? In 1991, the SBC asserted that "Scripture *condemns* . . . homosexuality."[15] These justifications raise the question of whether gay and lesbian Christians are welcome in the Southern Baptist Convention. Certainly there is no sermon from any *national* meeting of the Convention encouraging their presence, let alone their inclusion.

However, in the spring of 1992, two major events occurred in Southern Baptist church life in North Carolina that indicate some signs of tolerance on the local church level. In March of that year, Pullen Memorial Baptist Church of Raleigh voted to endorse the church as a site for a same-gender union of two men, one of whom was a member of the church. Nearly two-thirds of the church's membership voted to authorize the union and to permit Rev. Mahan Siler to perform the service. Further, after months of study, discussion, and deliberation involving the entire church, nearly 100 percent of the membership voted to accept homosexuals as members, presuming they met other appropriate membership conditions. These events were headline news items in the secular press and throughout the denomination.

Then on April 5, Olin T. Binkley Memorial Baptist Church of Chapel Hill voted to license a gay divinity student to the ministry. This procedure—which is often followed by ordination—was authorized by 57.5 percent, more than a majority, of the congregation. The decision was preceded by eight months of study by the congregation, a deacon motion of support, and four hours of deliberation before the actual vote by the assembled church.

The official and informal response to the actions of these churches was swift and punitive. In May, the Raleigh Baptist Association met twice to consider Pullen's actions and voted Pullen out of the association. The discussion in these two meetings was dominated by abominational rhetoric and fearsome calls upon believers to obey the selective laws of Leviticus. In April and May, letters to the *Raleigh News and Observer* concerning the decisions of Pullen and Binkley were similar in tone, for the most part, although some were supportive of the two churches. The ejection of Pullen was the association's first in its 109-year history. In May, the General Board of the North Carolina Baptist State Convention ejected both Pullen and Binkley from the state convention. By a secret ballot, the Board also voted not to accept any funds from either of the two churches.[16]

At the national meeting of the Southern Baptist Convention in June, Messengers changed the denomination's constitution to refuse the inclusion of any church that "affirms" homosexuality. This decision effectively legitimized the exclusion of Binkley and Pullen. Although that exclusion was not formalized until a year later at the SBC meeting in Houston, Pullen and Binkley were effectively no longer members, and the denomination declined to accept any money from them. The national SBC's action was the *first imposition of a sexuality criterion* as a requirement for church membership since the formation of the denomination.

Two months later in August 1992, the Associated Baptist Press (ABP) reported that the Covenant Baptist Church in Houston had cut its ties with the national Convention. The minister, Rev. Jim Leach, told the ABP that accepting the expulsion of the Convention would be the same as "surrendering to a religious hierarchy, and we're too Baptist to do that."[17] Covenant Baptist Church is now aligned with American Baptist Churches, USA, as is Pullen Memorial Baptist Church. Leach's statement is reminiscent of Roger Williams's commentary about the Massachusetts Bay Colony in the 1630s. The Bay's restrictive actions against Williams's church in Salem prompted him to predict that a "presbytery of churches" would inevitably and negatively affect the liberty of the individual church. In light of the recent developments in the SBC, Williams's prediction seems accurate, which Leach's only confirms.

In September 1992, the Riverside Baptist Church of Washington, D.C., also withdrew from the SBC because of the constitutional change forbidding ties with any church that "affirms homosexuality." According to Riverside pastor Michael Bledsoe, national SBC positions on such issues as the priesthood of believers were also a consideration. But the church has maintained its relationships with the American Baptist Churches, USA, and the Progressive National Baptist Convention. Rev. Bledsoe was quoted as saying in *Baptists Today*: "I'd say the continued erosion of historic Baptist principles and the recent action by the SBC . . . left us no choice. We had to get out of the SBC so we could remain Baptist."[18]

The Covenant Baptist Church and the Riverside Baptist Church decisions have apparently not been duplicated by many Southern Baptist churches. Resolutions of support from other churches for Covenant's decision, if any, have not been published in *Baptists Today* or in any other denomination publication. Perhaps other Baptist churches have supported the Convention's decision without making their opinions public. Perhaps some congregations have been afraid to openly consider the issue. In any case, the record is silent.

The sermon record at the various national meetings from 1979 to 1993 is silent regarding any pulpit discourse on homosexuality, and laypersons needing such discourses will search in vain. If there are any in the national Messenger meeting sermon archives from 1979 to 1993, we have been unable to find them. Nevertheless, the inclusion issue—and its related topics—is significant in terms of membership guidance and instruction. Does a silent pulpit constitute an example of leadership communication? Is this silence a model for encouraging the acquisition of knowledge? If the pulpit could be used as a tool for dispelling mistrust, would it breach the wall of silence?

There are several reasons that explain this rhetoric of silence. First of all, even in secular communication, there is a pervasive fear of uttering the "H word" or any word related to it, such as "gay" or "lesbian," because they are too connotative or negative. For example, the school board of Nash County, North Carolina, has adopted a sex education curriculum that forbids teachers from using the word "homosexual."[19] Furthermore, words of a specific sexual nomenclature, even when appropriate in secular discourse, are taboo for the pulpit, whether by tradition or policy. Currently, the "H word" is too terrible to speak because it carries with it a Darth Vader–like perversity far in excess of any ordinary denotative meaning. For those who fear change, these words have fearsome identities and connotations.

For some Baptist loyalists, *sermonizing* about homosexuality would infer the acceptability of it to persons in the pew. Worse, reconciling sermons might be viewed as promoting and therefore legitimizing allegedly aberrant behavior as appropriate for Baptist laypersons, and thus desecrate the pulpit itself. If SBC presidents sermonized about inclusion in their churches, such language would tacitly acknowledge the *presence* of gays and lesbians. By avoiding public or private discussion, loyalists maintain the myth that Christian gays and lesbians do not exist. From the loyalist perspective, if Christian gays and lesbians do exist, they are likely insignificant numerically within individual church congregations. Consequently, there is little justification for the denomination to produce instructional or devotional materials for this population, ostensibly because there are so few of them. This kind of circular reasoning justifies the rhetoric of silence.

The third explanation for the rhetoric of silence is that the historical record of annual convention sermons is not a *proactive* communication outlet on controversial morality issues. Except for evangelistic themes, the annual convention pulpit has rarely, if ever, been an initiator of debate. It has certainly not been the promoter of dialogue among the victimized, which suggests that it has been neither an energizer nor a catalyst of social problem solving.

The traditional argument against the pulpit as a location of inquiry can be simply stated: the pulpit is not the *appropriate* place for such discourses. Yet, that argument is facile, for it ignores contrary historical facts. In the nineteenth century, Southern Baptist preachers used the church pulpit to endorse slavery with justifications that argued for the subjugation of human beings as property. In the twentieth century, some Southern Baptist preachers have likely supported segregation, either by saying nothing against it or by supporting it outright. The fact is that the Southern Baptist Convention was born from its *defense* of slavery in 1845. One hundred and fifty years later, the denomination has reversed its approval of slavery, thus suggesting that it might be ready to move forward into the post–Civil War era.

Furthermore, the promotion of required or sanctioned prayer in the public schools is grist for current preaching discourse. Various state Baptist newspapers contain letters to the editor arguing for required school prayer. Consequently, it is difficult to conclude that SBC pulpits, whether on a local basis or at national meetings, have been devoid of *all* social issue-oriented sermons.

Nevertheless, pulpit silence on inclusion is supported by the absence of discussion in official SBC printed materials. Inclusion topics are not among published Sunday School teaching materials, youth materials, layperson periodicals, or devotional guides. Laypersons desiring to read neutral materials supporting a meaningful inquiry on homosexuality must turn to secular sources of varying quality. These publications may reflect political agendas, so finding appropriate study resources is often difficult.

Pulpit preaching does not occur in a vacuum, for SBC ministers presumably speak and listen within the environment of parishioner needs and opinions. If the membership urges a discussion of inclusion for all persons within the context of loving one's neighbor as John 15:12 urges, then such advice is likely to be heard from the pulpit. Congregations that have been jointly led by clergy and laypersons, such as those of Pullen and Binkley, have argued with moderation and adopted an inclusion position. Both congregations have proved that ministers and laypersons together can successfully overcome the rhetoric of silence with dialogue and deliberation.

But laypersons may feel uncomfortable or disinterested in discussing the inclusion of homosexuals as members.[20] As Mahan Siler of the Pullen church wrote in his church newsletter, "Even daring to discuss openly this subject as a congregation is to open ourselves to volatile, divisive possibilities. Homophobia permeates our society."[21] Furthermore, since the

1960s, any number of Baptist congregations have found it difficult to discuss racism and the inclusion of African Americans as members as well.

In the 1990s, however, there is another formidable obstacle to a layperson's dialogue about the inclusion of homosexuals: control of access to the channels of information. Even if the laity knew about the universe of information about Christian gays and lesbians, wished to move towards the spirit of love in John 15:12, and had the ability to promote a debate of inquiry, it would still be a difficult process. Currently, access to the official channels of pulpit, electronic, and print communication are controlled by those who favor exclusion. There is no reason to believe that these channels would be open to the laity even if they requested the time or space for an inclusion discussion.

Individual congregations, such as Pullen's and Binkley's, have moved forward by virtue of their own laity deliberations, and they have taken a position favoring inclusion. Contrary to some expectations, neither Pullen nor Binkley has lost much in the way of donations or numbers of members. While the *secular* press has shown an active interest in all sides of these church decisions, *denominational* press accounts have reported only the "official" response. Whether these latter reports have educated members about inclusion is arguable; rather, they seem to indicate only an attempt by the denominational press to present the precise facts of the Pullen and Binkley church decisions.

SBC pulpit ministers preach within the context of prevailing secular and denominational opinions, and laypersons and church congregations speak in the same context. To positively affect that context, pulpit ministers will need to encourage an open communication climate, one free of recrimination. Such encouragement will help establish a healthier spirit for inquiry. Committed to an atmosphere free of abominational rhetoric, laypersons can participate in an enlightened dialogue with each other about the inclusion of Christian homosexuals. The Pullen and Binkley congregations have proved, albeit with preparation, that ministers and laypersons together can overcome the rhetoric of silence with dialogue and deliberation.

The tragedy of rhetorical silence on the issue of homosexuality in the SBC today is that it allows—perhaps encourages by default—the growth of ignorance and fear. Dispelling ignorance and fear in the face of hostile secular public opinion is never an easy task for contemporary rhetors. Nevertheless, if knowledgeable and skilled spokespersons avoid speaking compassionately about the victimized, than they abdicate their role as a persuader in enhancing all that is best in human nature. To avoid the inclusion debate allows believers to evade a fundamental issue of being a Christian: caring for those who suffer. Apart from the agony experienced by gays and lesbians, there is grief within their families. The Pontius Pilate attitude of refusing to examine and discuss inclusion constitutes more than a lethargy of the mind; it can be defined as a refusal to minister to those in need.

In this controversy, silence is reinforced by a denominational rhetoric of abomination, which focuses on the themes of blame, accusation, and declarations of moral judgments. Milton Rokeach, the author of *The Open and Closed Mind: Investigations into the Nature of Belief Systems and Personality Systems* suggests a helpful way to analyze this kind of language.[22] Rokeach characterizes such language as "dogmatism" and recommends that dogmatic personalities and institutions be recognized by their communication style. Dogmatic communication exhibits rigidity, suspicion, and polarization. It discourages new points of view, and it describes the world in a bifurcated manner, as divided into two easily identifiable groups. Differences between acceptable and unacceptable groups are major when the dogmatist refuses to accept the beliefs of the unacceptable group as true. By contrast, dogmatists view differences within accepted groups as slight and nonthreatening. Dogmatic communication reflects a world that is a dangerous and menacing place, with sinister forces at work everywhere. These communicators emphasize that the receivers of their communications should unquestionably accept the role of authority in decision making, relegating personal investigation only to confirming those tasks that the authority wishes the receiver to do.

The theme of abomination is often buttressed by various biblical proof texts, principally from the Old Testament, such as those in the Leviticus scriptures already described earlier. In Resolution 6, distributed at the 1988 San Antonio meeting, the case against homosexuality is hotly presented, and laypersons will recognize three principal parts to its construction: first, the cultural basis from which the advocates develop their argument; second, categorical assertions of blame; and third, a moral judgment that both condemns homosexuality as a "lifestyle" and as an "abomination in the eyes of God," with a sop-like assurance that homosexuals are not beyond the possibility of God's forgiveness. To endow the moral judgment with a sense of legitimization, scriptural references are provided.

> Whereas, The erosion of moral sanity continues to be a major problem of modern society; and
>
> Whereas, Homosexuality has become the chosen lifestyle of many in this moral decline; and
>
> Whereas, The Bible is very clear in its teaching that homosexuality is a manifestation of a depraved nature; and
>
> Whereas, This deviant behavior has wrought havoc in the lives of millions; and
>
> Whereas, Homosexuals are justified and even glorified in our secular media; and
>
> Whereas, Homosexual activity is the primary cause of the

> introduction and spread of AIDS in the United States which has not only affected those of the homosexual community, but also many innocent victims.
>
> Therefore, be it RESOLVED, That we affirm the biblical injunction which declares homosexuals, like all sinners, can receive forgiveness and victory through personal faith in Jesus Christ (1 Corinthians 6:9–11); and
>
> Be it finally RESOLVED, That we maintain that while God loves the homosexual and offers salvation, homosexuality is not a normal lifestyle and is an abomination in the eyes of God (Leviticus 18:22; Romans 1:24–28; I Timothy 1:8–10).[23]

All of the assertions in Resolution 6 may be true or false. Our purpose is not to rebut them, although the global assertiveness of the claims is exceptional. The use of biblical citations within the resolution is predictable, and, presumably, laypersons should accept those selected examples of literal proof text because they are provided by sanctioned authors representing Southern Baptists.

Most resolutions from advocacy groups are admittedly one-sided, and Resolution 6 is no exception. Furthermore, for those Messengers who contend that exclusion is fully justifiable, as well as for those who see no controversy to begin with, these resolutions merely confirm the obvious. The claims are not speculatively written, nor do they propose debate. As with this resolution, the promotion of inquiry for the purposes of learning such as that conceived by the classicists of ancient Greece and Rome, is a tertiary objective, if one at all. To encourage persuasion is unnecessary, for its supporters are already committed to the resolution as a final truth.

Resolution 6 is also valuable to its proponents because it provides them with a reaffirmation and strengthening of an already held position. Seeing it in print confers a sense of status that a momentary oral discussion among its supporters would not possess. For those who wish to defend a policy of exclusion, the resolution provides proof text citations from the most authoritative source of all rules governing secular human social conduct, the Holy Bible.

Developing one's argument from biblical proof text is highly effective, especially when it is applicable, clear, and historically relevant to the contemporaneous issue. On the matter of homosexuality and inclusion, the historical and contextual record is difficult to judge. Loyal denominationalists may argue that Leviticus condemns gay or lesbian sexual practices. Others can argue from their reading of Leviticus that Jesus never condemned homosexuals (and they certainly existed in his day). Still others argue that the homosexual activity condemned in the Bible focuses on promiscuous and abusive behaviors, including various forms of prostitution in temple worship. Baptist laypersons are often ill equipped for a serious analytical examination of the Scriptures. Consequently, a personal study of the Bible and appropriate commentaries might well be more rewarding rather than relying solely on the national Convention resolutions or a particular church minister as a source of instruction for one's own ideology.

According to Roy Honeycutt in the *Layman's Bible Book Commentary*, Leviticus presupposes a thoroughly religious interpretation of life and states that no area of human life rests outside the bounds of God's care.[24] To live according to the laws of Leviticus requires that life must be observed totally within an Old Testament lifestyle. If laypersons today agreed to such a requirement, inquiry into the inclusion issue would be unnecessary. In the Levitical system, only the sanctioned priest is central, and is perhaps indispensable, in providing counsel, advice, and absolute rulings about human morality. Automatically relying upon a Levitical priest or minister as a source of counsel and governance for the development of human relationships would raise serious questions for laypersons today for two reasons. Firstly, dissident Baptists prefer to seek their own codes of moral behavior rather than blindly accepting them from another human being. Secondly, unquestioned obedience to the laws of Leviticus requires members to return to an ancient culture in which the priest had a position of remarkable, perhaps dictatorial, influence over individual moral behavior. While loyalist Baptists may find comfort and security in such a system, dissident Baptists reject it. Instead, they prefer to concentrate on their own direct communication with the Almighty. Doing so, they have chosen to pursue a more personal association with the Creator.

In any case, Honeycutt asserts that the contextual focus of Leviticus is about the individual's relationship with God, *not* with the relationships of humankind with humankind. Resolution 6 reverses that focus. Instead, human relationships are stressed within a cultural dimension rather than the construction of a loving association with God. But for layperson's using Resolution 6 as their guide, developing caring relationships with others would prove difficult, since there is no real advice on how to do this. Furthermore, if one understands Leviticus as it is interpreted in Resolution 6, then developing a loving relationship with God is of a secondary concern as well. If loyalist laypersons utilize the resolution as their guide for Christian morality, the believer will presumably live a morally clean life by avoiding any contact with homosexuals. But precisely how adherence to the sternly condemnatory resolution will develop one's relationship with God is not mentioned, and we are left to await further resolutions from the denomination to resolve that important matter.

Resolution 6 reflects various features of the Rokeach dogmatism model. The language is rigid, for it fixes blame without alternative. Homosexuals are the cause of the "erosion of moral sanity" and responsible for a "moral decline" in "modern society." They are guilty of committing "deviant behavior," being of a "depraved nature" and "not normal." They have "wrought havoc in the lives of millions" because of their alleged "introduction and spread of AIDS." The resolution's accusations are monumentally assertive. They confer nearly mythological powers to a rather small member of human beings that probably constitute less than 10 percent of the population in the United States.

The resolve clauses are equally global in their moral judgment, for the Messengers "deplore homosexuality as a violation and perversion of divine standards" because it is "an abomination in the eyes of God." The resolution offers no substitute to these conclusions, and it reflects the deep suspicion, fear, and insecurity of a small group of people. Apparently, homosexuality represents such an abominable force that it arouses the deepest dread from the resolution's authors and to the lives that they lead. If we accept the resolution as an appropriate guide to life, then the world clearly becomes a threatening place to live because of the homosexual.

Understandably, all language contains some degree of connotation because the meanings of words are dependent upon the perceptions of the receiver. Nevertheless, this resolution is full of words containing emotionally charged associations. According to Richard Weaver's *The Ethics of Rhetoric*, words that elicit representations of a highly positive nature and that are specifically linked to powers we believe might influence us are "god terms." Weaver defines as "devil terms" those words that evoke undesirable or loathsome feelings.[25] By invoking and relying on devil terms such as "depraved nature," the resolution prompts us to view homosexuals as abhorrent and "an abomination in the eyes of God." The use of such language is especially helpful for its advocates in establishing a scapegoat for its problems. Establishing a scapegoat helps the organization to divert attention away from more substantive membership issues and fosters a difficult climate for open communication and democratic problem solving.[26]

In today's hostile communication situation, homosexuals have become the lepers of contemporary society. In the time of Jesus, the "L word" was fearsome; today, the "L word" has become the "H word." Lepers were thought to be incurably infectious, destined for death, to be avoided at all costs, and persons without value. In effect, they were the living dead the minute the priest determined their fate, and the community acquiesced in that decision. All of these observations seem applicable to homosexuals today, given the spirit and letter of Resolution 6. The resolution decides that these human beings "like all sinners" can "receive forgiveness . . . through personal faith in Jesus Christ" but totally avoids recommending any role for the layperson in bringing these persons to Christ. Such a course of action is consistent with Leviticus 18:29, which explicitly prescribes: "For whosoever shall commit any of these abominations, even the souls that commit them shall be cut off from among their people." Ostracism is therefore considered a legitimate action, fully authorized by the Old Testament.

Baptist laypersons, who have been commanded to submit to the authority of the pulpit minister by the 1988 Resolution 5, "On the Priesthood of the Believer," might expect their minister to lead them in a more helpful course of action. But that solution is also omitted from Resolution 6. Even Leviticus is merciful when instructing the leper (or anyone else thought to be similarly contaminated and therefore unclean) to see the priest for cleansing. Have today's priests abdicated that function, leaving it instead to the secular physician or the families of these social outcasts?

Why is there so little dialogue among Southern Baptists on the inclusion of gays and lesbians in church life? The fault cannot be placed totally on the individual SBC preacher who avoids mentioning the topic for fear of losing his position. The dogmatic SBC resolutions analyzed here exacerbate mistrust and blame, and they encourage silence. The human cost of this silence is enormous. From 1979 onward, the Convention pulpit hierarchy *could* have become model persuasion agents for a healthier course of denominational communication regarding inclusion. These ministers *could* preach a gospel of reconciliation and help heal divisions among Christians. Convention resolutions at the national meetings *could* present alternatives to ostracism and abuse. A denominational dialogue on the topic *could* be vigorously two-sided. But, regardless of the SBC hierarchy's role in the stifling of inquiry, it is the layperson who is most responsible for abdicating a therapeutic communication for those affected.

When will laypersons desire a responsible, helpful, and rational discussion about inclusion? That course of communication will happen when those in the pew overcome their fear of the unknown, when hostile secular opinions concerning the topic of inclusion are lessened, or when laypersons are persuasively encouraged to discuss healthier conclusions.

Yet, a climate for open deliberation in this polarizing and contentious dispute, especially among advocates that seem so far apart, will not occur easily. Effective discussion can begin only when there is an attractive middle ground on which both proponents and antagonists can meet together. If that middle ground can be found, then a much healthier sense of communication will prevail. Neither denominational opinion nor secular public opinion currently seems to recognize that any intermediate positions exist.

An example of this middle ground can be found by first looking at the

Pullen Memorial Baptist Church perspective. The church members believe that all humans are made in God's image; all humans are now and have always been objects of God's will; all humans are eligible to receive God's grace, compassion, and salvation; homosexuals are redeemable by God just as are heterosexuals; and God does not command us to love only those we like, agree with, or find attractive. Consequently, we are commanded to love everyone in the grace of our Lord Jesus Christ.

Resolution 6, on the other hand, is fundamentally different than the Pullen position, and it reflects a totally different set of beliefs. Intriguingly, however, the resolution and the Pullen approach are in fundamental agreement on one key point. Homosexuals and heterosexuals are loved by God and God offers *salvation to all*. This mutual point of agreement is valuable for contemporary advocates of open inquiry to build on in their deliberations.

A second approach is that of *toleration*. Roger Williams and his sturdy band of outcasts in colonial Rhode Island developed a sense of toleration that worked, even if it was intensely disliked by their pompous Boston neighbors.[27] From the perspective of the Boston oligarchy, Rhode Island was a moral sewer. The earliest laws on toleration from the Rhode Island governing authorities and Williams's advocacy centered on one key idea: Everyone should enjoy the freedom of discussion except for those promoting public disorder. For example, in 1666 two Quaker women appeared nude in a worship service in Newbury, Massachusetts. Claiming a divine inspiration to witness to the unbelieving colonists from Isaiah 20:3–4, they also paraded nude through the city streets of Salem. When these Quakers were ejected from Massachusetts, they went to Rhode Island, where they were welcomed by many, including Baptists. There are no recorded instances of Quaker nudism in colonial Rhode Island, although the record is clear that Williams disliked their witnessing tactics. However, neither Williams, nor anyone else in authority, ever urged that the Quakers be jailed or ostracized for their public behavior in Massachusetts.[28]

Toleration is not the same as acceptance or loving with open arms those whom you dislike. Toleration simply recognizes the existence of an idea or person without malice or discriminatory action in law. Toleration legalizes, but does not force, acceptance of different viewpoints. Historically, Baptists have learned that in the long run, recognizing those of different ideas, races, and social behaviors, while difficult, is within the best tradition of being an American. It is also within the best tradition of being a "Roger Williams" kind of Baptist.

A third potential middle ground for deliberation focuses on the *law*. Currently, some lawmakers want to remove all legal protections for gays and lesbians under the premise that they are not worthy of such protection, perhaps not worthy of being a citizen of the United States. Nevertheless, homosexuals work, pay taxes, serve in the military, and have been elected to any number of high political offices. They are often victims of discrimination, and Baptists reject discrimination in other areas of human endeavor, such as in the refusal to hire someone because of age or gender. Being fired from a job based on such pretexts commonly draw the ire of, or legal action from, laypersons. When those who would stifle inquiry on the inclusion issue fully recognize that discrimination of *any* kind is intolerable against *everyone*, the opposers will begin to tolerate the existence of homosexuals.

The reality is, however, that none of the approaches above are currently viable in the denominational forum of opinion. It is possible that many Southern Baptists agree on certain aspects of these options and that they may offer points of agreement that could be used for deliberation in the future. To be usable, however, any middle ground in a dispute must be attractive enough to invite discussion, and it must be broad enough to allow room for negotiation and maneuvering by advocates.

Fortunately, there is one other middle ground: the importance and preservation of the family. There is unity among Baptist groups on this key point, and that unity is evident, at least in denominational communications. A cursory examination of post-1979 Southern Baptist Convention resolutions will establish that there is official concern for the family. Sermons from national Convention meetings and Pastor's Conferences frequently deal with the topic. Individual churches promote "family days" in a number of ways, in and out of the pulpit. Secular public opinion, however, while divided on other social issues, still seems unified on the need to preserve the family. Monogamous relationships continue to be emphasized as a stability factor for raising children. These points of agreement are emphasized in published materials such as Sunday School literature, whether Southern Baptist, Cooperative Baptist, or American Baptist. Publishing companies such as Broadman, Smyth and Helwys, and others frequently bring out new titles on the family and its significance.

So, what would be the characteristics of a rhetoric of reconciliation from the pulpit and the denomination? First, laypersons and pulpit artists alike will need to eliminate the kind of bombast and recrimination similar to that in secular discourse regarding homosexuals. Using abominational rhetoric simply imitates society's talk that characterizes gays and lesbians as if they were the living representation of the demonic man from Gadarene, who was possessed by devils and accused Christ of intimidation. Furthermore, if the church wishes to emulate the secular world with such discourse, it will have lost its justification for existence. Christians are *in* the world, but not necessarily *of* the world, and the way laypersons talk about others reveals a sense of ministry or the lack of one. The apostle Paul provides us with a layperson's model of spoken ministry in

I Corinthians 13:1–8. There, he admonishes all humans to speak with the tongues of angels and to remember that "charity suffereth long, and is kind." Charity "thinketh no evil."[29]

Second, reconciliation rhetoric will be acceptable when laypersons recognize that homosexuality is a heterosexual issue. Distressed parents, brothers, sisters, and relatives of gays and lesbians are in need of therapeutic conversation, not unhelpful silence or verbal abuse. Christian heterosexual families can be equipped to communicate with those who are estranged, and if the denomination is unable to break its pious silence to help them, then laypersons will need to find assistance elsewhere. When the church focuses on the need for reconciling the whole family of Christ, a dialogue will begin. Such a dialogue will necessitate discussion with individuals of differing sexual orientation, which will require inner strength for some in overcoming bias or admitting ignorance. But healing ministries typically demand personal change.

Third, layperson rhetoric can be focused on the commandment of love as presented in John 15:12. An appropriate example of this kind of communication is that from Eric Raddatz of Wake Forest, North Carolina. A former drug addict, Raddatz speaks in churches, conducts seminars, and encourages discussions among healthy persons and AIDS victims. He has also begun a drive for the construction of homes for the dying victims of AIDS. Raddatz's motivation in carrying out this ministry is based principally on his father's death from AIDS, although he has also been encouraged by Rev. Tom Jackson, his local church minister. Raddatz, a Southeastern Baptist Theological Seminary student, asserts that "[w]e must be compassionate, not judgmental."[30] The eminent Rev. Paige Patterson has pledged his support and money to Raddatz's ministry to AIDS victims. Undoubtedly, Raddatz and his friends believe—and have put into action—the advice from John 3:17: "For God sent not his Son into the world to condemn the world; but that the world through him might be saved."

The 1990s have been tumultuous and hostile, and the new century will likely be that way as well. There are ways of lessening that hostility, however, and especially so on the issue of the inclusion of homosexuals into church life. Can laypersons avoid the dogmatism of abomination? Can laypersons confront the negative impact of silence? They can, and must, or else this issue will gnaw at the very fabric of the church, sapping its strengths and relegating it to the status of a secular institution.

9

The New Southern Baptists and a Purified South

All Scripture is given by inspiration of God, and a God of truth cannot inspire error.

—Rev. Adrian Rogers, former president of the Southern Baptist Convention

In the Name of the Father is an unfinished story, for every day brings new evidence of the denomination's assertiveness. In 1997, in preparation for the 1998 annual convention in Salt Lake, Messengers voted to devote special emphasis to the conversion of Mormons. The Messengers also reaffirmed their boycott of the Disney empire because the corporation allegedly extends health benefits to its gay employees.[1] On April 11, 1996, Mark Coppenger, president of the Midwestern Baptist Seminary, told a seminary audience that women as pulpit preachers are contrary to God's intent in creation and an "affront to home and family [and] an affront to the creation order." Their preaching in local churches was "one of the raging, raging heresies and confusions of the day." After quoting I Timothy 2:11–15, Coppenger allegedly proclaimed: "There are women pastors all over the place. Now I'm not saying that everybody who toys with this idea is utterly apostate, but I'm saying that they are playing with a very dangerous approach to understanding Scripture and the church."[2] *Implicitly*, Coppenger's statements are an acknowledgement of the increase in the ordination of women despite his advocacy against their inclusion.[3] *Explicitly*, however, Coppenger's remarks clearly indicate his position that anyone who interprets Scripture as allowing women to occupy the pulpit is at least ignorant, if not also guilty of apostasy. To Coppenger, the strictures against women in I Timothy are clear, for he understands Paul's writing in a literal manner. In this regard, his viewpoint is identical to that of former SBC president Adrian Rogers.

President Rogers's views reflect our conviction that the central persuasive theme of Convention pulpit rhetoric is the promotion of inerrancy and the exclusion of those undesirable members who might interfere with reaching that goal. The leadership has a particular objective, namely, the inclusion of the "chosen ones" and the exclusion of disaffected groups, particularly those in disagreement with the decrees and doctrinal statements of the Convention hierarchy.

The total membership of the Nashville-based Convention has been polarized since 1979.[4] Since then, inerrantists have consistently been elected by loyalists to national Convention offices. In 1988, at the SBC convention in San Antonio, a determined campaign was made by dissidents to elect a different slate of officers; but that effort failed by 692 out of 31,291 votes cast. A mutual and harmonious resolution of this division that would tend towards reunifying the denomination seems extremely doubtful, since neither side appears focused on such a persuasive goal.

We have explored this division by centering on several key points: the interrelationship of the rhetorics of fundamentalism, inerrancy, and exclusion; attractively designed pulpit appeals urging adherents to cleanse themselves—and Southern society—of the sins of liberalism, feminism, and the social gospel; the rationale for the exclusion of women from leadership; and, finally, the trend of the individual believer away from unswerving obedience to the dictates of mainline denominationalism. Of course, to many evangelical Christians today, a binding tie to a national denomination is simply not as important as it used to be. According to church consultant Lyle Schaller, many persons have "an increasing lack of trust in institutions in today's society."[5] Consequently, many dissident Baptists would not return to the SBC even if it acquiesced to their concerns.

The authors of this book have analyzed the Southern Baptist Convention as a closed communication system, open only to certain persons, that continues to rely on the pulpit as a tool of power. The SBC pulpit has always been, and will continue to be, at the center of the denomination. New communication technologies are being employed to enhance the visual attractiveness of the pulpit speaker, not to replace him. To study the Convention as a communication system capitalizes on its strengths, for this denomination is surely one that has cultivated and depended upon the spoken word for its existence and power. On that point, its history since 1845 is clear.

The battle for the loyalty of the Baptist believer has historically been waged from the pulpit, with words as the principal tool of persuasion. In today's SBC world of leadership discourse, persuasion involves adjusting an inerrant Bible to a believer and a believer to an inerrant Bible. In the new Southern Baptist Convention, there is every reason to believe the issue of inerrancy will continue to be a part of presidential pulpit rhetoric, regardless of the past struggles respecting those who have left the denomination. It is always possible that theological changes will occur within the Convention itself, but to argue that the spoken word from the pulpit will cease to be a powerful force in this denomination forgets the vitality of its oral tradition. Since 1845, Southern Baptists have recognized the pulpit and the preacher as an indispensable force. The influence of television may modify it, and interactive computer technologies may enhance it, but the oral tradition will endure.

The words we use do more than describe events; they help us shape our reality. We are loyal to our words, and they become badges of allegiance that reveal our loyalties. Words such as "fundamentalists," "charismatics," "evangelicals," "progressive evangelicals," "moderates," and "liberals" are important as a means of identifying what is valuable to us. These key words are important less because the ordinary believer can provide a lengthy discourse about their meanings than because they are an indicator of one's personal beliefs.

Convention pulpit leaders contend that they must preach the necessity for a purer, more evangelistically driven denomination to attract new converts, expand their membership, and correct the harmful drift of believers in the South. Without reticence, Dr. Timothy George, dean of the Beeson Divinity School of Birmingham, Alabama, expansively justifies the denominational takeover: "Without some kind of conservative resurgence, Southern Baptists would doubtless have followed the same path of spiritual decline and theological erosion evident in so many of the mainline denominations."[6]

The presidential pulpit preachers are striving to promulgate and attractively design an inerrantist ideology developed from the ultimate source of textual authority, the Holy Scriptures. Inerrantism is woven into a pulpit rhetoric of order that focuses on the need for a cleansed denomination, free of the sins that intrude upon a believer's spiritual needs and personal theology while on earth.

All of these preaching efforts have been blended into a dynamic and hard-charging sound from the pulpit. Historically, Southern Baptists have always had a *preacher* in the pulpit, not a pastor. The difference is vast. Pastors counsel, affirm, and soothe. Preachers—at least those SBC presidents since 1979—have been vocally adept and commanding in the pulpit. They have attractive voices, a full range of tone scales, and a vibrant perception of word emphasis and timing. Furthermore, they have an acutely refined awareness of nonverbal communication. Their gestures, their hand and body movements, are more than coordinated; they are artistically timed to enhance ideas and make them visually attractive. Southern Baptists *know* about the orality of the pulpit. They see it as necessary, appropriate, and utterly valuable to an understanding of the sermon. The Reverends Bailey Smith, Adrian Rogers, and W. A. Criswell, with their pulpit use of nonverbal communication and their easy-to-understand rhetorical style, all satisfy the Southern Baptist believer's need to be challenged and inspired.

Denominational pulpit leaders have also argued for a heightened leadership role for local Southern Baptist ministers in interpreting doctrine. In 1988, Messengers revised the historic doctrine of the priesthood of believers. This doctrine, long accepted by Baptists, emphasizes that believers need not have an earthly mediator between themselves and God. The new revisions were earthshaking in their impact, since members must now submit to doctrinal interpretations by local church ministerial authority.

Dissenters have challenged the resolution as being a reversal of Baptist practice and as approaching episcopacy by having a negative constraint upon the freedom of individual believers to define the doctrine for themselves. Baptist historian Walter Shurden has commented that the SBC "fundamentalist majority" has "revised" the doctrine to the "point of repudiation."[7] According to William Powell Tuck, formerly professor of preaching at the Southern Baptist Theological Seminary (1978–83),

> [T]hroughout the history of Baptists, the doctrine of the priesthood of believers has resounded like the pealing of church bells . . . this doctrine has affected every belief we hold. It undergirds our understanding of salvation by faith, the right of each person to interpret the scriptures for himself or herself, our church polity and government, our rejection of creeds, and our understanding of the church's ministry and who is a minister in the church.[8]

Tuck's position underscores the significance of the priesthood of believers, and Shurden has concluded that the new revision "perverts" the historical traditions and scholarly record on the doctrine.[9]

Furthermore, current SBC leaders have reshaped the denomination in at least two ways. Firstly, from their national convention sermons, the SBC presidents verbalize a conformist and doctrinaire leadership model. Those adherents whose ideology or practices prevent them from giving unquestioned adherence to this governance model have few choices for continued membership within the denomination. Membership waywardness from the new standard of denominational exclusivity is subject to penalty by the leadership autocracy.

Secondly, exiled or disaffected female SBC members have argued that the denomination is an autocratic, gender-exclusive communication system designed to retain the power of sanctioned male rhetors in leadership positions. Consequently, female adherents seeking major leadership positions must instead apply their talent and skill in one of the breakaway organizations, such as the Baptist Women in Ministry (a one-time SBC auxiliary group), the Cooperative Baptist Fellowship (CBF), the Alliance of Baptists, or the Baptist Peace Fellowship of North America. Historically, ordained female pulpit ministers in the denomination have been overlooked for key roles in convention policy making. Furthermore, it would now appear that these women must be submissive to an exclusively male leadership hierarchy or risk the punishments of dismissal, ostracism, or exile. Sympathetic male denominational leaders who support their activist-minded female counterparts risk the same fate.

There have been significant changes regarding missions and missionaries as well following the crucial 1979 elections. Mission activity was once prized as the principal goal of the organization, but various missionaries have apparently become disenchanted, resigned, or have not been reappointed. Since 1988, for example, the number of missionaries to Japan has consistently dropped.[10] Unconfirmed reports suggest that some SBC missionaries have shifted their efforts to the CBF.

It is difficult to discern the trends, if any, of once loyal SBC churches shifting their membership to new denominational affiliations, since some have dropped the word "Baptist" from their names. Some churches have realigned themselves with other Baptist organizations, such as the Alliance of Baptists or the CBF, which specifically focus on activities such as a mission's delivery of medical and agricultural supplies as its principal objective. As we have noted earlier, some former SBC churches have become aligned with the American Baptist Churches, USA, or they have accepted a dual alignment with the CBF, thus retaining a historical identification with their organizational roots. Still other churches have placed their denominational monies in escrow or refused to designate them to the national SBC headquarters in Nashville, Tennessee. Some SBC churches no longer send their full complement of Messengers to the national conventions, preferring instead to send either a reduced number or none at all.

The SBC pulpit leadership is not responsible for all these changes, since the last decade has been a period of extreme change in American Protestantism. During this time, with the assistance of advanced electronic communication technologies, large independent or nondenominational congregations that have often labeled themselves Baptist, but which have never been affiliated with the Southern Baptist Convention, have become exceptionally visible in the South. In addition, potential church members have had before them a large and growing array of nondenominational parachurch organizations and Bible study movements that offer a new or different choice for membership allegiance.

One explanation for these denominational changes of the last fifteen years centers on the interrelationships of culture and religion, which has been explored by Charles Wilson, Clifford Geertz, Liston Pope, and others. In *Religion and Philosophy in the United States of America*, William Leonard suggests that the "tensions" that exist among the contending parties in the struggle for power in the SBC are "symptoms of a wider and more complex identity crisis in both the denomination and the culture" and that "questions of theology cannot be separated from [the] parallel issues of cultural and denominational instability."[11] From Leonard's viewpoint, Baptists and Southerners have seen themselves as synonymous and interlinked as a single culture, separate from American Baptists and other denominations. According to him, Southern Baptists have struggled to retain their cultural establishment against pluralism, the social gospel, and denominational diversity, all of which some fundamentalists view as deviations from true orthodox truth and practice.

In actuality, there is a close connection between Southern Baptists and Southern culture, since Southern Baptists have focused on the cultural preservation of the region since the denomination's founding in 1845. After the Civil War, they supported the restoration of states' rights, white supremacy, and the restitution of property rights. The objective of their advocacy was to help reestablish the cultural identity of Southern Baptists as a group, something that its members ardently desired. Accordingly, they continued to communicate their religious beliefs and values within a cultural system devoted to the maintenance of Southernness, while emphasizing their commitment to a pulpit advocacy that stressed personal conversion and individual morality. That dedication was noticeable before 1979 regardless of the pulpit advocacy method.

Consequently, rhetorical critics of Southern culture and religion view power, gender, sexuality, and ethical pulpit communication as controversies that impinge upon the denomination's determination to reclaim its historic cultural role in the South. The battles between Convention pulpit leadership and dissidents may be viewed as an attempt to purge the "isms" of feminism, pluralism, or any form of liberalism as unwelcome darksome forces from Southern culture. Similarly, pulpit leaders stress the renewal and restoration of persuasive pulpit preaching as a necessity in the individual church. Male rhetors whose communicative talents and pulpit delivery skills are effective seem to be most desirable to the hierarchy. It is central to focus on the powerful presence of the Southern Baptist pulpit, not only as a method of explaining present rhetorical phenomena, but also to understand the historical uniqueness of the denomination in the South. While the controversies above may be viewed as powerful forces in society, the Southern Baptist loyalist pulpit has other competitors. Today's parachurch and megachurch movements often use other enhancing and attractive forms of persuasion rather than that of the skilled pulpit sermonizer. The expanded use of music, drama, social dance, and interpretive reading threaten to displace the pulpit preacher.

Arguably, there have been, and continue to be, dissident Southern Baptist sermonizers such as Rev. W. W. Finlator, the retired minister of Pullen Memorial Baptist Church in Raleigh, North Carolina, whose pulpit discourses often center on the resolution of social problems. Rev. Kenneth Chafin is an outstanding pulpit artist, as are Rev. Russell Dilday and Rev. Nancy Hastings Sehested.

None of these persons, however, are denominational loyalists. Finlator and Sehested have always been too concerned with social ministries to others to be acceptable to the Nashville oligarchy. Chafin and Dilday are now in exile from the leadership because of their sense of rhetorical independence. It is doubtful that major Southern Baptist pulpit sermonizers of the first half of the twentieth century ever effectively linked the goals of personal conversion to social gospel action. But in the 1970s, until the takeover by the loyalists in 1979, the denomination vigorously pursued various social goals, perhaps in response to changes that were then occurring nationally. It would now appear, however, that the Convention hierarchy has successfully deflected or downgraded these goals in their struggle to reorient the denomination in a more conservative direction and to purge the denomination of disaffected members.

At present, the leadership's pulpit and convention rhetoric seems focused on cleansing both the denomination and the country from the alleged sins of liberalism and heresy. One of the major rhetors in this mission is Rev. W. A. Criswell, pastor emeritus of the First Baptist Church in Dallas, Texas—the largest church in the denomination. With discourse reminiscent of an Islamic jihad, Criswell pejoratively described Baptist dissenters in his 1988 San Antonio Convention Sermon. He told nearly twenty thousand assembled Messengers that

> [b]ecause of the curse of liberalism today, they call themselves moderates. [But a] skunk by any other name still stinks. To my great dismay, we have lost our nation to the liberals, humanists and atheists and infidels. America used to be known as a Christian nation, but now we are a secular nation. [The liberals, humanists and atheists and infidels] have taken the doctrine of the priesthood of the believer and made it cover every damnable heresy you can imagine.[12]

Watching and listening to Criswell deliver his famous "Skunk Sermon" at the San Antonio convention was an exciting experience. His ability to effectively characterize dissidents as analogous to skunks was original, humorous, and vocally compelling, and Criswell drew a loud response from the crowd. At the same convention, Adrian Rogers, president of the Convention from 1987 to 1988, also condemned denominational dissenters for allegedly infecting the membership with their liberalism. Sermons by the Reverends Jerry Vines, Bailey Smith, and Paige Patterson contain similar comments about Southern Baptist dissenters.

The Southern Baptist presidents such as Criswell and Rogers are word-picture artists, but their rhetoric is not pre–Civil War ornamentation. Rather, these artists prefer a spoken language designed to influence one's understanding and emotion. Criswell's rhetoric, for example, is not that of the antebellum South with its flowery encomium and exaggeration. His skunk narrative contained intent, morality, and power. In creating outgroups with his narrative, he also blames dissenters and discourages disagreement.

Consequently, all these labels matter, and some of them are fighting words, a point that Mark Coppenger has implicitly acknowledged. According to him, the words "liberal" and "fundamentalist" have been "demonized."[13] Coppenger's concerns are legitimate and his "demonizing" reference suggests more than merely that these words might be used indiscriminately by those in the pulpit. Rather, he identifies the words "liberal" and "fundamentalist" as negative in scope and hurtful in their application. His choice of words for illustration is clarifying, because loyalists have been called "fundamentalists," and dissidents "liberals," by their adversaries. Coppenger is clearly calling critical attention to the issue of labeling in this rhetorical dispute between dissidents and loyalists. Unfortunately, his colleagues—the SBC presidents—do not appear to be concerned, because their rhetoric appears to be focused on a different objective—that of reclaiming the South for the denomination.

The pulpit rhetoric of Criswell, Patterson, and Smith suggests that of a denominational recapture of the lost "Southern cause," and it conjures up the pursuit of a national commitment to a loyalist agenda. Viewed from their perspective, the concerns of breakaways are immaterial, for there is little place for them in the new denomination. Since 1979, disaffected Baptists have testified repeatedly to their exclusion from national offices of influence and to the changed character and mission of the Convention. In effect, they have been disenfranchised by the restrictive policies of their own pulpit leadership.

Dissenting Southern Baptists have been particularly galled by the hierarchy's treatment of women leaders. In 1984, the controversial Resolution 3 was passed, which asserted that because Eve initiated sin in the Garden of Eden, women should be forever subjugated to men. The resolution also opposed the ordination of women to the church pulpit. Furthermore, it was agreed that the Home Mission Board would no longer financially support a church that hires a woman as pulpit minister.

Then, in 1987, the denominational exclusion of women from the pulpit took a more personalized approach. When the Prescott Memorial Baptist Church of Memphis called Nancy Hastings Sehested as their lead church pastor, the Shelby County (Tennessee) Baptist Association formally ejected the church from its membership. Such an action was unprecedented. In Fort Worth, the trustees of Southwestern Baptist Theological Seminary denied a faculty appointment for a local pastor because women served as deacons in his church, while the Home Mission Board declined to hire an applicant because women deacons served in his church and because he had failed to hold Sunday night services. In 1994, Rev. Molly Marshall, professor of theology from Southern Baptist Theological Seminary, Louisville, Kentucky, was fired by President Al Moehler because her theological views were allegedly antithetical to those of the Southern Baptist Convention. Adhering to the mandates of Resolution 3, the Home Mission Board has withdrawn funds or refused to disburse funds to those SBC churches who have chosen females as church pulpit ministers. These actions appear to contravene that part of the denomination's national constitution that reads: "The [Southern Baptist] Convention does not claim and will never attempt to exercise authority over any other Baptist body, whether church, auxiliary organizations, associations or conventions."[14]

Alienated Southern Baptists have also been fired or forced to retire in various Southern Baptist schools or seminaries. At Missouri Baptist College in St. Louis, chemistry professor Leroy Madden chose early retirement rather than teach Genesis as a science. After the Nashville leadership appointed a majority of inerrantists to the Board of Trustees of Southeastern Baptist Theological Seminary in Wake Forest, North Carolina, they promptly announced their intent to install a faculty obedient to the doctrine of inerrancy. The president of the seminary, Randall W. Lolley, and the dean, Maurice Ashcraft, subsequently resigned, and various dissenting faculty members left their positions. In 1994, Russell Dilday, president of Southwestern Baptist Theological Seminary, was fired from his post by the seminary trustees for various positions thought unacceptable to the SBC's Executive Committee. In addition, Mercer University of Macon, Georgia, has been verbally attacked by various Convention loyalists as an institution of "debauchery and lewdness."[15]

We have already evaluated the Convention's Executive Committee decision making regarding two churches in North Carolina. The Pullen Memorial Baptist Church in Raleigh, which once was aligned with the SBC, voted to allow itself to be used as a site for a ceremony of union between two gay men, one of whom was a member. The minister, Rev. Mahan Siler, performed the union after he was authorized to do so by the church membership. This action was followed by a meeting of the top officials of the North Carolina Baptist State Convention, who recommended that relationships be severed with Pullen Memorial Baptist Church.[16] T. C. Pinckney, a member of the national Executive Committee, recommended that members from churches that "condone homosexuality" not be seated at the national meetings, and the request was approved. Eventually, Pullen was also ejected from the Raleigh Baptist Association.

The same punitive action by the national organization has been applied to Olin T. Binkley Memorial Baptist Church in Chapel Hill, because Binkley approved the licensure of a gay divinity student from Duke University. The Binkley church may be the first Southern Baptist congregation in the country to publicly ignore a member's sexual orientation in the ministry licensing procedure. Due to the actions of both North Carolina churches, the Executive Committee formally excluded them from sending Messengers to the national convention, thus expelling them from the denomination. According to local news reports, a member of the Pullen congregation viewed these actions as "the autonomy of the local church versus an organization of churches trying to dictate what individual churches practice."[17]

All of these punitive actions have prompted disagreeing Baptists to look at the example of Roger Williams, the one-time Baptist dissenter of early New England who was banished from Massachusetts rather than accept a "superintendency" of churches. According to Williams, a "presbytery" of churches would ultimately "prejudice" an individual "church's liberties" because of its disposition to impose rules of membership. His prophecy from the seventeenth century has a timely ring in light of the denominational exclusions today.

Current SBC developments also focus on the pulpit leadership's political alliances with the far right. In 1979, new denominational leaders believed that the Convention and its leadership had moved in a leftward theological and political course. To move the denomination away from these alleged misdirections, two major actions were initiated. First, denominational leaders attempted to redirect the membership to a more certain theological and doctrinal unity by publicly announcing their adherence to biblical inerrancy, urging fellow believers to accept that doctrine and appointing only inerrantists as members to SBC boards, commissions, and agencies. Paige Patterson—once president of the W. A. Criswell Center for Biblical Studies in Dallas, Texas, and now president of Southeastern Baptist Theological Seminary in Wake Forest, North Carolina—is a leading inerrancy advocate, a protégé of Criswell, and one of the driving theological forces behind the loyalists. Patterson and Criswell have prominently used the electronic and print media to communicate with their supporters.

Second, these leaders and their nonclerical counterparts—including Paul Weyrich, Ed McAteer, and appellate courts judge Paul Pressler—have publicly endorsed various conservative political candidates and causes. In fact, Pressler is reportedly the architect of the denomination's movement to the political right, for it is certain that in 1979, he and Criswell engineered the takeover of the denomination. Additionally, some Southern Baptist leaders have reportedly helped formulate, direct, or participate in such conservative groups as the Moral Majority, the Religious Roundtable, the John Birch Society, and the Heritage Foundation.

How these religious and political leaders have jointly or separately worked to accomplish their goals is intriguing. In May 1979, Harold Lindsell, a one-time editor of the conservative religious periodical *Christianity Today* and then president of the Baptist Faith and Message Fellowship group, was interviewed by the editor of the *Memphis Commercial Appeal*. Lindsell favored a new, more conservative Convention, with the doctrine of inerrancy as its theological centerpiece. With the assistance of Lindsell; Paul Pressler; and the pulpit advocacy of Criswell, Patterson, and their confederates, the takeover was successful.

That same year, the Moral Majority organization was founded with similar theological agendas, and a group named Christians for Reagan was formed by Weyrich, McAteer, Howard Phillips, and Robert Billings. In August 1980, at the invitation of these leaders and of the prominent televangelists Jerry Falwell and Pat Robertson, fifteen thousand followers converged on W. A. Criswell's First Baptist Church in Dallas for a conference at which Ronald Reagan was the only presidential candidate to attend. From Criswell's pulpit, Weyrich told his audience that it was necessary that the denomination become politically active in the coming years. Only weeks after the Dallas conference, Billings was reassigned to the Reagan campaign as its official liaison to religious organizations. By the end of 1980, these individuals and organizations had secured their principal objectives—the White House and a national religious denomination. According to critics Flo Conway and Jim Siegelman,

> [This] cluster of ultraconservative forces is a diversified agglomeration of negativity. Atop traditional old right pilings of anti-communism, anti-socialism and anti-labor—which it tends to equate indiscriminately—it has built a platform of reaction to the social developments of the sixties and seventies: anti-busing, anti-welfare, anti-gun control, anti-abortion, anti-feminism, anti-gay rights and anti-sex education.[18]

Disenfranchised Baptists have not entered into these political alliances, perhaps fearing an entanglement of religion with politics, something that Roger Williams forewarned his followers to avoid. Present-day Baptist dissenters contend that the principal conflict is not only theological, but that it concerns lust for denominational control. To them, the controversy centers on the inappropriate utilization of power, that is, the disbursements of money from the Nashville headquarters to promote allegedly non-Baptistic priorities, personnel appointments of inerrantists to organizations, and the promotion of inappropriate political agendas contrary to historic Baptist practices of nonintervention with church-state relationships. Alienated Baptists also contend that a pluralistic denominational unity is more valuable than obedience to ideologies or creedalistic dogmatism. They regard the rightward political direction of the leadership as a reversal of the denomination's usual practice of nonaffiliation with any political party, dogma, or candidate for office.

It is hazardous to draw certain conclusions about this denominational conflict because of its rapidly changing nature, but the pulpit hierarchy is dedicated to the purgation of "theological and doctrinal pollution" from the Convention's membership, schools, and seminaries. Undoubtedly, this "purification" will allow these leaders to view the reclaimed denomination as more pure and less tainted. The power of the inerrantist autocracy to make appointments solely from the body of their own followers is a key element to the success of this strategy, and only inerrantists loyal to the Criswell-Patterson faction appear to receive consideration.

The pulpit leadership's messages of fundamentalism, exclusivity, and inerrancy are threateningly clear to dissidents. Dissenters have mounted a counterattack in defense of the diversity of individual freedom by joining the Baptist Alliance and the Cooperative Baptist Fellowship.[19] Others have joined the Baptist Peace Fellowship. None of these groups contend that they are separate Baptist denominations, but those loyal to the Nashville leaders would argue differently.[20]

Resistance by dissenters to the denomination's actions have also been evident in the resolutions, petitions, and decisions of various state Baptist conventions across the SBC. State Southern Baptist organizations have responded in various ways to the exclusionary actions of the Nashville oligarchy. Virginia, Hawaii, and the District of Columbia have elected women as presidents. Some Baptist state Conventions have decided not to increase the percentage of funds given to national Convention offices, decreased their giving, or directed their funds to other organizations such as those listed above. These actions appear to have been the result of their unhappiness with various denominational decisions.

This kind of dissatisfaction could be seen when Dr. Curtis W. Caine, a member of the denomination's Christian Life Commission (CLC), endorsed the practice of apartheid in South Africa in a commission meeting and labeled the eminent Dr. Martin Luther King Jr. a fraud, and the CLC did not disavow his remarks. The reaction to Caine's position from several state Baptist conventions was quite negative. Protest resolutions were forwarded to the Southern Baptist Sunday School Board from Tennessee, New York, Maryland, and Delaware, and Mississippi Baptists repudiated Caine's remarks. In another example of negative responses to SBC policies, North Carolina and Virginia moderates have organized a new seminary in Richmond (and very recently, at Wake Forest University in Winston-Salem, North Carolina) rather than to continue their support of Southeastern Baptist Theological Seminary, which is now controlled by SBC loyalists.

Ultimately, however, the denomination's message of exclusivity, and the rhetorical strategies of those who employ it, raise the issue of how the denomination will be identified in the South and in the nation. In the seventeenth century, Thomas Helwys, John Smyth, John Murton, and Roger Williams, as dissenters from the conformist, authoritarian tradition of England and colonial America, propelled Baptists into existence. They publicly and privately argued for freedom from ecclesiastical control, the tyranny of the Bishops, and the authority of the brethren. Their nonconformity was focused on the separation of church and state and the disallowance of earthly priests as interveners between the believer and God. Baptists were known as nonconformists who spoke for personal freedoms, regardless of personal consequences. Early Baptists were also vitally concerned about personal evangelism and bringing others to believe in Christianity.

The formulation of the SBC Cooperative Program in 1925 carried the denomination and its foreign and domestic missionary objectives forward onto the stage of world community. The goal was the personal conversion of the "lost" the world over, and money and missionaries were designated through the years to carry out this purpose. If the denomination's leaders, members, and missionaries were excessively zealous, and their rhetoric did not fully appreciate changing cultures, at least they had a *global* perspective of service to others and Christianity as they understood it. Their vision was clear, even if it was Southern in origin. Indeed, most cooperating Southern Baptist churches who are hesitant or have refused to leave the Convention will likely cite their commitment to the missionary program as a principal reason for their nondeparture.

Since 1979, however, the SBC pulpit hierarchy has steadily moved towards a less congregational, more authoritarian system of church relationships; they have aligned themselves with a number of far-right political causes and candidates; they have diminished past allegiances to historic Baptist positions on the priesthood of the believer and the separation of church and state; and they have set out on a crusade to conquer the evil of liberalism in order to lead the nation back to purity and simplicity. How the denomination will be identified in the next century is uncertain. Even more difficult to determine is how history will judge those individual Baptists who were afraid to make a decision regarding this conflict, preferring instead to quietly hear the urging of their conscience to leave but refuse to act.

The new Southern Baptist Convention is governed exclusively by males, and as the 1998 Salt Lake annual meeting proved, it is determined to stay that way. It has publicly endorsed the notion that women shall forever submit to their husbands and been roundly satirized for the idea in newspaper cartoons and talk shows. If Southern Baptist social practices reflect a bygone era, that seems undaunting to its presidents. Noticeably, these skilled sermonizers embrace the South of yesterday, replete with its myths of gender submissiveness and repressive fictions about sexuality. Thus, the SBC is steadfast about its adherence to antebellum Southernness, perhaps hoping that the denominational pulpit can somehow be used to return the nation to a clearer time in history.

Yet, as it marches resolutely backwards to an authoritarian future, the SBC is more than ready to meet the next century. It is united in its theology, secure in its finances, and electronically sophisticated enough to spread its version of the gospel anywhere in the world. SBC churches are expanding with new members. Above all, this denomination has a powerful and skilled group of pulpit persuaders. They are trained to adapt to their audiences, to reveal a thorough familiarity with the Holy Bible, and to interpret doctrine approved by the denominational presidents. The SBC will likely be a dominant force in American Protestantism in the next century. If you think differently, you underestimate the power and communication artistry of the new Southern Baptist Convention.

Appendixes

Notes

A Bibliographical Essay

Index

Appendix 1. A Baptist and His Bible, II Timothy 3:14–4:13

In beautiful human language resplendent with divine revelation Paul sets before us the Bible's doctrine concerning itself. He quickly takes us to the Counseling Room and shows us the intention of the Bible; the Classroom and shows us the inspiration of the Bible; then the Crisis Room and shows us the implications of the Bible.

I am interested that Paul refers to the Bible as "the Holy Scriptures." The word combination is unusual, found only here in the New Testament: ta hiera grammata. Paul normally uses the word graphe (Scriptures) as in verse 16 or ho logos, the word as in 4:2. But here he uses grammata which sometimes refers to the letters of the words themselves or to the document. The word for holy is also unusual. Not the normal hagios but hiera. This word is found only one other time. In I Corinthians 9:13 reference is made to the "sacred things of the temple." The sacred things were the utensils set apart for God in temple services. The word means sacred or pertaining to God. Only of the Bible can it be said that it is the Sacred Scriptures. The Bible is the only book set apart for God's special uses. This term attaches great reverence to the Bible.

"The Holy Scripture." Paul sounds like a Baptist! A Presbyterian, a Pentecostal and a Baptist preacher were discussing what denomination Paul would join should he return to earth. The Presbyterian said, "I am sure he would join the Presbyterians. He would love our scholarship." The Pentecostal said, "Oh, no, he would be a Pentecostal, praise God! Read his doxologies." The Baptist preacher was silent. The others asked,

---

"A Baptist and His Bible" was the Convention Sermon given at the 1987 SBC annual convention by Dr. Jerry Vines, pastor of the First Baptist Church in Jacksonville, Florida. Reproduced courtesy of Dr. Jerry Vines.

Vines received his education at Mercer University, Macon, Georgia; New Orleans Baptist Seminary, New Orleans, Louisiana; and Luthur Rice Seminary, Jacksonville, Florida. He pastored in Georgia and Alabama before becoming copastor of First Baptist Church, Jacksonville, Florida, in 1981. His books include *I Shall Return . . . Jesus*, 1977; *God Speaks Today*, 1979; *Great Events in the Life of Christ*, 1979; *Interviews with Jesus*, 1981; *A Practical Guide to Sermon Preparation*, 1985; *An Effective Guide to Sermon Delivery*, 1986; *Wanted: Soul Winners*, 1989; *Wanted: Church Growers*, 1990; *Fire in the Pulpit*; and *Acts Alive* (Sunday School Lessons).

"What do you think?" The Baptist preacher replied, "Oh, I don't think he would change!"

"The Holy Scriptures." That is Baptist talk. Wherever you find a Baptist, somewhere nearby you will find a Bible. That Baptist will speak of the Bible in his hands with respectful tones. Baptists are early taught to love and respect the Bible. On a hot summer day, at Vacation Bible School, little Baptist feet carry little Baptist bodies into the awesome church auditorium. Billy Baptist stands before his little classmates and with trembling hands holds a Bible. Little Baptist voices sing, "holy Bible, Book divine, precious treasure, thou art mine." Baptists are known as a people of The Book. We are a Bible-readying, Bible-believing, Bible-loving and Bible-sharing people.

With Paul's words to young Timothy to guide us, think with me for a while about a Baptist and his Bible. First, he takes us into the Counseling Room and shows us:

I. The Intention of The Bible, vs. 14–15

But continue thou in the things which thou hast learned . . . That's continuation. The Bible is intended to help us live consistent Christian lives, moving to maturity. . . . the things which thou hast learned and hast been assured of . . . That's conviction. The Bible is intended to place our lives on a firm, assured foundation. And that from a child thou hast known the Holy Scriptures, which are able to make thee wise unto salvation . . . That's conversion. The Bible is primarily intended to bring people to salvation.

That's what the Bible did for young Timothy. When I was a boy most Baptist churches had a TEL Class named for Timothy, Eunice and Lois. His was a heritage of faith. Each day his godly mother, Eunice, and his godly grandmother, Lois, would take the sacred Scriptures and prepare the day's Bible lesson for Timothy. "What Bible lesson shall we teach tiny Tim today?" They were preparing his little heart. Then on a day Paul preached at First Baptist Church, Lystra. At the invitation time down the aisle came Timothy. He gave his hand to Paul and his heart to Jesus. What a testimony was his—from his mother's knee to his Master's knee! I can imagine a deacon went home that day and someone asked, "Did anything happen at church today?" "Not much. We had a long-winded preacher. Oh, yes, Eunice's boy, Timothy, joined the church. Not much." Not much? Paul's traveling companion was converted. Not much? The recipient of two Bible letters was born again. Not much? The angels in heaven were rejoicing because another sinner was converted.

That's what the Bible is intended to do—to make wise unto salvation. To know the Bible is not synonymous with salvation, but it does point us to the One who can save us. This is why Psalm 19:7 says, The law of the Lord is perfect, converting the soul. And John 20:31 says, But these are written, that ye might believe that Jesus is the Christ, the Son of God; and that believing ye might have life through his name. The vehicle of the Written Word brings us to the Living Word and thus to salvation.

Wise unto salvation. How smart do I have to be to be saved? First, I have to know I am a great sinner. The Bible confirms what experience screams in my soul. All have sinned and come short of the glory of God. (Romans 3:23) Mary Baker Eddy claimed that her book, Science, Health and the Scriptures, could cure appendicitis. I don't know about that, but this book can cure "devilities!"

Second, I have to know that God has provided a great Savior. The Bible points to Jesus. He is the central theme of the Bible. Acts 10:43 says, To Him give all the prophets witness . . . The Old Testament predicts Him; the New Testament presents Him. The Old Testament anticipates Him; the New Testament announces Him. If you want to know about the stars, read a book on astronomy. If you want to know about the Bright and Morning Star, read the Bible. If you want to know about the ages of the rocks, read geology; if you want to know about the Rock of Ages, read the Bible. If you want to know about the roses and the lilies of the fields, read botany; if you want to know about the Rose of Sharon and the Lily of the Valley, read the Bible.

I find my Lord in the Bible,
Wherever I choose to look.
He is the theme of the Bible,
The center and heart of The Book.
He is the Rose of Sharon
He is the Lily fair.
Wherever I open my Bible,
The Lord of the Book is there.

This is why Acts 4:12 says, Neither is there salvation in any other; for there is none other name under heaven given among men, whereby we must be saved.

What other book can change lives? Did you ever hear a man say, "I was a thief. One day I read a math book and it really straightened me out." Or, "I was impure, I read in a geometry book, and it surely cleaned me up." Or, "I was a liar. I read a book on anatomy and I have been telling the truth ever since." Or, "I was a drunk. I read a chemistry book and it sobered me up." But I can take you places where I have preached this Book and show you drunkards made sober, liars made truthful and adulterers made pure. James 1:21 says, Receive with meekness the engrafted word, which is able to save your souls. There is no debate here. We all understand what the Bible is intended to do.

Because we understand the Bible's intention, Baptists get concerned when there is any hint of attack upon it. We get upset when there is any undermining of its authority, questioning of its reliability or denying of its accuracy. This Book has to do with man's eternal destiny. To attack the Bible is like tampering with medicine for a sick man; like poisoning the bread of a hungry man.

The noted preacher, Henry Ward Beecher, was invited to be the guest of an Atheist Club presided over by Robert Ingersoll, the noted infidel. He went and listened to a brilliant speech by Ingersoll, who attacked Christianity unmercifully. Ingersoll sat down amidst thunderous applause. He turned to Beecher and invited him to say a few words in defense of the Bible. Beecher rose slowly to his feet: "Gentlemen, forgive me if I seem a bit shaken. I saw something shocking on the way to the meeting. I saw a poor, blind man with a cane, groping at the curbside. A young lad came along, offering to help him across the street. As he took the blind man's arm a hulk of a man came along, bullied the boy, broke the bland man's cane, pushed the blind man in the mud and went on his way laughing." A silence fell over the meeting. Then Ingersoll leaped to his feet, eyes blazing: "The bully," he roared, "Do you know who he is, Beecher?" "Yes, I know who he is. It is you! Mankind is poor, blind, and wretched. He has little enough to lean on as it is and few to help him on his way. What do you do, Ingersoll? You come along, break his faith in the Bible, push him in the mud and go on your way laughing. I tell you, Ingersoll, you are the man!"

How can anyone say we must trust our soul to Christ for eternity, then turn around and try to obliterate the very document which tells us about him? We honor the book and earnestly contend for it because we know what it is intended to do.

Next, Paul takes us to the Classroom and shows us:

II. The Inspiration of the Bible, vs. 16–17

For a while we are going to step into the Classroom. I am so thankful to God for the men who taught me during my seminary days. I am grateful for Dr. Gray Allison who instilled in my heart a burning desire to win the lost to Christ. I will never forget the day Dr. George Harrison showed me the beauty of Christ in the tabernacle. I left his classroom with glory in my soul. I shall never forget the week Dr. J. Wash spent meticulously dismantling the documentary hypothesis. At the conclusion of the week, this godly professor, with tears in his eyes, raised his Bible above his head and said, "Young men, the documentary hypothesis makes your Bible nothing more than a scrapbook!" I wish every young man called to preach could sit in classrooms with teachers such as these.

I return to the classroom again. Not as a scholar, but as a student. Not as a teacher, but as a learner. I am trying to understand the inspiration of my Bible. What I am after is what someone has called a "simple biblicism."

With breathtaking brevity of language, Paul says, All Scripture is given by inspiration of God. Actually he uses only three words in the original text: pasa, graphe, theopneustos. The last of these words, theopneustos, is translated by five words in the King James, given by inspiration of God. This is actually one compound Greek word, coming from theos, God and pneo, to breathe. The word seems to have been coined by the Holy Spirit to give us a glimpse into the mystery of inspiration. The word is a verbal adjective used in a passive sense. The emphasis is that God alone is the agent in the Bible's inspiration. The Bible is the produce of the creative breath of God. "God-breathed." That's the best way to translate it. Not man-breathed; God-breathed.

A. God-breathed. This means supernatural inspiration.

"All Scripture is God-breathed." The Bible owes its origin and contents to the divine breath of God. In creation God picked up the lifeless clay that was Adam, breathed into his nostrils the breath of life, and man became a living soul. (Genesis 2:7) In inspiration, God picked up the lifeless pages of man's composition and the Bible became a living book. Hebrews 4:12 (RSV) says, For the Word of God is living. . . . This book pulsates with life. It breathes, bleeds, sings and weeps. Charles H. Spurgeon said, "If you cut this book into a thousand pieces, every part would grow and live." Just as a little child puts a seashell to its ear and can hear the blowing of the waves in the sea, so we with childlike faith hear the breath of God blowing through the pages of the Bible.

Supernatural inspiration doesn't eliminate the human element in the Bible. The personalities of the human authors are everywhere apparent. We see the burning sarcasm of Isaiah. We witness the moving pathos of Jeremiah, the deep philosophy of John and the crisp logic of Paul. Amos writes like a farmer, Simon Peter like a fisherman. Luke writes like a doctor, James like a preacher. Each writer was sovereignly prepared by the Holy Spirit to be the ideal penman for that portion of Scripture. Does God want a selection of Psalms like David's? He prepares a David to write them! Does He want a series of letters like Paul's? He prepares a Paul to write them!

Human authorship must never be separated from the divine inspiration of the Bible. The human aspect is only one aspect under the category of its divine character. Actually there is a dual authorship in the Bible. II Peter 1:21 says, . . . Holy men of God spake. . . . Yes, but, as they were moved (borned along) by the Holy Spirit. Like a vessel gently carried along by the wind, so the Holy Spirit was the guiding, moving force in the Bible's composition. Acts 1:16 makes this dual authorship very plain:

This Scripture must needs have been fulfilled which the Holy Spirit by the Mouth of David spake. The Holy Spirit is speaking in Scripture. He speaks by the mouth of David.

The tendency today in much scholarship is to so emphasize the human authorship of the Bible that the divine is minimized. We are told that since the Bible is touched by fallible, error-prone men, it must be fallible and prone to err. The logic doesn't follow. If God can overcome man's tendency to err at one point, why not at every point. The divine human nature of the Bible is analogous to the divine human nature of Christ. Christ was fully God and fully man, yet, without sin. He was touched by our humanity, but not tainted by our depravity. The Bible was given by men superintended by the Holy Spirit so that what they wrote was without error. "God-breathed." A God of truth does not breath error.

Others tell us that the Bible is accurate on salvation matters but not on matters of science or history. Obviously, the Bible is not a science book. But, when it touches on science, it does so truthfully. Neither is the Bible a history book. But, its historical statements are reliable. If you can't believe what the Bible says about the creation, how can you believe what it says about salvation? If you can't trust it concerning history, how can you trust it concerning eternity? We would do well to ponder the words of Jesus: If I have told you earthly things, and you believe not, how shall ye believe, if I tell you of heavenly things? (John 3:12) Take, for example, a physics book. A physics book is not a math book. However, there are mathematical statements in it. If I constantly find mathematical errors in the physics text, how can I trust its statements concerning physics?

Further, how do we separate salvation matters from other matters? Take the virgin birth. If the virgin birth is not historical and biological fact, then it is theological fiction. Or consider the resurrection of Christ. If there was not a time when and a place where the resurrection occurred, what kind of resurrection was it. Salvation matters are so embedded in historical matters that you cannot consistently attribute inspiration to the one and deny it to the other. Every line, every sentence, every word and every letter was placed in our Bible by the supernatural inspiration of God.

B. God-breathed. This means verbal inspiration.

"All Scripture is God-breathed." The word is graphe, meaning from grapho, to write. The obvious reference is to the words. The words of the Bible are God-breathed. Some tell us that the words are not necessarily inspired, but only the thoughts. I am no scholar, but no one has ever explained to me how it is possible to have thoughts without words. Try it sometime. Think a thought without words. What kind of thought did you think? Were no words involved?

Words are vehicles of thought. I heard about two Indians talking. The first one said, "Ugh." The second replied, "Ugh." The first one said,

"Ugh." The second one replied, "Ugh, ugh." The first one said, "Don't change the subject!"

Remove the words from the page and the thoughts disappear. There can be no music without notes; no math without numbers; no geology without rocks; no thoughts without words. I Corinthians 2:13 sets forth the verbal inspiration of the Bible: Which things we also speak, not in the words which man's wisdom teaches, but which (words) the Holy Spirit teaches. Where do you find words the Holy Spirit teaches? In the Bible.

Did Jesus teach verbal inspiration? You decide. Man shall not live by bread alone, but by every word that proceeds out of the mouth of God. (Matthew 4:4) Not some of the words, nor part of the words, but every word. Heaven and earth shall pass away, but my words shall not pass away. (Matthew 24:35)

Jesus goes further than that. Matthew 5:18 is the strongest statement about inspiration ever made. He begins by saying, "verily." This is a strong word of affirmation. Then he says that not "one jot" will pass from the law. A jot is the smallest letter in the Hebrew alphabet. It is merely a breath mark, the stroke of a pen. Nor "one tittle" shall pass away. A tittle is a little horn on a Hebrew letter. It is only about 1/32nd of an inch. Don't forget your tittle! You can change a Hebrew letter by its omission. When I was taking Hebrew I tried to keep flies off my test paper. I might mistake a fly's leg for a tittle and flunk the test! Jesus also said, In no wise shall pass from the law. Actually a double negative is used here for emphasis. You could read the statement this way: "under no circumstances never." Now, let's put it all together. Jesus said, Until heaven and earth pass away the smallest letter of the Hebrew alphabet and the smallest part of a letter shall under no circumstance never pass from the law till all be fulfilled. Such is our Lord's view of inspiration.

We love the words of the Bible: salvation, justification, sanctification; faith, love, hope. "Sing them over again to me, wonderful words of life. Let me more of their beauty see, wonderful words of life."

C. God-breathed. This means total inspiration.

"All Scripture is God-breathed." pasa. Dr. Herschel Hobbs has given the best explanation of the meaning of the word pasa I have read. He says, "It means that every single part of the whole is God-breathed." That's where I stand. That's where Southern Baptists have always stood. Jed and his wife were riding the pick-up to town on a Saturday morning. His wife turned to him and said, "Jed, when we first married, we didn't sit this far apart." Jed looked up and said, "I ain't moved." I'm standing where Southern Baptists have always stood. When Southern Baptists stand where they should be standing they'll be standing where I'm standing! We affirm total inspiration.

At the turn of the century an old thief quietly entered the country. He had already robbed Germany of spiritual authority and moral conscience. He first appeared in the Garden of Eden, calling into question the authorship, accuracy, and acceptability of God's Word. This old thief began entering and robing in the north, leaving a trail of stripped denominations, faith-depleted schools and powerless churches.

He moved steadily down the eastern coast. A very crafty thief, he appealed to man's intellectual pride. His goal? To snatch the Bible from the man in the pew. He travels under many aliases. I want to unmask him. The name of the old thief is Destructive Criticism. Not reverent, believing scholarship, but destructive, faith-wrecking criticism. That criticism which clips faith's wings with reason's scissors. That kind of destructive scholarship which submits the warm wonder of the Word to the cold, merciless analysis of unbelief.

This old thief is a demolition expert. He has many tools in his tool chest. None are constructive; all are destructive. He has a heretical hammer, driving into the Bible the nails of anti-supernaturalism and the anti-miraculous. He explains away every account of miracle as natural phenomena or primitive folklore. He has a critical saw, dividing Scripture and the Word of God. He puts asunder what God has joined together. According to the old thief some of the Bible is, some isn't, the Word of God. The Bible is only inspired in spots. Only those who use his tools can tell you which spots are the inspired spots! He also has a cynical crowbar, ripping the Bible from the hands and hearts of simple believers.

But, old thief, your tools are fatally flawed. Your heretical hammer won't do. To reject the miraculous and supernatural in the Bible is to deny the Bible its own nature. You can't kick God out of His Book anymore than you can kick Him out of His universe. I believe in the miracles of the Bible. I really believe Jonah was swallowed by a great fish. How the fish stood him, I don't know, but I believe it. I do believe Daniel survived a night in the lion's den. He had a lion's mane for a pillow and used its tail to swish away mosquitoes. Early the next morning the frantic king called, "Daniel, are you there?" "Yes, what's for breakfast?"

I don't have all the answers to all the difficulties in the Bible. I can't place my peanut brain alongside God's infinite mind and not expect to have some problems. But, my list of difficulties has been progressively getting smaller. When I run across a difficulty in the Bible, I do not suppose the error is in the text, but rather in my understanding. "Where did Cain get his wife?" I don't know and I don't care. If she suited Cain, she suits me. I don't understand all the Bible, but I believe it all. I believe it all from Genesis to Maps!

Old thief, your cynical saw is dull. You can't separate the Word of God from Scripture. Note that Paul uses Scriptures (2:15), Scripture (3:16), and the Word (4:22) interchangeably in this passage. When Scripture speaks—God speaks. Jesus said, Thy word is truth. (John 17:17) Not contains truth, but is truth. When you try to separate the Word of God from Scripture, there is no stopping place. The Bible cannot be put on trial every few days while theologians hold symposiums to pool their ignorance.

When you force the Bible to pay tribute at every little "toll gate" of rational opinion, eventually you give away every part of the Bible. You begin by giving up the Genesis account of creation; next you dissect the historical parts of the Bible; then the miracles have to go; before it is over you are picking and choosing from the very words of Jesus. Perhaps you have heard about the Jesus seminar. This group of scholars is planning to put out a color-coded New Testament. The intention is to show us which of the words in the New Testament were actually the words of Jesus and which were put in His mouth by the church. Have you heard about the garbage barge in the Atlantic? I would suggest this color-coded New Testament be put on the garbage barge so all who purchase it will recognize it for the garbage it is. When you start trying to separate the Word from Scripture you wind up with a fictitious creation, three Isaiahs, exaggerated miracles and a speechless Jesus. Before it is over you have a Bible full of holes instead of a whole Bible!

Old thief, your critical crowbar won't do. This is the most serious flaw of all. Only the so-called critical scholars are supposed to be qualified to explain what the Bible means. At the Inerrancy Conference in Ridgecrest in May, 1987, Clark Pinnock was quoted as saying to reporters, "Adrian Rogers does not really know the Bible and Roy Honeycutt does. How do you deal with people who don't know the Bible?" (Florida Baptist Witness, June, 1987) Let me say, first of all, I do not believe Roy Honeycutt would ever say that. He is too much a gentleman. Further, I don't think Dr. Honeycutt would believe that. Poor Adrian Rogers. He doesn't have to be a Bible ignoramus all his life. Why doesn't he subscribe to my "tape of the month" plan! Look carefully at what is suggested in Pinnock's statement: The preacher doesn't know the Bible; the professor does. The two are pitted against each other. Do you know what that sounds like to me? The priesthood of the scholar. Baptists affirm the priesthood of the believer. We do not believe our preachers and professors should be pitted against each other, but be in partnership with one another, helping us find out what God has said in the Bible. That's the Baptist way and I like it!

We believe the Bible was given for common men. The Holy Spirit can take an unlettered man and give him amazing insight into the Bible. One of the greatest Bible students I ever knew was a man named Ed Shellhorse. Ed never owned a car until he retired. He worked all his life in a fabric mill. He read the Bible many hours each night after work. His insight into the Scriptures was amazing. The same Holy Spirit who inspired common men to write the Bible can illuminate common men to understand it.

I must make a choice. On one side is the old thief, destructive criticism.

On the other side is the infallible Son of the Living God. What about the stated authors of Bible books? For instance, Moses and the Pentateuch? The old thief says, Moses could not possibly have written it, because writing was unknown in that day. The Lord Jesus says, For had ye believed Moses, ye would have believed me: for he wrote of me. But if ye believe not his writings how shall ye believe my words? (John 5:46–47)

Were Adam and Eve really persons? The old thief says they were merely representative and never existed in fact. The Lord Jesus says, Have ye not read, that He which made them at the beginning made them male and female. (Matthew 19:4)

Did the miracles of the Bible actually occur? For instance, the ark and the flood? The old thief says this was merely a local legend which found its way into the Bible. The Lord Jesus says, They were given in marriage, until the day that Noah entered into the ark, and the flood came and destroyed them all. (Luke 17:27)

Is the Bible totally inspired? The old thief says only the salvation parts. The Lord Jesus says, O fools, and slow of heart to believe all that the prophets have spoken: (I didn't say it, Jesus did. If you don't believe all the prophets said, you have a head and a heart problem) and beginning at Moses and all the prophets, he expounded unto them in all the Scripture the things concerning Himself. Jesus affirms every major section of the Old Testament. He quotes from the first chapter of Genesis and the last chapter of Malachi. Virtually everything the old thief denies Jesus affirms. When you read the words of Jesus, it's as if He anticipated every modern attack against the Bible. At no time did he ever raise the slightest suspicion concerning the Scriptures.

The matter of the total inspiration of the Bible must be decided on the basis of lordship, not scholarship. I do not mean by this that it is unscholarly to believe in total inspiration.

Robert Dick Wilson was professor of semitic languages at Princeton Theological Seminary. He was considered the greatest biblical linguist of modern times. To answer the destructive critics he learned all the cognate languages of the Bible, and all the languages in which the critics had written. He learned Hebrew, Greek, Aramaic, French, German, Latin, Egyptian, Coptic, Syrian. He made himself at home in 45 languages and dialects. To answer a single sentence of a noted critic, he read all the extant ancient literature of the period under discussion in numerous languages. He collated no less than 100,000 citations. From the material he got at the basic facts, which when known, proved the critic was wrong! Critics then and now can't handle him. This is what he said: "After forty-five years of scholarly research and biblical textual studies and language study, I have come to the conclusion that no man knows enough to assail the truthfulness of the Old Testament." (Knights Illustrations for Today, page 22)

Yet, I repeat, ultimately the question of total inspiration must be decided on the basis of lordship, not scholarship. The decision must be one of the heart, not of the head.

I don't know about you, but I have heard enough from the old thief. I feel like the dear old grandmother who couldn't hear well. Her grandchildren insisted she go to the doctor. The doctor said, "I can solve your problem. All you need is a minor operation. I'm seventy-nine years old and I've heard enough!" I will study my Bible with more reverent, faith-building methods. I will study it textually, historically, grammatically, contextually, theologically and practically. I will study it on the basis of a "simple biblicism" which never calls into question the supernatural, verbal, or total inspiration of the Bible. Let the critics pick over the bones of the Bible. Bible-believing Baptists will continue to feast on the meat of the Word.

Finally, Paul takes us to the Crisis Room and shows us:

III. The Implications of the Bible, vs. 4:1–13

What one believes about the Bible's intention and inspiration has certain implications. From these verses in chapter four let me mention just a few of these implications. The Bible has:

A. Expositional Implications.

"Preach the Word," says Paul. Preach it faithfully, as a herald declares the message of his king; preach it incessantly, in season and out of season; preach it effectively, reprove, rebuke, exhort; preach it persistently, even though men might not endure sound doctrine.

Preaching is central in the worship of Baptist churches. Go into the average Baptist church on Sunday and you will find a pulpit in the middle. Chances are you will find a Baptist preacher standing with a Bible in his hand, preaching from the top of his head, the bottom of his heart and probably to the top of his lungs! I really believe there is no preaching like Southern Baptist preaching. The best preachers in America are in the pulpits of our Southern Baptist churches. Did you hear about the Southern Baptist preacher having coffee with his wife on a Monday morning? He was feeling good about his sermons the previous day. He leaned back and with a sigh said, "You know, there are only a few great preachers left." "Yes," his wife replied, "And there is one less than you think there is."

What the preacher believes about the Bible is crucial to the task of exposition. A low view of inspiration erodes the very foundation of preaching. Decide the Bible is not totally the Word of God and there will be no responsibility to study its text minutely and to preach its message authoritatively. Our most famous Southern Baptist evangelist, Billy Graham, punctuates his sermons with the now well-know phrase, "the Bible says." Obviously, the source of his authority and power is "thus saith the Lord."

I was interested to read again the account of the building of Solomon's temple. The whole thing went up without a fuss. Wouldn't you like to see Baptist churches build something without a fuss? The stones, hewed under ground, fit exactly. When the temple was dedicated hundreds of animals were sacrificed. A great white-robed choir and a magnificent orchestra performed. When it was all done they took the old Ark of the Covenant and put it in the Holy of Holies of the new temple. They stayed with the old ark. We don't need a new Bible. My preacher brother, preach the old Book, it will do the job. I think of so many dear people who go to church hungry and are given only bones to gnaw. People want to hear again the old, old truths from the old, old Book.

Though its cover is worn,
And its pages are torn,
And though places bear traces of tears.
Yet, more precious than gold,
Is this Book worn and old
That can shatter and scatter our fears.

Preacher man, I'm going to hit you with a hard lick. A sweet Quaker brother found a burglar in his home. There the burglar stood, arms full of stuff, ready to run. The Quaker cocked both triggers of his double-barreled gun and said, "I would not hurt thee for anything, but I'm about to shoot where thou standest!" I'm getting ready to shoot where you stand. If you don't believe the Bible, don't take a salary for preaching it. If you don't believe the Bible, do the world a favor and get a milk route. You will do more good. Our people come in on Sunday from a world of cynicism and doubt and unbelief. They have enough question marks in their lives; what they need are some exclamation points!

My days in college were great days. However, I had to make a decision about some of the things I was hearing concerning the Bible. I knew I would never be as scholarly or smart as those professors who were questioning the authority of the Bible. Thirty-one years ago now, as an eighteen year old boy, I decided to accept the Bible by faith and try to preach it. For me, the proof of the pudding is in the eating. I know the Bible is the Word of God.

I know the Bible was sent from God,
The old as well as the new.
Divinely inspired the whole way through,
I know the Bible is true.

The Bible has:

B. Evangelical Implications vs. 4:5

Paul says, "Do the work of an evangelist." Not all have the gift of the evangelist, but all should do the work of evangelism. Evangelism and missions are at the heart of all Southern Baptists do. Southern Baptists became great because of preachers and missionaries and evangelists and denominational leaders and lay people who carried New Testaments into the homes of lost people and led them to Christ. Our problems started the day we got away from personal witnessing. Every preacher and layman, denomination servant and scholar, missionary and institutional representative should do the work of an evangelist.

You can't have doubts about the Bible and be a soul-winner at the same time. The evangelist can't evangelize if he has misgivings about this evangel. As you go into the homes of the lost, what you believe about the Bible is absolutely crucial.

Step with me into a modest home. The carpet is smelly; beer cans are scattered around; the family is holding together by a thread. We are looking into the face of a man whose eternal destiny is on the line. He is an alcoholic; his son is on drugs; his girl is pregnant. "Sir, let me share with you some verses from Romans. But we are not sure Paul wrote it. Maybe the disciples forged his name to lend credibility to their work. This book of Romans says, all have sinned. We are sinners because of the fall of Adam and Eve in Eden. But we aren't sure there was a garden of Eden or that Adam and Eve ever existed. It also says, Christ died for our sins. But don't make more of that than you should. He died to set an example for you to follow. He is reported to have said, Come unto me and I will give you rest. Could I interest you in having an existential encounter with the spirit of Jesus which is alive in the universe somewhere?" The man replies, "No thanks, but if you have the phone numbers of AA, Drug Rehab or Planned Parenthood, I would like them."

If you don't have a trustworthy Bible, you are out of business in the homes of lost people. Let's get on with our evangelical imperative. Let's fill the highways and byways with Baptists and their Bibles, sharing the good news with a lost world.

The Bible has:

C. Eschatological Implications vs. 4:6–13

Paul's thoughts now turn eschatological, to last things. Not prophetically, but personally. He is facing his own death. I am ready to be offered (poured out like a drink offering) . . . the time for my departure (loosing of tent cords) is at hand. What did Paul want in the last days? Verse 13 tells us. He wanted his "cloak," something warm for his body; his "books," something stimulating for his mind; but "especially the parchments." He wanted the Word of God for his soul.

I wonder what Old Testament portions he wanted as soft pillows on his death bed? Was it Job 19:25–26, For I know that my Redeemer liveth, and that He shall stand at the latter day upon the earth; and though after my skin, worms destroy this body, yet in my flesh shall I see God. Or was it Psalm 23:4, Yea, though I walk through the valley of the shadow of death, I will fear no evil; for thou art with me; thy rod and thy staff, they comfort me.

I don't especially like funerals, but like all preachers, I don't refuse to conduct them. When I stand before a broken-hearted family I need something to bring them comfort. I have a Book! I have never seen it fail. I have seen the Word of God brush tears from eyes and pour the balm of Gilead on hurting hearts. Romans 15:4 says, Whatsoever things were written before time were written for our learning, that we through patience and comfort of the Scriptures might have hope.

If you have no trustworthy Bible, you have nothing to give hope to those who are facing death. A paster sowed seeds of doubt about the Bible in the minds of his congregation. A critically ill member sent for him. "Shall I read from the Bible and pray with you?" "Yes," said the dying man. His wife brought his Bible. As the pastor opened it he found certain books missing. Some chapters were gone, verses were cut out. It was a shamefully mutilated Bible. The startled pastor exclaimed: "Have you not a better Bible than this one?" Accusingly the dying man said, "When you came to our church, I had a whole Bible. You told us certain books were fictional and I cut them out. You told us some chapters were not true, and I removed them. You said certain verses were not accurate, so I cut them out, too. There is little of my Bible left except the two covers." When you come to die what kind of Bible do you want? Look to your left—see the death beds of those who die denying any part of the Bible. Show me the triumph death of one who rejected the Scriptures. There are no smiles of hope, no shouts of joy, only darkness and despair and doubt. Now, look to the right—see the death beds of those with the whole Bible in their hands. See the radiance on their faces. Listen to the shouts of victory!

> There is just one Book for the dying,
> One Book for the starting tears,
> And one for the soul that is going home,
> For the numberless years.
> There is just one Book.

Years ago, in the days of the old Camp Meetings, a preacher set out after the evening service to find his way along the edge of a dangerous cliff to the cottage where he was to spend the night. He had no lantern; flashlights were then unknown. An old farmer, sensing the preacher's predicament, lighted a bundle of pine branches, handed them to the preacher saying, "Take this, it will light your way home." The preacher said, "But what if the wind blows it out?" "It will see you home." "But what if it burns out before I get there." "It will see you home."

Do you see this Book? It is a lamp unto your feet and a light to your path. There will be times when winds of unbelief may seem to almost put out its glow. Storms of skepticism may threaten to engulf it. There may even be times when you are tempted to lay it aside and make your way unaided. At times it may look old fashioned alongside the psychedelic flashlights of this age. But, my Baptist brothers and sisters, hold on to your Bible. It will see you home!

Appendix 2. A Conservative Southern Baptist Affirmation

One unfortunate aspect of controversy is the inadvertent misunderstanding that frequently develops in the vortex of discussion. The brief statement of affirmations, prayerful desires, and goals which follows is an attempt to clarify the position of the past four presidents of the Southern Baptist Convention. While we recognize that we cannot speak for others, much consultation leads us to believe that this statement is representative of the heart-beat of most conservative Southern Baptists. While the statement is neither definitive nor exhaustive, our prayer to God is that it will serve to clarify to the minds of all Southern Baptists that which we have been attempting to say over the last ten years. As leaders elected by Southern Baptists, we sincerely feel that we should not and could not appoint anyone to positions of leadership who does not embrace the essentials outlined herein. We wish also to express in the strongest possible terms our unabated love for and devotion to our beloved Southern Baptist Convention of cooperating Christians laboring together to present the Gospel to every soul until Christ returns. God bless you every one.

I. Affirmations

1. We affirm the Baptist right to set parameters for the institutions and agencies which are supported by Baptists and agree with The Baptist Faith and Message as adopted by the Southern Baptist Convention's session in Kansas City in 1963. We are in agreement with the confession's statement that it contains a "consensus" of beliefs among Southern Baptist and is a statement of "those articles of the Christian faith which are most surely held among us."[1] We, therefore, affirm doctrinal unity in functional diversity.

2. We agree with and affirm Article One, "The Scriptures" as interpreted by Dr. Herschel Hobbs' testimony before the Southern Baptist

"An Inerrantist Manifesto," presented by SBC president Adrian Rogers and former SBC presidents James Draper, Charles Stanley, and Bailey Smith, press conference document, 24 February 1988.

Convention's meetings in Houston (1979) and in Los Angeles (1981), respectively, as meaning the m [*sic*] errancy of the original autographs. We understand (with Dr. Hobbs) the Scripture as having "God for its author, salvation for its end, and truth, without any error, for its matter" as being a synonymous phrase for inerrancy.[2] We further affirm the Glorietta Statement of the Southern Baptist Theological Seminary Presidents that the Bible "is not errant in any area of reality." Finally, we affirm the Southern Baptist Convention's overwhelmingly adopted report of the Peace Committee including the delineation of the nature and extent of our confidence in the accuracy and authority of the Bible.

3. We affirm evangelism as the attempt in every way possible to present the gospel of Jesus Christ to everyone in the world. It is the responsibility of every Christian and every church to obey the Great Commission and to seek "to extend the gospel to the ends of the earth."

4. We affirm the cooperative method of world missions is biblically based. Churches acting in cooperation and in concert can do some things better together than separately and alone. One of the things which can be done more efficiently in a cooperative way is the training, equipping, and supporting of missionaries for the worldwide missionary enterprise.

5. We affirm the autonomy of the local church as expressed in The Baptist Faith and Message and we believe that all Southern Baptist denominational organization is lateral, not vertical, in nature. Thus, Southern Baptist organizations, at whatever level, are groups of voluntarily cooperating local churches and nothing should be done to compromise the autonomy of the local congregation.

6. We affirm the separation of the institution of the church and the institution of the state. We believe, however, in the inseparability of religious convictions and political issues such as abortion, gambling, and pornography. The Baptist belief in separation of church and state does not absolve the individual Christian from the obligation to "oppose, in the spirit of Christ, every form of greed selfishness, and vice" and to "work to provide for the orphaned, the needy, the aged, the helpless, and the sick."

7. We believe in the institutions and agencies of the Southern Baptist Convention as they understand and comply with the beliefs enunciated above and as they respect local church autonomy.

8. We believe in the priesthood of every true believer, the competency of each individual to know and experience God for himself, and the absolute freedom of religion for all people. We recognize no official distinction between laity and clergy while at the same time recognizing the distinctive call of God to the ministry.

9. We affirm that this cherished belief in the priesthood of the believer guarantees access for all men to God through the blood of Christ appropriated by faith. We further affirm that the same doctrine underscores the

Christian's responsibilities in intercessory prayer and witnessing. We also affirm that to interpret this precious doctrine as license to believe anything and still be considered a Baptist is to misconstrue this liberty altogether.

10. We affirm that Jesus Christ, the virgin-born God-man, is the center of all faith. True doctrine centers in Jesus and his vicarious substitutionary death on the cross and subsequent resurrection from the dead. There is no salvation outside of faith in Christ.

II. Prayerful Desires

1. Our prayerful desire is for the institutions and agencies of the Southern Baptist Convention to work and teach in accord with The Baptist Faith and Message, especially concerning the article on "The Scriptures."

In this regard we agree with The Baptist Faith and Message that in "Christian education there should be a proper balance between academic freedom and academic responsibility. Freedom in any orderly relationship of human life is always limited and never absolute. The freedom of a teacher in a Christian school, college, or seminary is limited by the preeminence of Jesus Christ, by the authoritative nature of the Scriptures, and by the distinct purpose for which the school exists."

2. Our further prayerful desire is that nothing will ever be done intentionally in and by the institutions and agencies of the Southern Baptist Convention to shake anyone's confidence in the full reliability and infallibility of the Bible.

3. Our further prayerful desire is that institutions and agencies of the Southern Baptist Convention recognize local church autonomy in fact, as well as in theory, acknowledging with The Baptist Faith and Message that all such institutions and agencies "have no authority over one another or over the churches."

4. Our further prayerful desire is to encourage the institutions and agencies of the Southern Baptist Convention as they take every positive step to emphasize and prepare every possible part of our Convention for the task of worldwide evangelism.

5. Our further prayerful desire is for fair and balanced treatment in the denominational press. When issues and disagreements arise within our fellowship, all sides are to be presented fairly and fully.

6. Finally, our prayerful desire is that those who represent Southern Baptists on the boards of institutions and agencies be selected from among those who affirm Article One of The Baptist Faith and Message as set out above.

III. Goals

1. Our goal is to have our prayerful desires (as enumerated above) come to realization within the Southern Baptist Convention.

2. Our goal is to be cooperative with the institutions and agencies of the Southern Baptist Convention without being forced to support what we consider to be unconscionable. At the same time we recognize the right and privilege of every Southern Baptist to believe as led by his conscience.

3. Our goal is to make Southern Baptists ever more aware of the dangers of neo-orthodoxy, liberalism, and the misuse of the historical-critical method to the basic doctrines of the Christian faith and to the worldwide mission outreach.

4. Our goal is for the Southern Baptist Convention's institutions, agencies, churches, and people to be used and blessed by God to lead a nationwide revival and spiritual awakening.

5. Our goal is for the foreign and home mission efforts of the Southern Baptist Convention to be used and blessed by God to lead a worldwide expansion of the church of the Lord Jesus Christ through spiritual awakening and revival.

Notes

Introduction

1. Supportive male dissident rhetors risk the same punishment as their activist-minded female counterparts. According to Jim Barnette, pastor of Harrods Creek Baptist Church, Crestwood, Kentucky, in *SBC Today*: "My denomination has been oppressed by a Dallas oligarchy. . . . I feel as though the decree of banishment has already been read to me." See letter to the editor, *SBC Today*, 5 April 1991, 8.

2. As is often the case with words important to institutions and their members, the label Messenger is peculiar to the SBC in so far as we can determine. The label applies only to those members in good standing from cooperating SBC churches who are named or elected by their churches as official representatives to the national meetings. Regardless of church membership size, a church may send no more than ten persons as Messengers to the annual meetings.

3. "The Rev. Blow Gives A Sermon on the Mouse." *Dallas Morning News*, 19 June 1996, A10.

4. *Raleigh News* and *Observer*, 4 August 1997, 1A.

5. *Raleigh News and Observer*, 4 August 1997, 1A.

6. Harry S. Stout, *The New England Soul: Preaching and Religious Culture in Colonial New England* (New York: Oxford University Press, 1986), 3–4.

7. Richard Weaver, *Language Is Sermonic: Richard Weaver on the Nature of Rhetoric*, ed. Richard L. Johannson, Rennard Strickland, and Ralph T. Eubanks (Baton Rouge: Louisiana State University Press, 1970), 224.

8. Wayne Thompson, *Responsible and Effective Communication* (Boston: Houghton-Mifflin, 1978), 17.

9. Thompson, *Responsible*, 17.

2. Uncertain Times: Trouble in Zion

1. Unless otherwise indicated, we have used the authorized King James version of the Bible throughout the book for scriptural verse citation. See *Authorized King James Version of the Holy Bible* (Chicago: Spencer Press, 1946).

2. In this discussion of the traditions of Southern Baptist life, the authors have drawn on Walter Shurden's comments quoted in William Leonard, *God's Last and Only Hope: The Fragmentation of the Southern Baptist Convention* (Grand Rapids: William B. Erdmans Publishing Co., 1990), 32–35.

3. See Leonard, *God's Last*, 35, for more on this issue.

4. Leonard, *God's Last*, 35–36.

5. Leonard, *God's Last*, 36.

6. Nancy Ammerman is quoted in Martin E. Marty and R. Scott Appleby, ed., *Fundamentalisms Observed* (Chicago: University of Chicago Press, 1991), 1.

7. Leonard, *God's Last*, 73.

8. See Leonard, *God's Last*, 73.

9. For more on this, see Leonard, *God's Last*, 134.

10. See Leonard, *God's Last*, 6, for additional support of this idea.

11. For example, see Rev. W. A. Criswell, "The Infallible Word of God," Convention press release from the Southern Baptist Convention Pastor's Conference, 13 June 1988, 16. In this study, we have cited and studied *only* the Convention press release copy of Criswell's "The Infallible Word of God" sermon rather than the copy in the Southern Baptist Historical Commission Archives, Southern Baptist Sunday School Board. Regrettably, Criswell has refused us permission to reproduce the archive's copy, thus depriving our readers of the opportunity to study that version of the sermon.

12. Criswell, "The Infallible Word of God," 16.

13. Weaver, *Language Is Sermonic*, 22.

14. As cited in Rev. Adrian Rogers, [no title], audiotape of sermon from SBC Pastor's Conference, 10 June 1979 (Nashville: Southern Baptist Historical Commission Archives, Southern Baptist Sunday School Board). All of the SBC Convention Sermons and President's Addresses from 1979–94 were videotaped or audiotaped, or are in printed texts in the Southern Baptist Historical Commission Archives, Southern Baptist Sunday School Board in Nashville, Tennessee, and we have used them throughout this book as sources of evidence. For further assistance on these resources, see the bibliographical essay at the end of this book.

15. Rev. James Robison, [no title], audiotape of sermon from SBC Pastor's Conference, 10 June 1979 (Nashville: Southern Baptist Historical Commission Archives, Southern Baptist Sunday School Board).

16. *USA Today*, 3 June 1992, 7.

3. Preaching the Word: The Nature of Persuasion in the Southern Baptist Holy War

1. Martin E. Marty, "Fundamentalism and the Scholar," *Key Reporter* (spring 1993): 1.

2. Weaver, *Language Is Sermonic*, 201.

3. Rev. Jerry Vines, "A Baptist and His Bible," text of SBC Convention Sermon, 11 June 1987 (Jacksonville, FL: First Baptist Church), 4.

4. Rev. Edwin Young, [no title], text of SBC President's Address, June 14, 1994 (Nashville: Southern Baptist Historical Commission), 4.

5. Ernest Bormann, "Fantasy and Rhetorical Vision: The Rhetorical Criticism of Social Reality," *Quarterly Journal of Speech* 58 (December 1972): 396–407.

6. Nancy Ammerman is quoted in *Fundamentalisms Observed*, 1.

7. While these sentiments appear in nearly all of the national convention sermons that we have studied, Criswell, Young, Rogers, and Vines (see appendix 1) are especially good sources for study on this point.

4. All Scripture Is Given by Inspiration of God: An Apologia for Inerrancy

1. The volume referred to is Dr. James T. Draper, *Authority: The Critical Issue for Southern Baptists* (Old Tappan, N.J.: Fleming H. Revell, 1984). We have placed appropriate page references to Draper's book in the chapter rather than make repeated endnotes.

2. Joseph R. Gusfield, introduction to *On Symbols and Society*, by Kenneth Burke, ed. Joseph R. Gusfield (Chicago: University of Chicago Press, 1989), 32.

3. Gusfield, introduction to *On Symbols and Society*, 33.

4. "The Chicago Statement on Biblical Inerrancy, 1978," reprinted in the Convention edition of *Southern Baptist Watchman*, 1993, 5.

5. Readers may wish to know that all the SBC presidents since 1979 believe that the Holy Bible is inerrant and that they use a number of synonyms for the word. The Rogers passage at the beginning of the chapter exemplifies this point, for he often uses the label "inspired" or "inspiration" in his sermons.

6. Matt. 23:23 AV.

7. Emphasis added; Lewis Carroll, *The Best of Lewis Carroll* (Secaucus, N.J.: Castle Press, 1983), 238.

8. Rogers, untitled audiotaped sermon, 10 June 1979.

5. Tongues of Fire: The Inerrancy Rhetoric of Southern Baptist Presidents

1. Rev. Morris H. Chapman, "Faith Is the Victory," videotape of SBC President's Address, 4 June 1991 (Nashville: Southern Baptist Historical Commission Archives, Southern Baptist Sunday School Board). Chapman currently serves as the president of the Executive Committee, Southern

Baptist Sunday School Board, Nashville, Tennessee. Chapman is now tantamount to the status of CEO of the Convention.

2. Chapman, "Faith Is the Victory."

3. Chapman, "Faith Is the Victory."

4. See Bormann, "Fantasy and Rhetorical Vision."

5. Rev. Morris H. Chapman, "Search the Scriptures," text of videotape of SBC Convention Sermon, 14 June 1989 (Nashville: Southern Baptist Historical Commission Archives, Southern Baptist Sunday School Board).

6. Associated Baptist Press (ABP) news release, 8 September 1993 (Jacksonville: Associated Baptist Press Offices).

7. Chapman, "Search the Scriptures."

8. Chapman, "Search the Scriptures."

9. Adrian Rogers spoke this line in his introduction to Jerry Vines's videotaped SBC Convention Sermon, "A Baptist and His Bible," 16 June 1987.

10. Rev. Jerry Vines, "A Baptist and His Bible," text of videotape of SBC Convention Sermon, June 16, 1987 (Nashville: Southern Baptist Historical Commission Archives, Southern Baptist Sunday School Board).

11. Vines, "Baptist and His Bible."

12. Vines, "Baptist and His Bible."

13. Vines, "Baptist and His Bible."

14. Vines, "Baptist and His Bible."

15. Rev. Adrian Rogers, "The Decade of Decision and the Doors of Destiny," text of videotape of SBC President's Address, 10 June 1980 (Nashville: Southern Baptist Historical Commission Archives, Southern Baptist Sunday School Board).

16. Rev. Bailey E. Smith, text of videotape of SBC President's Address, "The Worth of the Work," 9 June 1981 (Nashville: Southern Baptist Historical Commission Archives, Southern Baptist Sunday School Board).

17. Rev. James T. Draper, "Southern Baptists: People of Deep Belief," text of videotape of SBC President's Address, June 14, 1983 (Nashville: Southern Baptist Historical Commission Archives, Southern Baptist Sunday School Board).

18. Rev. James T. Draper, "Debtors to the World," text of videotape of SBC President's Address, 12 June 1984 (Nashville: Southern Baptist Historical Commission Archives, Southern Baptist Sunday School Board).

19. Criswell, "The Infallible Word of God," 16.

20. Rev. Morris H. Chapman, "It's Time to Move," text of videotape of SBC President's Address, 12 June 1992 (Nashville: Southern Baptist Historical Commission Archives, Southern Baptist Sunday School Board).

21. Rev. Edwin Young, "Side Streets," text of videotape of SBC Convention Sermon, 15 June 1993 (Nashville: Southern Baptist Historical Commission Archives, Southern Baptist Sunday School Board).

22. Young, untitled President's Address, 14 June 1994.

23. Rev. Russell Dilday, "On Higher Ground," text of videotape of SBC Convention Sermon, 13 June 1984 (Nashville: Southern Baptist Historical Commission Archives, Southern Baptist Sunday School Board).

24. Dilday, "On Higher Ground."

25. ABP news release, 13 June 1988.

26. ABP news release, 13 June 1988.

27. ABP news release, 14 June 1988.

28. Rev. Jerry Vines, "The Glory of God," text of videotape of SBC President's Address, 11 June 1990 (Nashville: Southern Baptist Historical Commission Archives, Southern Baptist Sunday School Board).

6. Objectionable Believers, Roger Williams, and the Southern Baptist Oligarchy

1. For an example, see "Southern Baptists Aim at Disney's Liberalism," *USA Today*, 19 June 1996, D1–2. According to denominational spokespersons, "In recent years, the Disney Company has given the appearance that the promotion of homosexuality is more important than its historic commitment to traditional values."

2. For an active sense of dissent to the SBC's decision to target Jews for evangelism, see the Letters to the Editor section, *Baptists Today*, 25 June 1996, 18.

3. According to Dennis Bailey, the history of dissent within churches of the last twenty years "suggests that churches are able to do little to control conflict or restrain free expression except with the voluntary relations of their own memberships." Although Bailey did not apply his generalization to the SBC, he well could have. Dennis Bailey, "'Come Now, Let Us Reason Together': Conflict and Consensus in Contemporary American Religion," (paper delivered at the annual meeting of the Southern States Communication Association, 7 April 1989), 3.

4. We are unable to determine accurately the number of academics fired, forced into retirement, or induced to leave under pressure by the SBC pulpit oligarchy. We find one example in 1987, when Paul Simmons, professor of Christian ethics at Southern Baptist Theological Seminary in Louisville, was charged with being too liberal by the SBC Executive Committee. In 1990, his dismissal was demanded by various school trustees. Simmons refused to retire, prompting the possibility of heresy charges being levied against him by denominational authorities in order to force his removal. In 1993, under fire from loyalists for using a sex education video in his graduate education class titled "The Church and Sexuality," Simmons announced his early retirement. ABP news release, 7 January 1993.

5. For a discussion of the definitions of exclusionary language, see

Gregory J. Shepherd, "Communication as Influence: Definitional Exclusion," *Communication Studies* 43 (winter 1992): 203–19.

6. Weaver, *Language Is Sermonic*, 224.

7. Martha D. Cooper and William L. Nothstine, *Power Persuasion: Moving an Ancient Art into the Media Age* (Greencastle, Ind.: Educational Video Group, 1992), 175.

8. While this viewpoint is vintage Weaver, see Celeste M. Condit, "Crafting Value: The Rhetorical Construction of Public Morality," *Quarterly Journal of Speech* 73 (1987): 82–87. See also Weaver, *Language Is Sermonic*, 211.

9. Gusfield, introduction to *On Symbols and Society*, 32.

10. Gusfield introduction to *On Symbols and Society*, 38.

11. Kenneth Burke, *On Symbols and Society*, ed. Joseph R. Gusfield (Chicago: University of Chicago Press, 1989), 298.

12. See Burke, *On Symbols and Society*, 294–95.

13. This is explained more fully in Kenneth Burke, *The Philosophy of Literary Form*, 2d ed. (Baton Rouge: Louisiana State University Press, 1967), 40. We have drawn upon Burke's "The Sacrifice and the Kill" for assistance in formulating this chapter.

14. John Winthrop, *History of New England* (New York: Charles Scribner's Sons, 1908), 1: 162–63.

15. Roger Williams, *Mr. Cottons Letter Lately Printed, Examined and Answered*, (London: 1644: reprint, ed. R. A. Guild, Providence: Narragansett Club Publications, 1867), 1: 43.

16. Williams, *Mr. Cottons*, 56–67.

17. Winthrop, *History of New England*, 162–3. The letters are contained in Roger Williams, *The Letters of Roger Williams*, ed. John Russell Bartlett (Providence: Narragansett Club Publications, 1874), 6: 73–77.

18. For a discussion of Williams's rhetorical and forensic education, see L. Raymond Camp, *Roger Williams: God's Apostle of Advocacy* (New York: Edwin Mellen Press, 1989), 24–43.

19. Cotton Mather, *Magnalia Christi Magnalia, of the Ecclesiastical History of New England, from Its First Planting in the Year 1620, of Our Lord, 1693, First American edition, from the London Edition of 1702* (Hartford: Roberts & Burr, Printers, 1820), 1: 117.

20. ABP news release, 29 May 1996.

21. See Peter Waldman, "Fundamentalists Fight to Capture the Soul of Southern Baptists," *Wall Street Journal*, 3 July 1988, 1A. Waldman's front page article details the punishments of various dissident SBC members.

22. From an unpublished transcript of Rev. Nancy Hastings Sehested's remarks made available to the authors in April 1994, at Knollwood Baptist Church, Winston-Salem, North Carolina.

23. ABP news release, 12 January 1993.

24. "FMB Chairman Compares WMU Action to Committing Adul-

tery," *Biblical Recorder*, 6 February 1993, 9. The same issue also outlines the rescission of a speaking invitation involving Dellanna O'Brien, who had been invited to speak to the 1995 Waccamaw, South Carolina, fall associational meeting. According to the *Biblical Recorder*, associational spokesperson Charles Thrower outlined the reasons for the withdrawal: "The main reason is that WMU is linking up with the Cooperative Baptist Fellowship . . . and . . . [Thrower disfavored] women speaking from the pulpit when they are listed as delivering a message."

25. When the SBC Convention Study Committee of Greenwood Forest Baptist Church, Cary, North Carolina, commended the WMU for its devotion to missions in a letter from committee chairperson Judy Teander-Green to former SBC president Adrian Rogers, it also labeled John Jackson's and Rogers's statements in *Baptists Today* as "divisive, inappropriate and mean-spirited." Rogers responded to the committee on April 20, 1993, "Would you please give me the direct quotation concerning me that you mentioned in your letter? Please don't tell me what you heard someone say that I said but what I said. If you have no quotation, then please tell me why you said what you said." Noticeably, Rogers did not take issue with the letter's observations. From the Archives of the Convention Study Committee, Greenwood Forest Baptist Church, Cary, North Carolina.

26. For a review and analysis of the resolution's text, see Anne P. Rosser, "Why Did the Southern Baptist Convention Approve a Resolution That Violates and Destroys the Authority and Integrity of Scripture?" *Folio* 2 (spring 1985): 7. For the complete text of Resolution 3 from the 1984 SBC convention, please see chapter 7.

27. Coppenger's remarks, delivered in a seminary chapel service on April 11, 1996, have been only partially reprinted. See *Baptist Peacemaker* 16 (1996): 16. Despite Coppenger's (and other SBC presidents') advocacy against women in the pulpit, the SBC does not identify the gender of ordained pulpit ministers. Additionally, Baptist state newspapers do not necessarily report the ordination of women for any church capacity. The SBC has never reported such statistics, and there is no reason to believe they intend to do so now. We suggest that if such statistics were accurately kept and publicly reported, it might acknowledge an ineffective campaign against women's ordination.

28. Miller's ideas are summarized in "New National WMU President Outlines Role of Women in SBC," *Biblical Recorder*, 20 July 1991, 1.

29. "New National," 9.

30. "New National," 1.

31. "New National," 9–10.

32. The concept of "devil words" is discussed in Richard M. Weaver, *The Ethics of Rhetoric* (Davis, Ca.: Hermagoras Press, 1985), 222–32.

33. The depth of their fear for dissidents as agents of persuasion is

apparently substantive, if Criswell's 1988 sermon at the SBC Pastor's Conference in San Antonio is an accurate guide. See the *San Antonio Light*, 14 June 1988, 1A.

34. According to Mark Coppenger, president of Midwestern Baptist Seminary, the Bible assures the "equality and value" of men and women but distinguishes an "identity of role" between the sexes. See *Baptist Peacemaker* 16 (1996): 16.

35. Currently, Southern (and American) Baptists are also encountering difficulty with the issue of homosexuality. For example, in 1992, two North Carolina SBC churches were expelled by the denominations state and area organizations, actions never taken before by these organizations in recent history. See "Analysis Highlights Major News Stories among Tar Heels," *Biblical Recorder*, 9 January 1993, 6, and "Analysis of Recorder Issues Reveals Major SBC Stories," *Biblical Recorder*, 16 January 1993, 1, 6.

7. By Scripture and Argument: An Apologia for the Ordination of Women

1. Larry L. McSwain, "Anatomy of the SBC Institutional Crisis," *Review and Expositor* 88 (1991): 25.

2. Quoted from J. P. Ford, "Gender and Image: Baptist Clergy Woman's Important New Book," *Folio* 8 (spring 1991): 1.

3. Leonard, *God's Last*, 152.

4. C. I. Scofield, ed., *The New Scofield Reference Bible* (New York: Oxford Press, 1969), 1297.

5. See ABP news release, 29 July 1993.

6. See ABP news release, 31 October 1997.

7. See ABP news release, 29 July 1993.

8. ABP news release, 29 July 1993.

9. See ABP news release, 29 July 1993.

10. See Special Study Committee, First Baptist Church, Columbia, South Carolina, "The Role of Women in the Church," 9 November 1983 (Columbia, S.C.: First Baptist Church, the Dargan-Carver Library; also the Southern Baptist Convention Historical Commission Archives, Southern Baptist Sunday School Board).

11. Special Study Committee, "Role of Women," 5–11.

12. See Special Study Committee, "Role of Women," 4. See also Leonard Swidler, *Biblical Affirmations of Woman* (Philadelphia: Westminster Press, 1979), 75–76.

13. See Jann Aldredge Clanton, "Why I Believe Southern Baptist Churches Should Ordain Women," *Baptist History and Heritage* (July 1988): 50.

14. For more, see Walter Bureggemann, "Of the Same Flesh and Bone, (Gen. 2:23a)," *Catholic Biblical Quarterly* 32 (1970): 239–42.

15. See William E. Hull, "Woman in Her Place: Biblical Perspective," *Review and Expositor* 72 (Winter 1975): 14.

16. See Leonard, *God's Last*, 153.

17. See Scofield, *New Scofield Reference Bible*, 1244–45.

18. Clanton, "Why I Believe," 51.

19. See Shirley Stevens, *A New Testament View of Women* (Nashville: Broadman Press, 1980), 57.

20. Clanton, "Why I Believe," 52.

21. Clanton, "Why I Believe," 52.

22. For a full review of the history of women in ministry, see Betty McGary Pearce in consultation with Nancy Hastings Sehested, Anne Thomas Neil, and Reba Sloan Cobb, "A History of Women in Ministry," *Folio* 3 (summer 1985): 9–10.

23. See "Southern Baptist Women: Behind the Scenes or Ahead of the Pack?" *Florida Baptist Witness*, 11 May 1995, 16.

24. The report is summarily noted in *Folio* 2 (summer 1984): n.p.

25. Sara Frances Andrews, "Who Are Baptist Women in Ministry?" *Western Recorder*, 26 January 1993, 6.

26. "Gender Discrimination Suit Filed," *Folio* 3 (fall 1995): 3.

27. Dorothy Kelley Patterson, "Why I Believe Southern Baptist Churches Should Not Ordain Women," *Baptist History and Heritage* (July 1988): 61–62.

28. Also see Ford, "Gender and Image," 10.

8. The Rhetorics of Silence and Abomination: The Troublesome Issue of Homosexuality

1. *Raleigh News and Observer*, 15 October 1995, 9G.

2. In 1985, for example, around 2.1 million American couples lived together out of wedlock. By 1997, that number had doubled. ABP news release, 30 July 1998.

3. According to the Associated Baptist Press, "more than 109 million adults were married and living with their spouse in 1997 [which is] roughly 56 percent of the adult population." On the other hand, the same news release indicated that "in 1997, 19.3 million adults were divorced, about 10 percent of the population." See ABP news release, 30 July 1998. We have been unable to secure marriage and divorce statistics regarding Southern Baptists.

4. ABP news release, 30 July 1998.

5. See ABP news release, 30 July 1998.

6. In the 1996 edition of *Beyond Acceptance*, authors Carolyn Welch Griffin, Marian J. Wirth, and Arthur G. Wirth explore the current thinking of all mainline religious groups in America—except, rather notably, Southern Baptists—regarding the acceptance of gays and lesbians in re-

ligious life. While Southern Baptist officialdom may seem to embrace Griffin, Wirth, and Wirth's definition of having a "rejecting-nonpunitive" attitude towards gays and lesbians, to us, SBC practices appear closer to that of these authors' description of "rejecting-punitive." See Welch Griffin, Marian Wirth, and Arthur G. Wirth, *Beyond Acceptance* (New York: St. Martin's Press, 1996), 71–72.

7. *Raleigh News and Observer*, 4 August 1997, 1A.

8. However, according to the *Raleigh News and Observer*, the American Psychiatric Association has declared: "There is no evidence that any treatment can change a homosexual person's deep seated sexual feelings for others of the same sex." See *Raleigh News and Observer*, 4 August 1997, 8A. The Family Research Institute disagrees, for it alleges that homosexuality is "totally learned." On the basis of a 1983 study of 147 homosexuals, the Institute claims that homosexuality is principally a matter of preference, arising from "early homosexual experience(s) with adults/and or peers." See the unpaginated pamphlet from the Family Research Institute, Inc., Washington, D.C., 1991.

9. *Baptists Today*, 30 September 1993, 7.

10. We have drawn this legislative information from the *Chronicle of Higher Education*, 26 October 1994, 1.

11. For example, see the debate between U.S. Senator Jesse Helms and newspaper columnist Ann Landers. Helms wrote Landers and claimed that "as has been made clear by many medical authorities long ago, the ultimate origin of all such AIDS-tainted blood has been homosexual contact." Landers rebutted him, replying, "Your statement . . . is patently incorrect. The Center for Disease Control does not know where the virus originated, but it infected both homosexuals and heterosexuals alike." Helms, she contended, has actively opposed the provision of funds and resources against AIDS. *Raleigh News and Observer*, 15 October 1995, 2E. On 28 October 1995, Helms complained that Landers was guilty of an "intentional distortion" of his voting record on AIDS. See *Raleigh News and Observer*, 28 October 1995, 17A. Helms did not, however, deny Landers's point about the origin of AIDS.

12. *Baptists Today*, 20 August 1992, 17.

13. See *Baptists Today*, 21 January 1993, 9.

14. See *Baptists Today*, 21 January 1993, 1.

15. *Annual of the Southern Baptist Convention, Nineteen Hundred and Ninety-One, Atlanta, Georgia*. Distributed by the Executive Committee (Nashville: Southern Baptist Convention, 1991), 73.

16. See *Baptists Today*, 28 May 1992, 3; see also *Biblical Recorder*, 9 January 1993, 8.

17. ABP news release, 20 August 1992.

18. *Baptists Today*, 24 September 1992, 18.

19. *Raleigh News and Observer*, 18 December 1994, 1.

20. Al Waddill, a member of University Baptist Church of the Columbus, Ohio, Baptist Association (Southern Baptist), spoke to his association membership. The *Baptist Peacemaker* reported that he "described the despair of his adolescence at the silence regarding gay sexuality in his Southern Baptist congregation." *Baptist Peacemaker*, (summer 1995), 17.

21. *Pullen Memorial Baptist Church Newsletter*, 14 September 1990, Raleigh, North Carolina.

22. For a lively discussion, see Milton Rokeach, *The Open and Closed Mind: Investigations into the Nature of Belief Systems and Personality Systems* (New York: Basic Books, 1960), 41–47. Communication scholars have published extensively in this area since at least 1971. See, for example, Craig Allen Smith, "Communicative Characteristics of Dogmatism and Authoritarianism in Written Messages," *Central States Speech Journal* 29 (1978): 293–303, and Smith's companion piece, "Special Report: Communicative Characteristics of Dogmatism and Authoritarianism in Oral Messages," *Central States Speech Journal* 29 (1978): 304–7.

23. *SBC Bulletin of the Southern Baptist Convention*, 15 June 1988, 5. The bulletin was distributed to Messengers on the floor of the annual meeting in San Antonio, Texas.

24. See Roy Honeycutt, *Layman's Bible Book Commentary* (Nashville: Broadman Press, 1979), 3: 18.

25. Weaver, *Ethics of Rhetoric*, 222–23. See page 222 where Weaver notes that in World War II, terms such as "Nazi" and "fascist" were condemnations, just as "communist" negatively described the Russians in the 1950s.

26. In his essay entitled, "Elvis Presley as Redneck," Will Campbell comments on our compulsion to try to fix blame on someone else for our own social problems. Regarding racism, he writes: "*We* are not racists, *they* are racists." His point is that it is usual to blame unseen others, rather than to engage in the kind of discussion and persuasion that confronts problems like inclusion. See Will Campbell, "Elvis Presley as Redneck," *Baptist Peacemaker* (fall–winter 1995): 1.

27. See chapter 6, "Preacher, Diplomat and Debater: Williams' Advocacy of Soul Liberty," in L. Raymond Camp, *Roger Williams*, 146–73.

28. Williams spoke out against public nudism because he believed that it was impractical for civil and sober people to practice public nakedness. See Camp, *Roger Williams*, 191.

29. I Corinthians 13:4–5.

30. *Biblical Recorder*, 27 March 1993, 9.

9. The New Southern Baptists and a Purified South

1. For a justification of the boycott on different grounds than those

advanced by the SBC, see the editorial in the *Kearney [Nebraska] Daily Hub* (5 August 1997, 4A), which describes some Disney movies as "sludge." In particular, the editorial asserts that the movie *Priest* is guilty of "displaying" hostility to the Roman Catholic Church and laments the film *Pulp Fiction* for its use of splattered brains as "slapstick." The editorial charges that the "entertainment industry's violent and smutty 'amusement' bears some blame for our nation's mindless crime, epidemic illegitimacy, and high divorce rate."

2. *Biblical Recorder*, 18 May 1996, 3, 14.

3. For example, in the same *Biblical Recorder* issue with Coppenger's statements, see an opposing view in a letter to the editor from reader Jim Kirstein: "It is appropriate for women to teach and have authority (over men) in the church whenever God's appointment and their spiritual maturity warrant it. Let the voices of women who are gifted and called by God be heard in our churches. Let them be ordained as pastors and deacons." *Biblical Recorder*, 18 May 1996, 2.

4. Securing an accurate count of Southern Baptists is difficult. According to Dr. Thomas Ascol, pastor of the Grace Baptist Church in Cape Coral, Florida, "only half of our 15 million members can in any sense be counted as active (that is, they contributed financially or attended at least one service last year). Even the secular media recognizes the deception of our inflated membership statistics." Ascol cites the *Wall Street Journal*, 25 April 1990, 16A, to substantiate his claim. According to him, the *Journal* "exposed the facade." See Ascol's essay, "Southern Baptists at the Crossroads[,] Returning to the Old Paths," *The Founders Journal*, (winter/spring 1995) 1. The Ascol count, now dated, does not reflect the point that over two thousand SBC churches have left the denomination. Those churches now comprise the Cooperative Baptist Fellowship, Alliance of Baptists, and other splinter groups. However, the SBC has added so many new churches that the departure by the dissidents is unnoticeable.

5. *Biblical Recorder*, 27 April 1996, 3.

6. *Founders Journal* (winter/spring 1995): 26.

7. Walter Shurden, *Proclaiming the Baptist Vision: The Priesthood of All Believers* (Macon, Ga.: Smyth and Helwys, 1993), 131.

8. William Powell Tuck, *Our Baptist Tradition*, (Macon, Ga.: Smyth and Helwys, 1993), 62. Chapter 5 is a very helpful source on the historical background of the doctrine.

9. For more, see Shurden, *Proclaiming the Baptist Vision*, 149.

10. See *Biblical Recorder*, 18 May 1996, 1. We have found it difficult to establish the reasons and numbers of individual missionary changes since 1979. Published denominational materials do not provide a clear indication of the rationale for missionary departures from their work locations at home or abroad.

11. William Leonard, "Southern Baptists and Southern Culture: A

Contemporary Dilemma," in *Religion and Philosophy in the United States of America* (Essen: Verlag Blanc Eule, 1987) 2: 478–79.

12. Quoted from the *San Antonio Light*, 14 June 1988, 1A. It is intriguing that the skunk reference is not in the Convention press release sermon copy, suggesting that Rev. Criswell was inspired to add the remark to the sermon while delivering it.

13. *Biblical Recorder*, 27 January 1996, 5.

14. *Annual of the Southern Baptist Convention, Nineteen Hundred and Ninety-Seven, Dallas, Texas*, distributed by the Executive Committee (Nashville: Southern Baptist Convention, 1997), 5.

15. *Wall Street Journal*, 7 March 1988, A1, A15.

16. See *Baptists Today*, 28 May 1992; and *Biblical Recorder*, 9 January 1993, 8.

17. Letters to the Editor section, *Raleigh News and Observer*, 8 May 1992, 10, and 10 May 1992, 12.

18. Flo Conway and Jim Siegelman, *Holy Terror* (New York: Delta Books, 1984), 114–15.

19. The SBC has officially responded to these organizations. On 11 April 1996, Eliu Camacho-Vazquez, the executive director of the Caribbean office of the Home Mission Board warned local Puerto Rican Baptist churches that any church that associates with the Fellowship will forfeit financial assistance from the HMB. Most of the thirty-two congregations in Puerto Rico depend upon such assistance. Furthermore, the executive director denounced the dissident CBF as one that promoted lesbianism and "errors" in the Bible. While President Larry Lewis of the HMB declined to accept the sentiments as an "official statement of the HMB," it is noticeable that Camacho-Vazquez admitted he developed his views from materials published by the Southern Baptist Convention. See *Baptists Today*, 2 May 1996, 3.

20. The former global missions director of the CBF, Keith Parks, has argued that the Fellowship should not declare itself a new denomination. Additionally, he contended that those who "have found sanctuary" in the CBF "should not be labeled disloyal to the SBC." Perhaps not, but the SBC doesn't agree, and neither do we. Denominational loyalists are the most likely to defend its ideology, theology and practices and to exclude those who disagree. It is not the focus of this book to examine the motivations of those who have become affiliated with the CBF, but it is clear to us that the CBF's policies and positions range from being cosmetically different to being in total disagreement with those of the SBC. See the *Biblical Recorder*, 18 May 1996, 1.

Appendix 2. A Conservative Southern Baptist Affirmation

1. Unless otherwise indicated, all quotations are from Herschel H.

Hobbs, *The Baptist Faith and Message* (Nashville: Convention Press, 1971). [Note is in original text.]

2. Harold C. Bennett, "God's Timeless Message," in *God's Awesome Challenge* (Nashville: Broadman Press, 1980), 35. [Note is in original text.]

A Bibliographical Essay on the Rhetorics of Fundamentalism, Inerrancy, and Exclusion in the Southern Baptist Convention, 1980–1994

The authors include here those sermons, speeches, conference talks, resolutions, and other rhetorical artifacts that are regarded as essential to an understanding of the conflict within the Southern Baptist Convention since 1980.

We do not claim to present or to assess all of the defining rhetorical moments in the controversy within this book. Undoubtedly, many of the best rhetorical moments were seen and heard by a fortunate few in scattered locations across the Convention rather than by the masses of Messengers at state, regional, and national conclaves. Clearly understood, the advocates of the fundamentals of the Baptist persuasion are legion, and their various preaching styles are relevant only to their local congregations. Thus, the rhetorics of fundamentalism, inerrancy, and exclusion made sense to a wide number of churches because their pastors made these concepts clear to the understanding of their church members.

The authors are equally impressed with the superior rhetorical abilities of the known and unknown men who pressed their cases for the rhetorics of fundamentalism, inerrancy, and exclusion. To their credit, they set a standard for excellence by drawing thousands of adherents from thousands of local churches to rally around the fundamentals of the faith that the few moderate voices from the pulpit could only admire with regret and unsuccessfully challenge.

Criteria for Inclusion in the Bibliographic Essay

1. Sermons and press releases on inerrancy and other defining issues, such as the role of women in the church and in church leadership.

2. Defining moments: critical national SBC events that set the tone for months and years to come, namely, SBC President's Addresses and Convention Sermons, speeches at the SBC Pastor's

Conferences, and other mediated events where the most impact could be delivered.

3. Authentic and complete texts: wherever possible, the authors have used video and/or printed texts from the Historical Commission of the Southern Baptist Convention in Nashville, Tennessee, with the gracious assistance of chief archivist, Bill Sumners, and his staff. Although other texts have been quoted throughout the book, this section contains only those rhetorical artifacts with complete texts. We have noted where we have only sermon speech texts and where we have used only videotape. We especially note where we have both speech text and videotape of a cited sermon or speech. In rare cases, we have access only to an audiotape and no text, while, in other cases, we omit a text of some consequence for which we have no record, but understand its impact upon listeners.

4. There are five categories of texts from Southern Baptist Conventions. In order, they are:

The President's Address

The Convention Sermon

Entries from the annual preconvention Pastor's Conference

Convention theme interpretations

The Southern Baptist Forum (SBF) (a 1983 entry in the Convention public communication formats whereby laity and professional church figures spoke by invitation on the current issues in a given year)

5. Encompassing all of these categories, only those convention presentations that addressed the issues of the loyalist movement have been included in the essay. Although the rhetorical themes, arguments, and resulting emotional appeals of fundamentalism, inerrancy, and exclusion appeared nearly every year, there were notable exceptions when the convention addresses were relatively silent on these three themes, while loudly expressing that year's convention theme. In the years 1985 to 1994, the obligatory sermons addressed the church and denominational expectations of preaching, teaching, understanding, and being motivated to return home to do the work of Christ's Church, no matter how difficult.

There are a number of loyalist "champions," namely, Dr. W. A.

Criswell, First Baptist Church, Dallas, Texas; Dr. Bailey Smith, evangelist, Atlanta, Georgia; Dr. Adrian Rogers, Bellevue Baptist Church, Memphis, Tennessee; and Dr. Jerry Vines, First Baptist Church, Jacksonville, Florida. Without question, Vines's sermon, "A Baptist and His Bible," is the finest sermonic exposition of the loyalist movement. Equally so, Dr. Russell Dilday's "On Higher Ground," the Convention Sermon in 1984, was the finest expression of the moderate or centrist position on the controversy.

Other than Dilday's pleas for a return of the priesthood of the believer to combat the struggle, the Convention's political machine did not permit other spokesmen to address the 1980–94 convention attendees with divergent views on inerrancy, fundamentalism, exclusion, or any of its attendant claims.

The statements included here make up the finest hours of rhetorical pomp and circumstance to herald, year after year, the drumbeat of rightward thinking—the Bible is inerrant and infallible. A Baptist, his church, and his Convention must join together "to throw the rascals out" and wrap the loving arms of inclusion around those who swear allegiance to the inerrant Word. For those who were excluded, by whatever means, the shadow of a true, error-free Bible would be their sealed indictment.

Hereafter, bibliographical entries will be abbreviated as follows:

1.Text—The sermon or speech text is included exactly as submitted to the Southern Baptist Historical Commission Archives, Southern Baptist Sunday School Board, Nashville, Tennessee. All of the speech texts have been photocopied as they were submitted to the archives. There are some sermons that appear only on videotape. In some instances, the speaker at issue did not have a written text or title or if he did, he chose not to submit the text to the archives.

2. Videotape—Since 1975, the Radio and Television Commission has videotaped the proceedings of the annual national conventions. Wherever noted, the particular speech/sermon included in the essay is on videotape and has been edited from the original master tapes for evaluative purposes. Moreover, the sermons cited in the various chapters of this book have been evaluated by viewing the sermon while following the printed text to check for textual variance and fidelity, that is, "adlibbing" and the oral reading of the text. We have noted in the narrative of the various chapters when we have viewed the videotape, read the sermon, or relied on a text-only analysis with whatever secondary research available to inform us about the live speech event.

3. Speaking Event Identification

A. Theme Interpretation (TI). Each year, the central theme of the annual convention is subdivided as to its various subthemes. We have included several examples throughout the fifteen years of discourse represented here.

B. Pastor's Conference (PC). Held prior to the annual convention, the Pastor's Conference is the "love feast" of rhetorical excitement and excess for the several thousand pastors and other professionals in attendance.

C. President's Address (PA). In the following year after his election, the president of the Convention addresses the conference on the first full day of business at 11:35 A.M. Usually, the address is broad, conciliatory, and open in its expressions for cooperation and consensus. In the second year of a two-year term (guaranteed by willing supporters), the seasoned president is often proactive and provocative in his quest to leave his mark on the Convention and Southern Baptist life.

D. Convention Sermon (CS). An invited and cherished assignment, the Convention Sermon may well be the plum of all rhetorical events at the convention. In the voices of statesman and evangelists, the speakers in this venue have a level playing field to say whatever they like. The most volatile entry in this category was Dilday's 1984 address "On Higher Ground," the singular national response to the loyalist rhetoric of the denomination.

E. Southern Baptist Forum (SBF). Begun in 1983 in the various speech/sermon convention schedules, this series often produced rhetorical flourishes and firebrand oratory commenting on the national scene by laity and professional churchmen alike. In many instances, both pastors and laity have changed positions and even professions. We have noted the professional affiliation of the speakers at the time of their address.

Part 1: 1980–1984

The first four years were stormy for the inerrancy movement. The President's Address (PA), Convention Sermon (CS), and sermon/talk from the annual Pastor's Conference (PC) comprise the earliest and best indicators of the major national expressions of loyalist rhetoric. The period ends with Dilday's "On Higher Ground," the 1984 SBC Convention sermon—a heraldic finish to a period of loyalist beginnings with the first, and perhaps the finest, expression of the moderate/centrist view of Southern Baptist life and polity.

1980 Adrian Rogers, "The Decade of Decision and the Doors of Destiny" (PA), 10 June 1980, (text, videotape).

Edwin Young,"Side Streets," June 11, 1980, (text, videotape).

1981 Bailey E. Smith "The Worth of the Work" (PA), 9 June 1981, (text, videotape).

Bill Bennett, "Message" (PA), 7 June 1981, (text).

1982 Bailey E. Smith, "Southern Baptists' Most Serious Question" (PA), June 15, 1982, (text, videotape).

William E. Hull, "Who Are Southern Baptists?" (CS), 16 June 1982, (text).

1983 James T. Draper, "Southern Baptists: People of Deep Belief" (PA), 14 June 1983, (text, videotape).

Ron Herrod, "The Basics That Bind Us" (PC), 13 June 1983, (text).

1984 James T. Draper, "Debtors to the World" (PA), 12 June 1984, (text, videotape).

Russell Dilday, "On Higher Ground" (CS), 13 June 1984, (text, videotape).

Part 2: 1985–1990

The second period of five years was marked by the finest array of Convention presidents at their rhetorical best. From Charles Stanley's 1985 address through a trio of stirring sermons by Adrian Rogers to the best expression of the loyalist's rhetoric—Jerry Vines's 1987 "A Baptist and His Bible," these years were a period of gains and glory for the fundamentalists. Even the gifted Joel Gregory's 1988 "The Castle and The Wall," perhaps one of the finest moderate sermon texts and vocal presentations ever heard in Baptist circles, was only momentarily influential.

The period ended with Jerry Vines's "The Glory of God"—a marvel of rhetorical pulpiteering concerning His perfect Word. These years sealed the fate of the moderates, effectively driving them out of the convention, if not out of the Southern Baptist family. In these five years, thousands of

Southern Baptist dissidents were cast out into a wilderness unbounded by the life-long understanding of denomination, all in the name of the Father.

1985 Charles Stanley, "Healing Hurts in the Family of God" (PA), 11 June 1985, (videotape).

Charles G. Fuller, "Too Much to Lose" (CS), 12 June 1985, (text).

Thomas Elliff, "Settled in Heaven" (PC), 10 June 1985, (text).

1986 Charles Stanley, [no title], (PA), 14 June 1987, (text, videotape).

Adrian Rogers, "The Church Triumphant" (CS), 11 June 1985, (text, videotape).

1987 Adrian Rogers, [no title—sermon on doctrinal unity and functional diversity] (PA), 15 June 1987, (text, videotape).

Jerry Vines, "A Baptist and His Bible" (CS), June 1987, (text, videotape).

1988 Adrian Rogers, "Salty Saints in a Sick Society" (PA), 14 June 1988, (videotape).

Joel Gregory, "The Castle and the Wall" (CS), 15 June 1988, (text, videotape).

W.A. Criswell, "The Infallible Word of God" (PC), 13 June 1988, (text).

1989 Jerry Vines, [no title—sermon on a settled agreement over the Bible and an emphasis on personal evangelism] (PA), 13 June 1989, (videotape).

Morris H. Chapman, "Search the Scriptures" (CS), 14 June 1989, (text, videotape).

1990 Jerry Vines, "The Glory of God" (PA), 11 June 1990, (videotape).

Fred Wolfe, "Despise Not the Day of Little Things" (CS), 12 June 1990, (videotape).

Part 3: 1991–1994

Beginning with Morris Chapman's 1991 President's Address "Faith Is the Victory" and the withdrawal of David Vestal from the field of battle by his 1990 loss to Chapman, this period is marked by success, plans for the future, and the final campaign to compete political control—the push to victory within state associations, state newspapers, and denominational seminaries. Since 1991, the loyalists have been counting their winnings because the game is over.

Sure of their vision and goals, the first generation of SBC leadership uneasily began the process of turning over the reins of power to the younger generation, an unsettling task for many. To be sure, the mainstream was still in charge, as in Morris Chapman's 1991–92 addresses and Ed Young's pleas for courage and advance planning for a brighter Southern Baptist future in his 1993 and 1994 President's Addresses. By now, the moderates and so-called liberals were absent from the Convention family. The period of rhetorical activity covered in this book ends on an unusual note with the only lay speaker in the Canon, Zig Ziglar, with his 1994 "A Layman Speaks to the Pastor." In this final entry in the Canon, Ziglar instructs writer and reader alike as to what a listener wants to hear from his pastor.

Throughout this book, we have tried to sit where the listener sits. We began with the special narrative in chapter 1 on the archetypal First Baptist Church, Daycross, Georgia. Here, we end our odyssey with a gifted rhetor in his own right telling his pastor, Jack Graham, of the First Baptist Church, Fort Worth, Texas, what he needs to hear from him.

The messages of this essay and within this book have been understood to comprise a body of persuasion that set standards and drew battle lines that included some and exiled others. In all of these messages, the attractiveness of a perfect God and a perfect Word has had a lasting rhetorical stamina. In these instances, year after year, the preached Gospel of the Word never failed to win the hearts and minds of its hearers. It is the singular accomplishment of the twenty-year history and counting of the loyalist movement that all of the dozens of speakers at annual meetings always attracted listeners to the only true light of God's Word.

1991 Morris H. Chapman, "Faith Is the Victory" (PA), 4 June 1991, (text, videotape).

Tom Elliff, "How to Get Back to God" (CS), 15 June 1991, (videotape).

1992 Morris H. Chapman, "It's Time to Move" (PA), 12 June 1992, (text, videotape).

Lewis Dummond, "The Quest for Balanced Truth" (CS), June 1992, (videotape).

1993 Edwin Young, "Side Streets" (CS), 15 June 1993, (text, videotape).

Jack Graham, [no title] (CS), 16 June 1993, (videotape).

1994 Edwin Young, [no title] (PA), 14 June 1994, (text, videotape).

Zig Ziglar, "A Layman Speaks to the Pastor" (PC), 13 June 1994, (text).

Printed Artifacts on the Rhetoric of Inerrancy

McCall, Duke K. "My Bible Is True," *Southwestern Baptist Theological Seminary Magazine*, June 1975, 11.

Pressler, Paul. "Firestorm Chats," interview by Gary North. Nashville: Southern Baptist Historical Commission Archives, Sunday School Board, 1988.

Rogers, Adrian, James Draper, Charles Stanley, and Bailey Smith. "An Inerrantist Manifesto," press conference document, 24 February 1988.

Index

Carl L. Kell is the director of Development and Alumni Affairs in the communication and broadcasting department at Western Kentucky University, where he also teaches rhetorical strategies in American and Southern popular culture. He has presented over fifty seminars and presentations on Southern rhetorical issues and is the coauthor, with Hal Fulmer, of "A Sense of Place—A Spirit of Adventure: The Rhetorics of South and West" in *Rhetoric Society Quarterly*. In his three decades of teaching, Kell has won numerous teaching awards.

L. Raymond Camp is a professor in communication at North Carolina State University. He is the author of *Roger Williams: God's Apostle of Advocacy* and the editor of *Persuasion in the Public Forum: Pulpit, Bar, and Council*. In 1993, he received the Mary Jo Welch Award for Outstanding and Continuing Service to the Profession from the Carolinas Communication Association. He has also received the Outstanding Teacher of the Year Award from his department.